The Most Notorious Serial Killers in History

Crimes, Patterns, and the Minds Behind the Murders: 51 Profiles of the World's Deadliest Predators

Julian Smith

Introduction

A quiet street. A friendly neighbor. A respected doctor. A youth leader. A traveling drifter. A celebrity fan holding a book. None of these images immediately bring to mind the idea of a serial killer. And yet, history shows again and again that some of the most shocking crimes were committed by people who did not look like monsters at all. As they say, you could walk right by them in the supermarket and not have any idea.

That unsettling truth sits at the heart of this book.

The *Most Notorious Serial Killers in History* isn't just a collection of crimes. It's a look into the patterns, motives, and warning signs behind some of the most infamous cases ever recorded. These are stories that have shaped law enforcement, influenced forensic science, and changed how society understands violence. They are also stories about trust, deception, vulnerability, and the systems that sometimes fail to protect people.

The individuals covered in these pages operated in different eras and countries. Some were active in crowded cities. Others chose isolated rural settings. Some targeted strangers. Others attacked people who trusted them. A few were public figures. Many lived quiet lives that seemed completely ordinary.

What they share is not a single personality type or background. What they share is a pattern of repeated, intentional violence carried out over time. That pattern is what defines a serial killer. It is also what makes these cases so important to study.

This book is organized into 51 profiles. Each focuses on one individual. Within each profile, you will find a consistent structure designed to make complex information clear and easy to follow.

First, each chapter introduces the person and explains why the case became historically significant. This provides context. Some of these cases changed police procedures. Some introduced new forensic methods. Others sparked public fear on a national scale.

Next, the profile looks at early life and background. Childhood experiences don't excuse criminal behavior. But understanding upbringing, environment, and early warning signs helps paint a fuller picture. Patterns often begin long before the first known crime.

From there, the book explores psychological traits and behavioral patterns. This section looks at known diagnoses when available, along with traits such as manipulation, narcissism, obsession, or desire for control. The goal isn't to sensationalize. It's to understand how certain patterns repeat across cases and how they differ from one individual to another.

Each profile also outlines the crimes themselves in a factual and responsible way. The focus stays on patterns and impact rather than graphic detail. Victims aren't reduced to statistics. They're acknowledged as real people whose lives mattered.

After that, the chapters examine the investigation. Many of these cases reveal fascinating lessons about police work. Some offenders were caught quickly. Others avoided capture for years or even decades. In several cases, advances in DNA technology or forensic genealogy finally brought long awaited justice.

The legal outcome is also covered. Trials, confessions, appeals, and sentencing provide insight into how justice systems respond to extreme violence. Some were executed. Some received life sentences. A few died before facing full legal consequences.

Finally, each chapter reflects on the legacy of the case. What changed afterward? What was learned? How did this case shape public awareness or law enforcement policy? These final sections connect past events to present realities.

Readers may notice similarities in victim selection, geographic movement, or investigative errors. Others may see striking differences. These patterns are part of the value of studying serial crime in a structured way.

Why read a book like this at all? It's a fair question.

Some people are drawn to true crime out of curiosity. Others are interested in psychology. Some want to understand how investigators solve complex cases. Still others are trying to make sense of how extreme violence can exist within ordinary society.

This book speaks to all of those motivations. It offers a balanced approach that avoids glorifying offenders. It doesn't present killers as masterminds or antiheroes. Instead, it treats them as case studies. The emphasis stays on understanding behavior, recognizing patterns, and learning from history.

One of the most important lessons across these pages is that serial killers rarely appear in dramatic form. Many blend into their surroundings. They have jobs. They have families. They participate in communities. Warning signs are often subtle.

Another important theme is vulnerability. In many cases, the victims were people living on the margins. Runaways. S** workers. Immigrants. The elderly. The isolated. These cases remind readers that social inequality can increase risk. They also highlight the importance of taking every missing person seriously.

Readers will also see how forensic science has evolved. Early cases often relied on witness descriptions and basic detective work. Later cases used fingerprint databases. Eventually DNA testing became a turning point. In the modern era, genetic genealogy has solved cases that once seemed impossible.

As you move through the chapters, you may begin to recognize recurring patterns. A need for control. A desire for recognition. A history of manipulation. A belief in superiority. Yet no two profiles are identical. Each individual had a unique combination of background, personality, and circumstance.

The book spans more than a century of history. From Victorian era mysteries like Jack the Ripper to modern cases solved through advanced technology, the timeline reveals how both criminals and investigators adapt over time. Society changes. Methods change. But certain human tendencies remain constant.

It's important to remember that behind every profile are real victims and grieving families. This book aims to respect that reality. The focus remains on education and understanding rather than shock value. Violence isn't described in graphic detail. The emphasis is on facts, context, and impact.

If you are a student of criminology, this book offers structured case studies. If you're interested in psychology, it presents a wide range of behavioral profiles. If you are simply curious about history's most notorious crimes, it provides clear and organized narratives.

You will see how small investigative breakthroughs led to major arrests. You will learn how missed warning signs allowed certain offenders to continue. You will understand how community advocacy sometimes forced authorities to take action.

The goal isn't to leave readers feeling disturbed without purpose. The goal is to leave readers informed. Knowledge doesn't eliminate crime, but it helps societies respond more effectively.

Serial killers represent an extreme and rare form of violence. They don't define humanity. But studying them reveals important truths about psychology, power, deception, and resilience. It also highlights the strength of investigators, survivors, and families who refuse to give up.

This book invites you to look beyond headlines and into the deeper structure of each case. It offers clarity without sensationalism. It presents facts without exaggeration. And it organizes complex information in a way that is accessible, structured, and easy to follow.

As you turn the page to the first profile, remember that these stories are not myths. They happened. They shaped communities. They changed laws. And in many cases, they changed how the world understands crime itself.

Welcome to *The Most Notorious Serial Killers in History*.

Overview

Ted Bundy – Charming law student who preyed across multiple states

Jeffrey Dahmer – Isolated Milwaukee man obsessed with possession and control

John Wayne Gacy – Suburban contractor hiding murders beneath his home

Dennis Rader – Self-named BTK killer who communicated with media

Gary Ridgway – Quiet truck painter linked to Green River deaths

Aileen Wuornos – Drifter who shot men along Florida highways

Richard Ramirez – Satan-obsessed burglar who invaded homes at night

David Berkowitz – .44 caliber gunman who terrified 1970s New York

Edmund Kemper – Highly intelligent murderer targeting college students

Albert DeSalvo – Man who confessed to Boston Strangler killings

H. H. Holmes – Con artist tied to suspicious deaths in Chicago

Andrei Chikatilo – Soviet-era predator who eluded capture for years

Pedro López – Convicted killer of young girls in South America

Harold Shipman – Trusted physician who secretly poisoned patients

Jack the Ripper – Unidentified killer stalking Victorian London streets

Robert Hansen – Alaskan outdoorsman who hunted human victims

Israel Keyes – Calculating traveler who buried evidence nationwide

Samuel Little – Long-overlooked offender with decades of victims

Herb Baumeister – Businessman whose property concealed grim discoveries

Joel Rifkin – New York laborer responsible for numerous deaths

Leonard Lake – Survivalist plotting captivity from remote compound

Charles Ng – Accomplice involved in calculated abductions and killings

Arthur Shawcross – Paroled offender who resumed violent crimes

Paul Bernardo – Canadian criminal in infamous partnership murders

Karla Homolka – Wife and accomplice in high-profile Canadian case

Peter Sutcliffe – Yorkshire Ripper targeting women across northern England

Robert Pickton – Pig farmer connected to missing Vancouver women

Dean Corll – Houston electrician responsible for youth abductions

Wayne Williams – Convicted in Atlanta child homicide investigations

Henry Lee Lucas – Notorious drifter known for widespread confessions

Ottis Toole – Transient offender tied to multiple violent acts

Belle Gunness – Farm widow who lured suitors for profit

Nannie Doss – Serial poisoner who killed within her family

Elizabeth Báthory – Aristocrat accused of brutal historical crimes

John Bunting – Australian mastermind behind Snowtown killings

Fred West – Builder involved in concealed household murders

Rose West – Partner in Gloucester's notorious murder case

Juana Barraza – Former wrestler targeting elderly women in Mexico

Yang Xinhai – Rural Chinese attacker convicted of mass killings

Mikhail Popkov – Former officer linked to numerous Russian murders

Robert Ben Rhoades – Long-haul trucker preying on stranded women

Donald Harvey – Hospital orderly convicted of patient deaths

William Bonin – Freeway Killer abducting young male victims

Patrick Kearney – Methodical California killer known as Trash Bag Murderer

Joseph DeAngelo – Golden State Killer identified through genetic genealogy

Bruce McArthur – Toronto landscaper hiding crimes in plain sight

Dennis Nilsen – London civil servant who killed vulnerable men

Carl Panzram – Early American drifter leaving violent confessions

Anatoly Slivko – Soviet youth organizer convicted of multiple murders

Lonnie Franklin Jr. – Grim Sleeper targeting women in Los Angeles

Mark David Chapman – Assassin who murdered former Beatle John Lennon

Contents

Ted Bundy

Few serial killers have disturbed the public imagination as deeply as Ted Bundy. Operating across multiple states during the 1970s, Bundy was intelligent, well-spoken, and outwardly charismatic, traits that defied the typical image of a monster. He exploited social trust, manipulated appearances, and committed murders that were methodical, ritualized, and terrifying in their intimacy. His case became one of the most studied in criminal psychology, not only for the sheer volume of victims, but for what he revealed about the gap between appearance and reality. Bundy was not a mindless killer. He was a calculating predator who understood, and weaponized, human empathy. In the end, he confessed to 30 murders, though experts believe the true number was significantly higher. His legacy is not merely one of violence, but of psychological and cultural disruption.

Born Theodore Robert Cowell on November 24, 1946, in Burlington, Vermont, Bundy's early life was shaped by deception. For the first several years of his life, he was raised to believe that his grandparents were his parents, and that his mother, Louise Cowell, was his sister. His biological father remains unknown. This concealment was not uncommon in mid-20th-century America for children born out of wedlock, but in Bundy's case, the secrecy seemed to imprint deeply. Eventually, he learned the truth, and though he would speak of it with studied nonchalance, the psychological effects of this revelation, compounded by emotional detachment and uncertainty in his early home life, have remained a point of analysis for decades.

As a child, Bundy displayed conflicting tendencies. Some accounts describe him as polite and quiet; others, including recollections from classmates and neighbors, recall early instances of disturbing behavior. He was fascinated by knives, often seemed emotionally disconnected, and was prone to manipulating other children. There are also reports of him surrounding his aunt with knives while she slept. While many of these stories are difficult to verify, they support the notion that Bundy's darkness emerged early, if quietly.

His adolescent years were marked by increasing social isolation. Though bright, he struggled with connection. He later admitted that he felt like a misfit, unable to understand social cues or establish genuine friendships. Despite this, he maintained a public mask of normalcy. Bundy attended the University of Puget Sound before transferring to the University of Washington, where he studied psychology. He had aspirations in law and politics and interned at a Seattle suicide crisis hotline alongside future true crime author Ann Rule. To those around him, Bundy appeared ambitious, intelligent, and charming. Few would have suspected the turmoil underneath.

Psychologists and profilers have long examined Bundy's duality. He was able to dissociate from his actions, compartmentalizing his sadism from his daily life. Experts have suggested psychopathy, narcissistic personality disorder, and antisocial traits, all of which appear consistent with his behavior. Bundy understood how he appeared to others, and he used that appearance as a weapon. His confidence, good looks, and disarming demeanor enabled him to approach victims in broad daylight, often feigning injury or authority to gain their trust. He was, in essence, a social chameleon, adapting to whatever persona would best serve his predatory goals.

Bundy's modus operandi relied heavily on psychological manipulation. He frequently used ruses to lower his victims' defenses, pretending to have a broken arm, asking for help loading items into his car, or impersonating a figure of authority.

Once isolated, he would overpower them, often using blunt force to subdue them before transporting them to secondary locations where the violence escalated. His crimes included abduction, s**ual assault, mutilation, and murder. He sometimes returned to crime scenes, engaging in n*crophilic acts, which suggests an obsession with total control and domination.

Most of Bundy's victims were young women between the ages of 15 and 25, often white and brunette, typically wearing their hair parted in the middle. This apparent consistency in victim profile led some to speculate that they resembled his early girlfriend, an elegant, dark-haired woman who ended their relationship abruptly, leaving Bundy devastated. Whether this connection is meaningful or coincidental is debated, but the pattern is undeniable.

The confirmed timeline of his murders begins in 1974 in Washington state, where young women began disappearing from college campuses. The first known victim was Lynda Ann Healy, a student at the University of Washington. Her bed was found made with blood on the pillow and no signs of struggle, suggesting she had been attacked in her sleep. Over the following months, more women vanished, sometimes in broad daylight. In July of that year, two women (Janice Ott and Denise Naslund) disappeared from Lake Sammamish State Park within hours of each other. Witnesses reported a man named "Ted" asking for help while wearing a sling. This was a crucial turning point: the predator had a name and a description.

Despite mounting reports, Bundy eluded capture. He moved to Utah and continued killing, later committing crimes in Colorado and Florida. His ability to blend in, coupled with law enforcement's lack of centralized databases, allowed him to cross state lines and confuse investigators. The country had not yet developed the forensic and interagency coordination needed to detect patterns in transient offenders. Bundy exploited that gap ruthlessly.

It was in August 1975 that Bundy was first arrested in Utah for possession of burglary tools, leading authorities to connect him to local disappearances. Though he was initially charged with kidnapping, the investigation quickly widened. Bundy escaped custody twice, once from a law library and again from a jail cell in Colorado.

The second escape was particularly audacious: he dropped through a ceiling panel and walked out of the building. By the time authorities noticed he was missing, Bundy was already en route to Florida.

In January 1978, Bundy broke into the Chi Omega sorority house at Florida State University. Within minutes, he had bludgeoned and strangled two women to death and severely injured two others. Less than a month later, he abducted and murdered 12-year-old Kimberly Leach. These crimes were more frenzied and chaotic than his earlier ones, suggesting a loss of control and increasing desperation. Bundy's time on the run was ending.

He was arrested on February 15, 1978, after being pulled over in a stolen vehicle. This time, there was no escape. Bundy was eventually tried for the Chi Omega murders in Miami, and the trial became a national media event. It was one of the first criminal cases in the U.S. to be televised gavel-to-gavel. Bundy, always confident in his charm, insisted on representing himself in court.

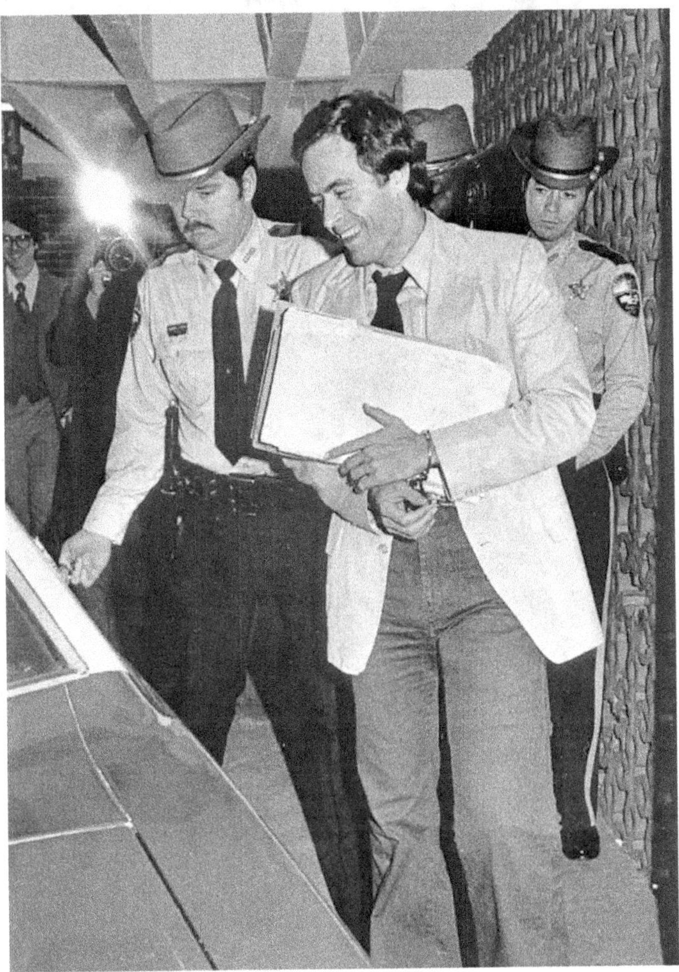

(Bundy in custody)

He treated the trial as theater, at one point proposing marriage to a witness on the stand, Carole Ann Boone, a former coworker who believed in his innocence and later bore his child while he was on death row.

Despite Bundy's attempts to manipulate the courtroom and the media, the evidence was overwhelming. Bite mark analysis (shown on the next page), eyewitness testimony, and physical evidence led to convictions. He was sentenced to death for the Chi Omega murders and later received two additional death sentences for the murder of Kimberly Leach.

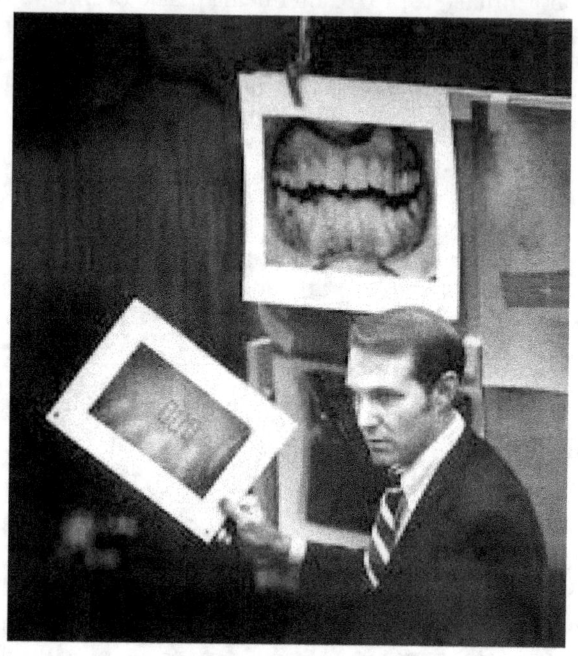

Bundy spent nearly a decade on death row, using the time to appeal his sentence, delay execution, and provide partial confessions to investigators in exchange for leniency, confessions that confirmed his involvement in dozens of killings but left others unacknowledged.

Throughout his incarceration, Bundy continued to fascinate and terrify the public. He gave interviews to journalists, criminologists, and law enforcement, offering insights into the mind of a serial killer that were both chilling and revealing. He was articulate and composed, but his words often revealed a deep lack of empathy. When finally facing execution, Bundy attempted to shift blame to viewing lewd content, suggesting it fueled his violent fantasies. Most viewed this as a last-minute attempt to redirect culpability.

On January 24, 1989, Ted Bundy was executed in the electric chair at Florida State Prison. Outside the prison, crowds gathered, some cheering and holding signs that read "Burn, Bundy, Burn." His death marked the end of one of the most disturbing chapters in American criminal history, but the questions he raised remain.

Bundy's case had profound implications for criminal justice. It exposed weaknesses in law enforcement communication across state lines, led to the development of better interagency data sharing, and helped refine behavioral profiling techniques. The FBI's Behavioral Science Unit incorporated lessons from his crimes into the growing field of criminal profiling. Bundy became a case study in how charm, intelligence, and privilege could obscure violent pathology. He forced the public to reconsider assumptions about what evil looks like and where it can hide.

His story has since become a cornerstone of true crime literature, academic study, and popular media. Books, documentaries, and films continue to dissect his life, often with a mix of horror and fascination. Yet amid the analysis, it is vital to remember the victims, many of whom remain unnamed or unconfirmed. Bundy's greatest act of cruelty may not have been the violence he inflicted, but the fact that he denied so many families the closure of knowing what happened to their loved ones.

In the end, Ted Bundy's crimes were not simply a product of individual pathology. They reflected a time when serial murder was poorly understood, when social trust was easily exploited, and when the justice system was ill-equipped to track nomadic predators. Bundy manipulated all of these gaps. He was not a monster in the traditional sense, but something far more unsettling, a man who understood human behavior well enough to destroy it from within.

Jeffrey Dahmer

Jeffrey Lionel Dahmer remains one of the most chilling figures in modern criminal history. Known to the public as the "Milwaukee Cannibal" or the "Milwaukee Monster," Dahmer committed a string of murders between 1978 and 1991 that stunned the world not only for their violence but for their extreme depravity. Unlike many serial killers who operated in the shadows and left behind only traces, Dahmer was caught with an apartment that had become a chamber of horrors, filled with skulls, body parts, and photographic documentation of his crimes. His case sent shockwaves through the public, the legal system, and the field of forensic psychology.

Dahmer was born on May 21, 1960, in Milwaukee, Wisconsin, to Lionel and Joyce Dahmer. His early life, at least superficially, seemed unremarkable. His father was a chemist, and his mother reportedly struggled with mental health issues, though accounts of the home environment vary depending on the source.

(Dahmer in high school)

The family moved several times during his early childhood. Dahmer was a quiet and withdrawn child, described by neighbors and teachers as polite but emotionally distant. There was a growing sense of alienation, one that would deepen through adolescence and fester into something darker.

By the time Dahmer reached his early teens, he was already exhibiting troubling behavior. He developed an intense fascination with dead animals, often collecting roadkill and dissecting the carcasses in private. He claimed he was curious about how bodies fit together, how muscles and bones interacted, but the interest bordered on obsessive. He later admitted that the process gave him a sense of control, something he otherwise lacked in his life. His alcohol use began early, reportedly drinking heavily by the time he reached high school. He was isolated, socially awkward, and increasingly consumed by violent s**ual fantasies involving domination and death.

At age 18, Dahmer committed his first murder. In 1978, just three weeks after graduating high school, he picked up a hitchhiker named Steven Hicks. The two returned to Dahmer's house to drink. When Hicks attempted to leave, Dahmer bludgeoned him with a dumbbell and later dismembered the body. He buried the remains in the backyard and eventually scattered the bones after pulverizing them with a sledgehammer.

For nearly a decade afterward, Dahmer would not kill again. This dormant period is one of the more unusual aspects of his criminal trajectory. While many serial killers escalate quickly, Dahmer remained inactive, at least in terms of known murders, until 1987.

That year, while living in a Milwaukee hotel, he met Steven Tuomi at a bar. Dahmer brought him back to his room, and by morning, Tuomi was dead. Dahmer claimed to have no memory of the killing, stating that he woke up to find Tuomi beaten and lifeless. From this point forward, the murders began to occur with increasing frequency. Dahmer rented a room in his grandmother's house in West Allis, Wisconsin, and for the next two years, it became the setting for many of his killings. He murdered several young men during this period, luring them with offers of money or companionship, drugging them, and then carrying out acts of strangulation, mutilation, and, in some cases, n*crophilia.

His method evolved over time. He would often lure victims to his apartment, sedate them with sleeping pills, and wait until they were unconscious. Then he would strangle them, pose their bodies for photographs, and engage in acts of dismemberment. Dahmer kept skulls, genitals, and other body parts as trophies. He stored remains in refrigerators and freezers, and he admitted to cooking and eating portions of some victims. These acts were not driven by hunger but by compulsion, a desire to possess, consume, and fully dominate another person. In interviews, he described wanting to create "a permanent part" of the people he killed, to make them part of himself. He fantasized about creating obedient zombies by drilling holes into his victims' skulls and injecting acid or boiling water in an attempt to destroy specific brain regions while keeping them alive.

Dahmer's crimes escalated not only in brutality but in frequency. Between 1987 and 1991, he murdered at least 16 more victims. Most of the men were gay or bis**ual and from marginalized communities, including African-American and Southeast Asian backgrounds. Dahmer frequented gay bars and bathhouses to find his victims, often choosing those who were vulnerable, estranged from family, or unlikely to be reported missing. This element of his crimes sparked later accusations from critics that law enforcement had failed to intervene sooner because of institutional biases against both race and s**ual orientation.

Despite multiple close calls, Dahmer managed to evade capture. On several occasions, police were called to investigate suspicious behavior. In one particularly shocking incident in May 1991, a 14-year-old boy named Konerak Sinthasomphone was found naked and disoriented on the street. Neighbors called 911, but when police arrived, Dahmer convinced them that the boy was his intoxicated lover and they were having a domestic dispute. The officers escorted the boy back to Dahmer's apartment, where he was murdered shortly thereafter. The failure to intervene at this moment would later become one of the most widely criticized aspects of the case.

It all came to an end on July 22, 1991. Tracy Edwards, a 32-year-old man, escaped from Dahmer's apartment after being held at knife point. Edwards flagged down police and led them back to the apartment.

What the officers found inside was beyond comprehension. There were photographs of dismembered bodies, severed heads in the refrigerator and freezer, and a barrel containing acid and body parts. The apartment had been transformed into a slaughterhouse, a private realm of death and desecration.

Dahmer was arrested immediately. During interrogation, he confessed in chilling detail to 17 murders. He spoke without emotion, describing his actions with clinical detachment. He provided information about methods, motives, and locations. His openness shocked investigators. He seemed relieved to be caught, claiming he had lost control and was grateful it had ended. Psychologists would later debate whether this was genuine remorse or simply a form of emotional numbness, consistent with psychopathy and dissociation.

The trial began in January 1992 and lasted just over two weeks. Dahmer was charged with 15 counts of first-degree murder. He entered a plea of guilty but insane. The central issue was whether he could be considered legally sane at the time of the killings. The defense argued that his acts were so bizarre (cannibalism, n*crophilia, attempted zombification) that they must reflect severe mental illness. The prosecution countered that he took elaborate steps to conceal his crimes, indicating awareness of wrongdoing and legal culpability.

The jury found Dahmer to be legally sane and guilty on all counts. He was sentenced to 15 consecutive life terms, totaling 957 years. Later, he was convicted of a 16th murder in Ohio and received another life sentence. He was incarcerated at the Columbia Correctional Institution in Portage, Wisconsin.

While in prison, Dahmer reportedly converted to Christianity and was baptized. He spent much of his time in isolation but later joined the general population. On November 28, 1994, he was beaten to death in the prison gym by another inmate, Christopher Scarver. Scarver later stated that he believed Dahmer was unrepentant and had mocked prison staff and inmates by shaping food into limbs and drizzling ketchup to resemble blood. Dahmer's death closed the chapter on one of the most horrifying crime sprees in American history.

The public response to Dahmer's crimes was one of revulsion and fascination. The grotesque nature of the case (human remains found in a modest apartment, tales of cannibalism and n*crophilia) combined with his quiet, unassuming demeanor to create a cultural paradox. How could someone who appeared so normal be capable of such monstrous acts?

The media coverage was relentless. Journalists, authors, and television producers turned his life and crimes into a morbid spectacle. At the same time, activists and scholars used the case to highlight systemic failures, particularly the disregard for missing gay men of color.

From a criminological perspective, Dahmer's case prompted significant introspection. He didn't fit the classic mold of an impulsive or disorganized killer. His crimes were carefully planned, and his ability to manipulate victims suggested both intelligence and social cunning. Yet his fantasies were deeply disturbed and marked by a desire for control so total that it crossed into the surreal. The concept of creating compliant, soulless partners through chemical lobotomy placed Dahmer into a category of offender that defied traditional typologies. He was a n*crophile, cannibal, sadist, and fantasist, but he was also methodical, composed, and terrifyingly self-aware.

Dahmer's story has been dissected in academic literature, criminal psychology, and popular culture. It has inspired dozens of documentaries, books, films, and even art exhibits. His case has served as a touchstone for debates about mental illness, criminal responsibility, s**uality, and societal neglect. Forensic psychologists still analyze his behavior in graduate seminars. Law enforcement agencies study the failures in early investigation. Advocacy groups cite his victims to call attention to marginalized communities.

What makes Dahmer particularly unsettling is not just the violence he committed, but the intimacy of it. He didn't kill for profit, power, or revenge. He killed to erase loneliness, to possess others so completely that they could never leave. His crimes were rooted in psychological need rather than rage. That made him harder to detect, and harder to comprehend.

The apartment where he killed became infamous, but it was ultimately demolished. Victims' families sought to distance themselves from the spectacle and urged the public to focus on remembrance and justice rather than infamy. Some called for his brain to be studied to find neurological anomalies, but after legal battles between his parents, it was ultimately cremated.

Jeffrey Dahmer remains a symbol of hidden horror, a soft-spoken man whose atrocities were committed behind a locked door in a city that had no idea what was happening.

His case shattered assumptions about what a killer looks like and how long one can operate undetected. In the years since, he has become more than a criminal; he is a case study in the failure to see the evil that walks among us in plain clothes.

John Wayne Gacy

John Wayne Gacy was the embodiment of a nightmare hiding in plain sight. Outwardly, he was a respected member of the community, an active participant in local politics, a successful contractor, and even an entertainer who dressed as a clown for children's parties.

Beneath that carefully constructed facade, however, lay one of the most prolific and horrifying serial killers in American history.

Between 1972 and 1978, Gacy s**ually assaulted, tortured, and murdered at least 33 young men and boys, most of whom were buried beneath the crawl space of his suburban Chicago home. His case was not only a gruesome tale of abuse and death, but a sobering study in deception, manipulation, and institutional failure.

Born on March 17, 1942, in Chicago, Illinois, Gacy was the second of three children in a working-class family. His father, a World War I veteran and machinist, was an abusive alcoholic who subjected his son to frequent physical and verbal assaults.

Gacy struggled with poor health during childhood, including a heart condition that limited his participation in sports and isolated him from other boys his age. Despite his efforts to win his father's approval, he was often ridiculed, called "sissy," and accused of being weak. His early life was marked by feelings of shame, secrecy, and a growing disconnect between his public and private self.

As a teenager, Gacy demonstrated an eagerness to be liked and accepted. He became active in school and community activities and learned to adopt a friendly, accommodating persona that masked his inner turmoil. In his early twenties, he moved to Las Vegas, where he worked briefly at a mortuary. There, he slept on a cot behind the embalming room and later admitted to once climbing into a coffin with a deceased young man. The experience reportedly disturbed him deeply, prompting his return to Chicago. Soon after, he enrolled in business school and began to cultivate a life of apparent stability and upward mobility.

By the mid-1960s, Gacy had relocated to Waterloo, Iowa, where he managed several KFC restaurants owned by his father-in-law. He married, had two children, and was considered a model citizen. He joined the local Jaycees, a civic organization, and quickly rose through the ranks due to his charisma and drive. But behind closed doors, darker impulses were surfacing. In 1968, Gacy was convicted of s**ually assaulting a 15-year-old boy. He served 18 months of a 10-year sentence before being released on parole. His wife divorced him, and he returned to Chicago to rebuild his life, vowing never to be caught again.

Over the next decade, Gacy would do just that. He worked his way into the good graces of his new community, becoming a successful contractor who operated a remodeling business called PDM Contractors.

He continued his involvement in local politics, even posing for photographs with First Lady Rosalynn Carter during a Secret Service-vetted event, as seen below.

He hosted neighborhood parties, engaged in charity work, and donned the persona of "Pogo the Clown" to perform for children in hospitals. His public identity was designed to disarm suspicion and project an image of harmless eccentricity.

In reality, Gacy's house at 8213 West Summerdale Avenue had become a killing ground. He lured young men and boys, many of them runaways, drifters, or youths looking for work, into his home under various pretexts. Some he hired as employees; others he picked up from bus stations or offered rides.

Once inside, he would ply them with alcohol or drugs, engage them in conversation, or use a ruse involving handcuffs and a "magic trick." After rendering his victims helpless, Gacy would proceed to s**ually assault them, often accompanied by sadistic violence that included beating, strangulation, and torture.

Gacy developed a chilling ritual. He referred to his murders as "cruising," and often wore his clown costume before or after committing them. He used a ligature to strangle his victims, sometimes tightening it slowly to prolong their agony. In several cases, he buried the bodies himself in the crawl space beneath his house. As the number of corpses increased, he began to run out of room. When decomposition and odors became overwhelming, he dumped some victims in the Des Plaines River. But for years, there was no investigation, no suspicion, and no clue that something so monstrous was occurring beneath the surface of suburban normalcy.

Gacy's ability to go undetected for so long speaks to both his cunning and the vulnerabilities of his victims. Many of the boys he targeted came from troubled backgrounds or lacked strong family connections. In some cases, missing persons reports weren't filed immediately, or were dismissed by authorities. The public and law enforcement alike were reluctant to imagine that someone so respected and well-connected could be involved in anything criminal, let alone a series of disappearances. It was a failure of pattern recognition, one that would only be corrected when Gacy made a critical mistake.

In December 1978, 15-year-old Robert Piest disappeared after telling his mother he was going to speak with a man about a potential job. That man was John Wayne Gacy. Unlike previous victims, Piest came from a stable, attentive household. His mother immediately reported him missing, and police launched an investigation that quickly pointed to Gacy.

When detectives visited his home, they were struck by the overpowering stench but were told it was due to plumbing issues. They began surveillance and conducted background checks, discovering his previous s**ual assault conviction. Gacy, meanwhile, attempted to manipulate the situation, alternating between cooperation and evasion.

A breakthrough came when officers obtained a search warrant and uncovered damning evidence: driver's licenses, handcuffs, p***ography, and items belonging to several missing boys. On December 21, Gacy confessed to more than two dozen murders, calmly recounting the details as though describing someone else's crimes. He expressed little emotion and showed no signs of remorse. Over the following weeks, authorities unearthed the remains of 29 victims from beneath his house. Four others were found in the nearby river. It was the worst case of serial murder in U.S. history at the time.

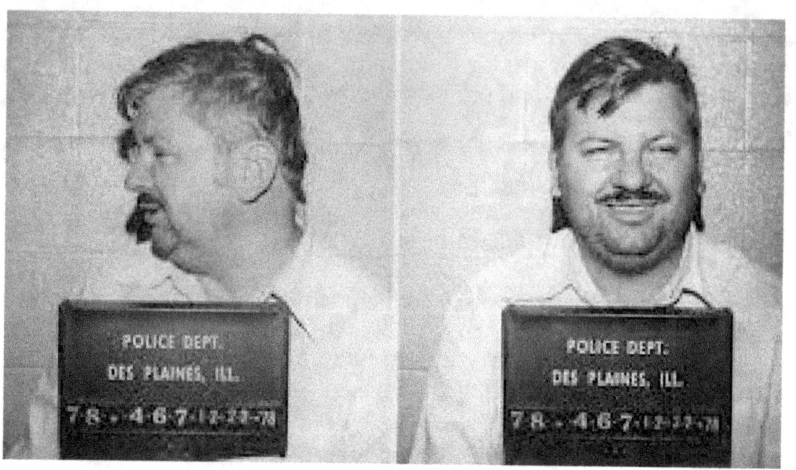

The trial of John Wayne Gacy began in 1980 and became a media sensation. Gacy pleaded not guilty by reason of insanity, with his defense team arguing that he was mentally ill and incapable of understanding the consequences of his actions. Prosecutors countered that Gacy's meticulous methods, efforts to hide the bodies, and continued business and social activities demonstrated clear awareness and intent. Psychiatric evaluations were divided, with some experts diagnosing him with antisocial personality disorder while others saw signs of psychosis. The jury ultimately found him guilty on all 33 counts of murder and sentenced him to death.

Gacy spent 14 years on death row at Menard Correctional Center. During his incarceration, he painted prolifically, producing hundreds of works of art, many of them self-portraits as Pogo the Clown. The paintings became collectibles, some selling for thousands of dollars, though others were destroyed in public protests. Gacy gave numerous interviews, often shifting blame to his victims, society, or his own mental illness.

His attitude veered between arrogance and defiance. In a 1994 interview, he stated, "I should never have been convicted of anything more serious than running a cemetery without a license."

On May 10, 1994, Gacy was executed by lethal injection. His last words were reportedly, "Kiss my ass." Outside the prison, crowds gathered to celebrate his death, some holding signs and chanting. His remains were cremated, and his possessions were auctioned, collected, or destroyed. In the aftermath, questions continued to surface about how Gacy had been able to maintain a double life for so long and how so many red flags had been overlooked.

The legacy of John Wayne Gacy extends far beyond his body count. His crimes forced law enforcement agencies to reevaluate how missing persons cases were handled, especially those involving young males. The case also contributed to the development of psychological profiling and the study of organized offenders – i.e., killers who maintain control over their public personas while committing atrocities in private. Gacy fit this mold precisely. He was methodical, manipulative, and adaptive. He knew how to project normalcy while operating a hidden world of violence beneath his feet.

Forensic teams studying the site of his home faced unprecedented challenges. The excavation of the crawl space required meticulous effort, often conducted by hand to preserve evidence and respect the integrity of the remains. The sheer volume of victims buried in such a confined area revealed the logistical horror of Gacy's operations. Victim identification took years, and as of the 2020s, several of his victims remained unnamed, though advances in DNA technology have helped identify others.

The case also opened painful wounds for families and communities. Many of Gacy's victims had run away from home, were estranged from families, or were exploring their identities in a world that offered little acceptance. Their disappearance often attracted minimal attention until it was too late. Gacy targeted them not only because they were vulnerable, but because he knew no one was looking closely enough. In this way, his crimes reflect broader societal failures, toward youth, toward marginalized groups, and toward the hidden traumas that often precede victimization.

Gacy's public persona as a clown added an almost surreal quality to his story. The image of "Pogo the Clown," meant to entertain children, became an enduring symbol of the darkness hiding behind smiles. It haunted a generation and inspired countless fictional villains.

Yet the reality was more frightening than the caricature. Gacy was not a monster in makeup. He was a man who made conscious choices to abuse, murder, and dehumanize others for his own gratification. His ability to pass as ordinary remains one of the most unsettling aspects of the case.

The house where Gacy committed his crimes was demolished, and the lot was left empty for years. Eventually, a new home was built, but the address was changed. The events that unfolded there left a permanent scar on the landscape and in the American psyche. Gacy's name is now synonymous with serial murder, with evil masked in the everyday, with the chilling possibility that anyone, no matter how friendly or familiar, can harbor darkness.

Dennis Rader

Dennis Rader spent decades living what appeared to be a respectable, unremarkable life. He was a father, a church council president, a Boy Scout leader, and a city compliance officer in a quiet Kansas suburb. But behind that ordinary exterior was a man who lived for the thrill of control, secrecy, and sadistic violence. Between 1974 and 1991, Rader murdered ten people in Sedgwick County, Kansas.

He gave himself a name (BTK, short for "Bind, Torture, Kill") and he terrorized Wichita with his chilling blend of calculated brutality and self-conscious notoriety. The sheer normalcy of his public life, paired with the sadism of his crimes, turned the BTK case into one of the most disturbing examples of compartmentalized evil in American criminal history.

Dennis Lynn Rader was born on March 9, 1945, in Pittsburg, Kansas, and grew up in Wichita. He was the oldest of four boys. His parents, Dorothea and William Rader, worked long hours, and Dennis later described feeling ignored and emotionally neglected. Though there is no record of overt abuse, Rader reportedly developed a need to assert control and sought power over others from an early age.

Like many serial killers, he displayed disturbing tendencies in childhood, including killing small animals, engaging in voyeurism, and harboring violent s**ual fantasies. He became fixated on bondage and control, often imagining women as helpless captives. These fantasies would not remain private forever.

Rader graduated from high school in 1963 and served in the U.S. Air Force from 1966 to 1970. Upon his return, he married Paula Dietz in 1971 and started building the image of a conventional life. He worked in various roles, including at a meat department and later at ADT Security Services, where he installed alarm systems, often in homes of women concerned about a growing local crime wave that, unbeknownst to them, he had started. He later earned a degree in criminal justice from Wichita State University and became a compliance officer for Park City, a suburb of Wichita. There, he was known for his strict code enforcement and occasionally authoritarian demeanor, often citing homeowners for minor infractions.

Rader's first known murders occurred on January 15, 1974. He broke into the home of the Otero family and systematically murdered Joseph and Julie Otero and two of their children, 11-year-old Joseph Jr. and 9-year-old Josephine. He had stalked them in advance and later described the killings with chilling detachment. He tied them up, suffocated and strangled them, and took trophies from the scene.

What made the crime particularly shocking was not just the brutality but the planning. Rader had chosen the victims, cased the home, and brought a "hit kit" with ropes, cords, and tools prepared. Afterward, he returned to his daily life without arousing suspicion.

Following the Otero murders, Rader killed Kathryn Bright in April 1974. He broke into her home, waited for her to return, and was surprised when she arrived with her brother, Kevin. Rader shot Kevin, who survived, and proceeded to strangle and stab Kathryn. This encounter was more chaotic than his first, and the lack of full control seemed to frustrate him. After this, he went quiet for several years but continued developing his fantasies, maintaining his "projects" (a term he used to refer to potential victims) and documenting his thoughts in meticulous detail.

Rader wanted recognition. In 1978, he sent a letter to a local TV station, taking credit for the Otero and Bright murders and revealing details only the killer would know. He signed the letter "BTK," cementing his identity as someone who craved infamy as much as he craved dominance. His communications were littered with references to bondage, control, and death. He mimicked the style of the Son of Sam letters from New York, clearly modeling himself after other notorious serial killers. The public nickname BTK caught on quickly, and Wichita was gripped by fear. Families began double-locking their doors, installing alarms, and looking over their shoulders.

Rader's next murders followed a similar pattern: stalking, breaking in, subduing, binding, torturing, and finally killing. He often took personal items from his victims (underwear, IDs, or jewelry) and kept them as trophies. In some cases, he took Polaroids of the bodies, posed them, or returned to the crime scenes in his imagination through writing or masturbation. His victims were mostly women, though the inclusion of the Otero children showed that age and gender were not absolute limits for him. He sought vulnerability and submission, and he enjoyed prolonging fear.

In 1985, he murdered Marine Hedge, a neighbor he knew from church. This time, he removed her body from the home and took it to the Christ Lutheran Church, where he was a member and president of the council. There, he posed her body, photographed her, and eventually disposed of her in a ditch. The use of the church as a backdrop for his crime stunned investigators when it was eventually revealed. It showed the extent of his compartmentalization, how he could blur the sacred and the profane without remorse.

Despite several murders and periodic letters to the press or police, Rader evaded capture for decades. He was methodical. He wore gloves, kept his victims' houses clean of fingerprints, and chose his targets with care. He appeared utterly normal. To his family and colleagues, he was a disciplined man, perhaps a bit rigid, but never dangerous. His ability to mask his depravity behind suburban normalcy became a central part of his story.

By 1991, after the murder of Dolores Davis, Rader stopped killing. Or at least, he stopped murdering known victims. His last known crime was carried out with the same precision as his earlier attacks, but as DNA technology advanced and databases improved, the chances of getting caught were increasing. Rader seemed to sense this, and for over a decade, BTK went silent. The murders faded into cold case files, though the psychological impact on Wichita never entirely disappeared.

In 2004, the 30th anniversary of the Otero murders brought renewed public interest. Rader, unable to resist the urge for recognition, resurfaced. He sent a letter to the Wichita Eagle, including photos of a crime scene and a copy of the victim's driver's license.

Over the following months, he continued communicating with media and police, sending packages, letters, and even a puzzle with clues about his identity. The communication escalated to the point that investigators launched a renewed task force. This decision would finally unravel the mystery.

In one of the most ironic miscalculations of his life, Rader asked police whether they could trace a floppy disk. Believing their answer of "no" to be honest, he sent one to a TV station. Investigators found metadata on the disk linking it to Christ Lutheran Church and to a man named Dennis. A simple search revealed Dennis Rader, the church council president. Surveillance confirmed his movements, and DNA obtained from his daughter's pap smear matched semen found at several crime scenes. It was over.

Rader was arrested on February 25, 2005. When confronted, he initially denied everything, but under questioning, he unraveled. He confessed to all ten murders with the same emotionless detail that had characterized his crimes. He described the planning, the stalking, the bindings, the killing… all delivered in a tone that was chilling in its calmness. He spoke of his "dark side," a compartmentalized part of himself he referred to as "Factor X." He said this force compelled him to kill and that it had parallels to other infamous killers like Jack the Ripper and the Hillside Stranglers.

At trial, Rader pled guilty to all charges. The judge allowed him to speak openly during his sentencing hearing, and he did so for over an hour, detailing each murder without visible emotion.

He described the victims' deaths, the preparations, and the aftermath all as though he were explaining a business project. His demeanor stunned courtroom observers. There was no apology, no genuine remorse, only the cold narration of someone who had studied his own behavior and taken pride in his control.

Rader was sentenced to ten consecutive life terms with no possibility of parole. He is incarcerated at El Dorado Correctional Facility in Kansas, where he remains under tight security, now in his 80s as of this is written. His cell contains only the bare essentials: a bed, toilet, sink, and a few permitted books. He continues to correspond with criminologists and journalists, offering insights into his behavior in exchange for attention. Though barred from profiting from his crimes, he has participated in interviews and provided detailed written accounts of his actions.

The BTK case reshaped public understanding of serial killers. Rader was not a drifter or a loner; he was deeply embedded in his community. His life was an example of what criminologists call the "organized offender," someone who plans meticulously, maintains social ties, and operates in plain sight.

His crimes spurred advancements in forensic investigation, DNA database management, and the use of criminal profiling. He also served as a case study in narcissism, compartmentalization, and ritualistic behavior.

What made Rader's crimes so uniquely disturbing was not just the violence but the contrast. He could deliver sermons and then commit torture. He could discipline city residents for overgrown lawns and then fantasize about strangling them.

He built a mask of normalcy so convincing that even his family had no idea. To the outside world, he was ordinary. Inside, he was planning his next bind, torture, kill.

Gary Ridgway

Gary Leon Ridgway, better known as the Green River Killer, is one of the most prolific serial murderers in American history. Operating primarily in Washington state during the 1980s and 1990s, Ridgway confessed to killing 71 women and was convicted of 49 murders, though authorities suspect the true number may be higher. Unlike many serial killers who attract attention through erratic behavior or theatricality, Ridgway operated quietly, consistently, and without drawing notice. His crimes haunted the Pacific Northwest for decades and revealed profound vulnerabilities in law enforcement's ability to track predators who blend seamlessly into society.

Ridgway was born on February 18, 1949, in Salt Lake City, Utah, and raised in a working-class neighborhood in SeaTac, Washington. His childhood was marked by emotional instability and confusion around s**uality and authority. His father worked as a bus driver and often complained about the presence of s** workers on his route, expressing contempt for them that Ridgway would later echo in far more extreme ways. His mother was described as domineering and manipulative. Ridgway would later recount complex feelings about her (revulsion, fear, and s**ual arousal) that blurred into fantasies of power and violence. He recalled one memory in particular, where she cleaned his genitals after he wet the bed, triggering deep and conflicting emotions that he didn't understand at the time.

He struggled in school, had a low IQ, and was socially awkward. Teachers and peers remembered him as unremarkable, even invisible. As a teenager, Ridgway stabbed a six-year-old boy, nearly killing him. The act was quickly dismissed as an isolated incident, but in retrospect, it revealed a chilling capacity for violence that would later define his adult life. Despite this, he managed to graduate from high school, join the Navy, and marry. While stationed overseas, he frequented s** workers, a habit that would later become intertwined with his homicidal compulsion.

After returning from the Navy, Ridgway settled back in the Seattle area. He worked as a painter at a truck manufacturing plant, a job he would hold for decades. Coworkers described him as reliable but strange. He read the Bible at lunch and often spoke about religion, yet he would also make inappropriate s**ual remarks and obsess over prostitutes. He married multiple times, fathered a son, and lived in suburban neighborhoods without attracting suspicion. His lifestyle was modest, his manner mild. That, in part, is what made him so dangerous.

The Green River killings began in 1982. Young women, many of them s** workers or runaways, began to disappear from the Seattle-Tacoma area. Bodies were discovered near the Green River, sometimes dumped, sometimes hidden in forested areas, posed or violated. Most had been strangled, often with ligatures or by hand.

Law enforcement soon realized they were dealing with a serial offender. The victims shared consistent characteristics: they were vulnerable, often engaged in s** work, and lived on the margins of society. The killer seemed to have intimate knowledge of where to find them and how to dispose of their bodies without being seen.

Ridgway developed a method that was both brutally effective and chillingly impersonal. He would pick up women, usually under the pretense of paying for s**, and drive them to secluded areas. He often used his son to make himself appear harmless or trustworthy. Once alone, he would attack, strangle, and then dispose of the body, sometimes returning later to engage in n*crophilic acts with the corpses. He would leave the bodies in clusters, almost as if marking territory, and frequently revisited these sites for s**ual gratification. His ability to revisit scenes without being noticed suggested both confidence and a strong psychological need for control and repetition.

The investigation into the Green River Killer was massive and frustratingly fruitless. In 1984, police created the Green River Task Force to coordinate efforts across

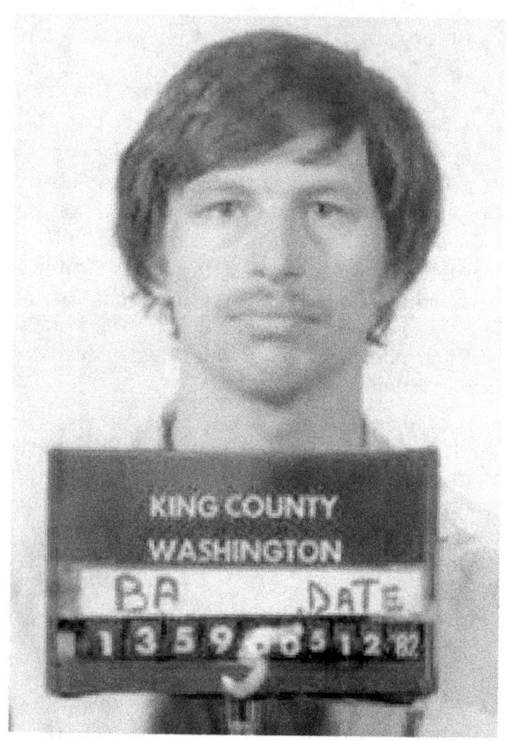

(Ridgway in 1982)

jurisdictions. Despite their growing resources, the case yielded little progress. They interviewed hundreds of suspects and combed through thousands of leads. Ridgway himself was interviewed early in the investigation, largely because he had been arrested in 1982 for soliciting a prostitute and had been seen with several missing women. He passed a polygraph test and cooperated with law enforcement. Nothing about him stood out, and with no forensic evidence to tie him to the crimes, he was released.

At one point, the task force enlisted the help of FBI profilers, including John Douglas, who offered a psychological assessment of the killer. The profiler described a man who would seem average, work a blue-collar job, and target women he perceived as immoral. This turned out to be eerily accurate, but without physical evidence or eyewitness accounts, the investigation remained stalled.

As the years passed, the murders slowed but didn't stop. Ridgway began spacing them out, choosing his victims more carefully. He later claimed he deliberately picked women who were less likely to be missed, who had no fixed address, no strong family ties, and no one to report them missing right away.

In 1987, police obtained a DNA sample from Ridgway, but at the time, forensic science had not advanced enough to use it effectively. It would remain in storage for years. In the meantime, Ridgway continued living a quiet life. He remarried, became active in church, and remained employed. He was, by all external measures, a typical middle-aged man. Yet he carried within him a compulsion to kill that he had learned to hide beneath layers of normalcy.

It wasn't until 2001, nearly two decades after the first murders, that technology finally caught up to the evidence. New DNA testing methods allowed authorities to re-examine biological material collected from several victims. The results were conclusive: DNA from three victims matched Ridgway. Additional evidence, including trace paint from his workplace found on victims' clothing, helped strengthen the case. On November 30, 2001, Gary Ridgway was arrested outside the truck plant where he had worked for over 30 years. The quiet man in the coveralls was, at last, exposed.

Under questioning, Ridgway at first denied everything, but the forensic evidence was overwhelming. Once he realized the depth of the case against him, he began to talk. What emerged was a confession that stunned even seasoned investigators. Ridgway admitted to killing at least 71 women, though he could not recall all their names. He spoke about the murders with detachment, describing the process with cold efficiency. He explained how he selected, lured, killed, and disposed of his victims. He expressed no real remorse, only regret that he had not been more careful in avoiding detection.

To avoid the death penalty, Ridgway agreed to a plea bargain. In exchange for life imprisonment, he provided detailed confessions and led investigators to previously unknown burial sites. His cooperation helped resolve dozens of cold cases and provided families with long-awaited answers.

In 2003, he pled guilty to 48 counts of murder, and in 2011, a 49th victim was confirmed and added. He is currently serving life without the possibility of parole at the Washington State Penitentiary.

The public reaction to Ridgway's arrest and confessions was a mix of horror, relief, and disbelief. That one man could commit such a staggering number of murders over so many years, while remaining virtually invisible, exposed deep weaknesses in law enforcement systems and societal attitudes. Many of his victims were s** workers, drug users, or transient young women, groups that often received less attention when they disappeared. Ridgway understood this and exploited it ruthlessly. He admitted that the less someone was likely to be missed, the more likely he was to target them.

Ridgway's psychology is particularly chilling because of how unremarkable he appeared. He was not especially charismatic, intelligent, or erratic. He was consistent, disciplined, and patient. He murdered not out of rage or passion, but out of habit and desire for control. He often killed multiple women in a single week and returned to work as if nothing had happened. He saw his victims not as people, but as disposable objects. This dehumanization made his crimes easier to commit repeatedly. He did not stalk celebrities, or seek fame, or leave messages for police. He wanted only to kill, and to do so efficiently and often.

Criminologists and psychologists have since studied Ridgway as a textbook case of the organized serial killer. His crimes followed a routine. He had a "type," a method, and a preferred geography. He kept trophies, revisited scenes, and adjusted his strategy when the heat turned up. He adapted over time, which allowed him to operate undetected for years. His case has informed modern policing strategies, especially around the use of DNA databases and the investigation of s** worker disappearances. It also led to new legislation in Washington around missing persons and inter-agency cooperation.

The human toll of Ridgway's crimes is almost impossible to quantify. Dozens of families spent years not knowing what happened to their daughters or sisters. Some victims were never identified. Others were known only by the location of their remains.

Ridgway's decision to dump bodies in rivers, forests, and ravines made recovery difficult and sometimes impossible. He deliberately spread them out to confuse law enforcement and to prevent a clear picture of his total victim count from ever emerging.

Despite his cooperation with police, Ridgway has remained largely unrepentant. He described his killings as an addiction, something he could not stop. He claimed that he wanted to rid the streets of s** workers and that he thought he was doing the world a service.

Yet these justifications ring hollow when weighed against the cold reality of his crimes. His own s**ual obsession and need for control were the true motives. He didn't kill out of anger. He killed because it brought him gratification.

Today, Gary Ridgway serves as a dark reminder that evil doesn't always come with fanfare. It can wear the face of the man next door, the coworker who shows up on time, the husband who volunteers at church. The scope of his crimes, combined with the duration of his killing spree, place him in a category few serial killers occupy. His victims were marginalized, and he exploited that status mercilessly. For decades, he remained hidden in the background, a predator camouflaged by routine.

His story is one of systemic failure and methodical cruelty. It challenges assumptions about who killers are and what they look like. It shows how easy it is to overlook the vulnerable, to dismiss the missing, to believe that evil always looks like a monster.

In Gary Ridgway's case, the monster looked like a neighbor, a husband, a man with a job and a quiet life. But behind that mask was one of the deadliest killers the United States has ever known.

Aileen Wuornos

Aileen Wuornos was one of the few female serial killers in American history, and the first woman in modern times to be labeled as such by the FBI. Her case unsettled the public because it challenged conventional images of both femininity and criminality. While most serial killers are male and prey on the vulnerable, Wuornos turned the pattern on its head: her victims were men, and her motives, at least in her own account, were rooted in self-defense and revenge. Her story became a battleground for debates over trauma, agency, and justice, and remains one of the most controversial in the annals of American crime.

Wuornos was born Aileen Carol Pittman on February 29, 1956, in Rochester, Michigan. Her early life was marred by violence, neglect, and abandonment. Her father, a convicted s** offender, was imprisoned at the time of her birth and later died by suicide. Her mother left when Aileen was still an infant, and she and her brother were adopted by their grandparents. Her grandfather was reportedly abusive, both physically and emotionally. She claimed that her grandfather beat her and that she was s**ually assaulted by men in her extended family from an early age.

By the age of 11, she was exchanging s**ual acts for cigarettes, food, or money. She was pregnant by 14, allegedly as a result of rape, and the child was placed for adoption. Shortly afterward, she was expelled from her home and forced to survive on her own in the woods and abandoned vehicles.

Throughout her teens and early adulthood, Wuornos drifted through a life marked by instability, violence, and street-level s** work. She was arrested multiple times for theft, assault, and prostitution. Her relationships were volatile and often abusive. In 1976, she briefly married a 69-year-old man in Florida, but the marriage quickly dissolved amid allegations that she attacked him with a cane. The rest of her life was spent on the margins of society, living in cheap motels, hitchhiking along highways, and relying on s** work to survive.

It was during this time, in the late 1980s, that she met Tyria Moore, a hotel maid with whom she formed a long-term romantic relationship. The two women lived together and traveled across Florida, relying on Wuornos's earnings from prostitution. According to Wuornos, Moore was her one true love, and their bond would later be pivotal in her arrest and conviction.

Between 1989 and 1990, seven men were found shot to death in Florida. Each had been killed with a .22 caliber handgun. The bodies were discovered in wooded areas off highways, stripped of their valuables and, in some cases, their vehicles. At first, investigators did not link the killings, but a pattern began to emerge: the victims were middle-aged white men, often traveling alone. The murders were spread across multiple counties, complicating jurisdictional coordination. The press dubbed the killer a "highway murderer," and as fear spread, so did speculation.

In January 1991, police arrested Wuornos at a biker bar in Volusia County. Moore had already been taken into custody and, in exchange for immunity, agreed to cooperate with authorities. In a carefully orchestrated plan, police set up a series of phone calls between Moore and Wuornos. During these conversations, Moore pleaded with Wuornos to confess, saying she was scared and wanted to be protected. Wuornos, believing that Moore was in danger of being charged, ultimately broke down and admitted to the killings. Her confession was raw, emotional, and conflicted. She claimed that the men had either attempted to rape her or had threatened her, and that she had killed in self-defense. Her statements, however, often changed and contradicted each other.

The evidence against her was strong. She was found in possession of items belonging to several of the victims, including their cars and personal effects. Ballistics matched the handgun she carried to the bullets recovered from multiple murder scenes.

Witnesses placed her with victims shortly before their deaths. Police also recovered fingerprints, receipts, and surveillance footage that linked her to the crimes. Despite the strength of the case, Wuornos remained defiant. She told reporters she had no regrets and even dared law enforcement to execute her.

Wuornos was charged with multiple counts of first-degree murder. In January 1992, she was tried for the murder of Richard Mallory, an electronics store owner whose body had been found in Volusia County.

The prosecution painted her as a cold-blooded killer who targeted men for money and stole their belongings after murdering them. The defense argued that she had been the victim of chronic s**ual violence and that she killed only in response to threats or attempted assaults. The trial included harrowing details from both sides, but the turning point came when the judge allowed evidence from other murders to be introduced under Florida's "Williams Rule," which permits the admission of similar crimes to show pattern or motive.

Wuornos was found guilty of first-degree murder and sentenced to death. Over the next two years, she pled no contest or guilty to five additional murders and received five more death sentences. In the case of one victim, Peter Siems, no body was ever recovered, so no charges were filed. While her early statements emphasized self-defense, her later interviews often expressed rage toward men, society, and even her own legal team. She accused her attorneys of exploiting her for fame and profit and claimed that the legal process was rigged from the start.

As she languished on death row, Wuornos became a cultural figure, both reviled and mythologized. Her case drew national attention, spawning documentaries, books, and eventually a feature film. Journalists and filmmakers explored the layers of trauma, mental illness, and violence that shaped her life. Some viewed her as a tragic figure, an abused child who never stood a chance in a world that discarded women like her. Others saw her as manipulative and dangerous, a predator who used her past as a shield for her crimes.

Her mental health deteriorated in the years following her conviction. She exhibited signs of paranoia, delusions, and mood instability. Court-appointed psychiatrists diagnosed her with borderline personality disorder, antisocial personality disorder, and possible psychosis.

She claimed she was being tortured in prison through food tampering and mind control. Despite these claims, multiple courts found her competent to stand trial and to be executed.

On October 9, 2002, Aileen Wuornos was executed by lethal injection at Florida State Prison. She declined a last meal, requesting only a cup of coffee. Her final words were, "I'd just like to say I'm sailing with the rock, and I'll be back like Independence Day, with Jesus. June 6, like the movie. Big mother ship and all. I'll be back." She was 46 years old.

The debate over Wuornos's legacy continues. To some, she was a symptom of a society that fails its most vulnerable, an abused, abandoned girl who became a killer because she had no other options. To others, she was a calculated murderer who used the claim of self-defense as a cover for greed and rage. What is undeniable is that Wuornos represents an extreme convergence of trauma, violence, and criminal behavior. Her life challenges assumptions about victimhood, gender, and justice.

Her crimes changed how law enforcement viewed female serial killers. Unlike poisoners or caregivers who killed for financial gain or attention (profiles more typical of female offenders) Wuornos hunted. She stalked, lured, and killed in isolated settings, often at night.

Her methods resembled those of male serial killers, and her motives (control, power, vengeance) aligned with them as well. In that sense, she stood outside traditional categories, a figure that both fascinated and disturbed investigators.

Aileen Wuornos remains one of the most studied and polarizing figures in American criminal history. Her name is now synonymous with the extremes of human suffering and rage, a case where society is forced to confront how far someone can fall, and how often they are pushed. Whether she was a cold-blooded killer or a woman who finally struck back, her story offers no easy answers, only difficult truths.

Richard Ramirez

In the summer of 1985, fear gripped California. A series of brutal, seemingly random home invasions had turned the region into a patchwork of terror. The intruder would break in at night, often entering through open windows or unlocked doors, and unleash a torrent of violence on whoever was inside. He used guns, knives, hammers, tire irons, and machetes. He killed men, women, and children. He raped, mutilated, beat, and taunted his victims. Sometimes he stole jewelry or electronics, other times he left with nothing. He showed no pattern except for cruelty, no preference but opportunity. Police called him the "Valley Intruder" at first, but as his crimes escalated and the media seized on his penchant for satanic symbols and sadistic declarations, a new name stuck: the Night Stalker.

Richard Ramirez was born Ricardo Leyva Muñoz Ramirez on February 29, 1960, in El Paso, Texas. He was the youngest of five children in a working-class Mexican-American family. His father, Julian Ramirez, was a former police officer in Juárez who later worked for the Santa Fe railroad. He was known to be harsh and hot-tempered, sometimes beating his children into submission. As a boy, Richard suffered multiple head injuries, including being knocked unconscious by a falling dresser and hit in the head with a swing. These injuries reportedly caused seizures and may have contributed to neurological and behavioral problems later in life.

Ramirez's early childhood was a chaotic blend of trauma, religious confusion, and exposure to violence. He was deeply influenced by his older cousin Miguel ("Mike") Ramirez, a Vietnam War veteran who showed him photographs of mutilated women, some of whom Mike claimed to have raped and killed during the war. Miguel also introduced Richard to drugs and taught him how to kill stealthily. In 1973, Mike murdered his wife in front of Richard, an event that profoundly shaped his psyche. Rather than rejecting the trauma, Ramirez seemed to absorb it, retreating further into darkness.

As a teenager, Ramirez began using LSD and developed an obsession with Satanism. He dropped out of high school and moved to California in his early twenties. He drifted between hotels, bus stations, and abandoned buildings in Los Angeles and the Bay Area, supporting himself through petty theft, burglary, and increasingly violent crimes. He was gaunt, disheveled, and often clad in all black, his teeth rotting from drug use and poor hygiene. He carried himself with a detached, almost predatory calm. People who crossed paths with him would later describe him as eerie, hollow-eyed, and silent.

The first confirmed murder attributed to Ramirez occurred on June 28, 1984, when he raped and murdered 79-year-old Jennie Vincow in her Los Angeles apartment. She had been stabbed repeatedly, her throat slashed so deeply she was nearly decapitated. Police noted the extreme savagery and lack of forced entry, but at the time, they had no idea this was only the beginning.

It wasn't until the spring and summer of 1985 that his killing spree exploded in frequency and notoriety. On March 17, Ramirez attacked 22-year-old Maria Hernandez outside her home in Rosemead. She survived after raising her hands to protect her face, and the bullet ricocheted off her keys. Ramirez entered the house and shot her roommate, Dayle Okazaki, killing her instantly. Just an hour later, he pulled 30-year-old Tsai-Lian Yu from her car and shot her in the chest. She died the next day. The randomness of the attacks and the lack of connection between victims confounded police and terrified the public. There was no clear motive, only a man moving through the darkness, striking wherever he pleased.

Ramirez soon began leaving behind signs of sadism and ritualism. At one crime scene, he drew a pentagram on a bedroom wall. At others, he raped victims and forced them to swear allegiance to Satan. He sometimes spared children, instructing them to "tell the police the Night Stalker was here."

He showed no fear of capture and seemed to relish the fear he instilled. Media coverage exploded, and panic spread. People began locking windows, arming themselves, and sleeping with lights on. The LAPD struggled to respond to the scale and randomness of the crimes. A task force was created, but the killer continued to elude them.

Over the next several months, Ramirez committed a wave of murders and assaults across Southern California. He attacked both men and women, couples and individuals, the elderly and the young. He entered homes at random, typically through open windows or unlocked doors, and unleashed chaos. His weapons varied – handguns, knives, a tire iron, a machete. He raped women, beat men to death, bludgeoned victims in their sleep, and sometimes lingered after the killings to eat food, rummage through belongings, or mark satanic symbols. The unpredictability made him all the more terrifying.

Despite the intensity of the investigation, Ramirez remained free through much of 1985. Law enforcement agencies from multiple counties struggled to coordinate. Evidence linking the crimes, such as shoe prints from a rare Avia sneaker and a series of pentagrams, was mounting, but no suspect had been identified. Breaks finally came when two key witnesses described a suspicious man and partial license plate numbers were traced to a stolen car. In that car, police found a fingerprint. When run through the system, it returned a match: Richard Ramirez, a drifter with a long rap sheet of arrests for burglary and drug possession.

On August 30, 1985, police released Ramirez's name and photo to the public. The next day, he was recognized on the street in East Los Angeles. Attempting to flee, he ran through backyards and tried to carjack a vehicle, but was surrounded and subdued by a group of residents. They held him down until police arrived. The man who had terrorized Southern California for over a year was caught by ordinary citizens. His capture felt like a public exorcism.

During interrogation, Ramirez showed little remorse. He confessed to numerous crimes but often spoke cryptically. In court, he was volatile – laughing, sneering, holding up a pentagram drawn on his palm, and declaring "Hail Satan." The press swarmed the courtroom. People lined up for seats at the trial. The atmosphere was part spectacle, part horror show. Ramirez's gaunt appearance, dark eyes, and devil-worship posturing turned him into an icon of evil for the media.

The trial began in July 1989 and lasted over four years. It became one of the most expensive and complex criminal trials in California history. He was charged with 13 counts of murder, five counts of attempted murder, 11 counts of s**ual assault, and 14 counts of burglary. The evidence against him was overwhelming. Witnesses identified him. Fingerprints and ballistic evidence linked him to multiple crime scenes. Survivors recounted harrowing encounters. The defense tried to delay proceedings with motions and psychiatric evaluations, but the facts were undeniable.

On September 20, 1989, the jury found Ramirez guilty on all charges. During the penalty phase, he taunted the court, saying, "You don't understand me. You are not expected to. You are not capable. I am beyond good and evil." He was sentenced to death and sent to San Quentin State Prison, where he would remain for more than two decades. Despite his crimes, Ramirez received love letters and fan mail while on death row. In 1996, he married a journalist named Doreen Lioy, who claimed he was innocent and misunderstood.

While incarcerated, Ramirez granted occasional interviews. He alternated between defiance and detachment, sometimes discussing Satanism, sometimes describing his crimes as expressions of power. He claimed to have no regrets.

Criminologists studying his case noted his lack of empathy, his compulsive behavior, and his fascination with death and domination. Ramirez fit the mold of the disorganized killer in some respects (acting on impulse, leaving evidence) but he also exhibited planning, predatory patience, and symbolic rituals, blurring traditional categories.

Over the years, investigators suspected Ramirez of additional crimes outside the known victims. Some unsolved murders from the early 1980s bore similarities in method and signature. Others questioned whether his crimes stretched into the San Francisco Bay Area or beyond. Though nothing was definitively added to his official tally, the possibility that his reign of terror was even longer than acknowledged continues to haunt those who followed his case.

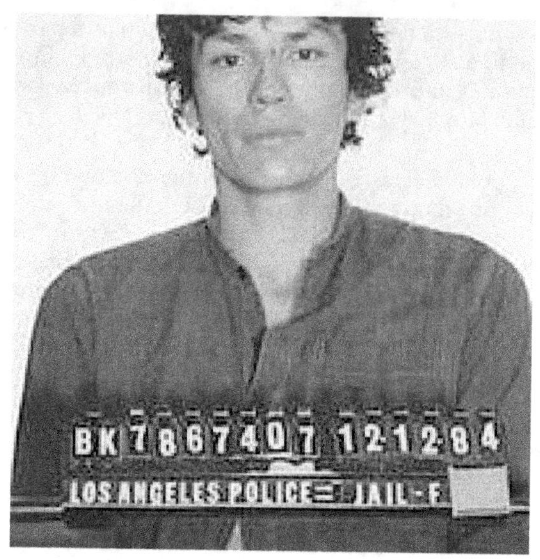

(Ramirez arrested for auto theft in Los Angeles in 1984)

(Ramirez in 2007)

On June 7, 2013, Richard Ramirez died at the age of 53. The official cause was complications related to B-cell lymphoma. He had also been diagnosed with chronic hepatitis C and other conditions related to his decades in prison. At the time of his death, he had spent over 23 years on death row without ever being executed. His passing closed one of the most brutal chapters in California's criminal history, but the wounds left behind remained raw.

The legacy of the Night Stalker case reshaped how law enforcement handles serial crimes, particularly those involving home invasions and geographically dispersed victims. It highlighted the need for interdepartmental coordination, forensic databases, and public communication.

The panic Ramirez instilled also changed public behavior, leading to a surge in home alarm sales, deadbolts, and security measures across the region. The randomness of his attacks shattered the illusion of safety in one's own home. Unlike other killers who stalked specific types or ages, Ramirez targeted whoever was available, making every locked door feel like a line between life and death.

His life and crimes have inspired countless books, films, documentaries, and cultural references. Yet beneath the mythology lies a grim reality: a predator whose violence was fueled by sadism, not ideology; by compulsion, not need. Ramirez didn't kill for money, revenge, or ideology. He killed because he could. He reveled in it. That is what makes him so chilling to this day.

Richard Ramirez remains one of the most infamous figures in American criminal history. He embodied a type of evil that felt both chaotic and purposeful, mindless and calculated. He didn't fit neatly into the boxes used by law enforcement or psychologists, and he didn't want to. He styled himself as a servant of darkness, but in truth, he was a man broken long before he became a killer, a product of trauma, influence, and personal choice. In the end, he needed no devil. He was one.

David Berkowitz

In the summer of 1977, New York City was teetering on the edge. The economy was struggling, the crime rate was surging, and the infamous blackout had plunged entire neighborhoods into darkness and chaos. But the deepest fear came from something harder to predict and impossible to contain: a gunman, seemingly choosing victims at random, was stalking the streets at night and killing with cold precision. He struck couples parked in cars, lone women walking home, strangers with no connection to each other. He left behind shell casings, cryptic letters, and fear. The media called him the ".44 Caliber Killer." The name he gave himself ("Son of Sam") would become part of American criminal history forever.

David Berkowitz was born Richard David Falco on June 1, 1953, in Brooklyn, New York. His mother, Betty Broder, gave him up for adoption shortly after birth. He was adopted by Pearl and Nathan Berkowitz, a middle-class Jewish couple living in the Bronx. They renamed him David, and by most accounts, his early years were relatively stable. But even in childhood, signs of internal conflict emerged. Teachers described him as disruptive, aggressive, and prone to angry outbursts. He had trouble concentrating, made few friends, and seemed drawn to violence from an early age.

As he entered adolescence, Berkowitz's emotional issues deepened. He became isolated and socially awkward, struggling to connect with others and often bullied for his appearance and behavior. The death of his adoptive mother when he was 14 had a profound impact. He became more withdrawn, more volatile, and more obsessive. His relationship with his adoptive father deteriorated, especially after the elder Berkowitz remarried and moved away. Left largely to himself, David began descending into what would later be described as paranoid delusions, compulsive behavior, and simmering resentment toward the world.

After graduating high school, Berkowitz briefly attended college before enlisting in the U.S. Army. He served in South Korea and completed his tour honorably, but the experience did little to stabilize him. Upon returning to New York, he worked various low-level jobs, eventually securing a position as a postal worker. He lived alone in a small apartment in Yonkers and kept to himself.

During this period, his behavior became increasingly erratic. He set numerous fires (more than 1,400, according to later confessions) and kept detailed logs of each blaze. He also began writing bizarre, threatening letters to strangers and local officials. These were early signs that his internal fantasy life was turning outward.

The killings began on July 29, 1976, when two women (Jody Valenti and Donna Lauria) were sitting in a parked car in the Bronx. A man approached, drew a .44 caliber Bulldog revolver, and fired. Donna Lauria died instantly; Jody Valenti was seriously wounded but survived. The randomness of the attack confused investigators. There was no robbery, no apparent motive, no clear suspect.

Over the following months, more shootings followed. Always at night. Always in or near parked cars. Always with a large-caliber weapon. Most of the victims were women with long dark hair, leading some to believe the killer had a specific type. Panic began to spread. Women began cutting their hair or dying it blonde. Couples avoided sitting in parked cars. New York had seen crime before, but this was different. This felt personal.

As the body count grew, the city's sense of safety collapsed. The killer's boldness escalated. He began taunting police and media. In April 1977, a letter was found near the body of one of the victims, addressed to NYPD Captain Joseph Borelli. In it, the killer referred to himself as "Son of Sam" and claimed to be acting under the orders of a demonic entity who spoke through his neighbor's dog. The letter was rambling, laced with bizarre references to ancient gods and evil spirits, but it was also deliberate, careful, and chilling. He signed it with a stylized symbol and promised more bloodshed to come. The press published excerpts, and overnight, the "Son of Sam" name stuck.

Over the next three months, he attacked again and again. He killed Stacy Moskowitz and wounded Robert Violante in Brooklyn. He murdered Christine Freund and injured John Diel in Queens. He left his mark across boroughs, confusing detectives and shattering the illusion that the city could contain the violence.

The investigation ballooned into one of the largest manhunts in New York's history. Thousands of tips poured in. The NYPD devoted over 300 officers to the case. Psychological profilers developed a picture of the suspect as a paranoid, socially isolated white male, likely living alone, with a fascination for fire and authority.

The break came not from forensic science, but from basic observation. On the night of his last attack, a witness saw a man near the scene loitering by a parked car. The car was ticketed for being too close to a hydrant. A sharp-eyed dispatcher noticed the ticket was issued just minutes before the murder. The vehicle was registered to David Berkowitz in Yonkers. When police checked his file, they found a record of previous gun violations and arson. They staked out his apartment and, on August 10, 1977, arrested him as he exited the building. In the backseat of his car, they found a .44 caliber revolver, a duffel bag with ammunition, maps, and another letter.

Berkowitz immediately confessed. "You got me," he reportedly said. "I'm Sam." He was 24 years old. During interrogation, he described hearing voices, particularly those of a demon named "Sam" who communicated through a neighbor's black Labrador retriever and commanded him to kill. He claimed he had no choice but to obey.

While many dismissed this as a performance, psychiatric evaluations revealed signs of severe mental disturbance, including paranoid delusions and disorganized thought patterns. Ultimately, however, he was declared fit to stand trial.

In May 1978, rather than face a public spectacle of a trial, Berkowitz pled guilty to six counts of second-degree murder and received six life sentences, 364 years in prison without the possibility of parole. During sentencing, he made a statement that he had been possessed by Satan. The courtroom remained quiet, but the world outside continued to obsess over him. Books, articles, and TV segments dissected his background, his crimes, and his alleged connection to the occult.

Berkowitz's claims about demonic possession were met with skepticism. Some believed he was mentally ill but fully responsible. Others suspected he was exaggerating or inventing the story to avoid the death penalty or to mythologize himself. Years later, he recanted portions of his original story, claiming that he had not acted alone and was part of a satanic cult that carried out the murders as rituals.

These claims, made in the 1990s, were never substantiated and have been widely dismissed by law enforcement. Still, the theory fueled conspiracy speculation and added another layer to the already bizarre narrative.

While in prison, Berkowitz underwent what he described as a religious conversion. He became a born-again Christian and began referring to himself as the "Son of Hope." He wrote letters to victims' families, expressed remorse, and gave interviews in which he distanced himself from the man he had once been. He participated in Bible study, counseled other inmates, and maintained a quiet existence behind bars. His transformation sparked debates about redemption, sincerity, and justice. Some believed he had truly changed. Others viewed his conversion as opportunistic and manipulative.

In a highly publicized decision, Berkowitz declined to attend his own parole hearings, stating that he accepted his punishment and had no desire to be released. He insisted he could do more good inside than out. He remained incarcerated at Shawangunk Correctional Facility in upstate New York. Despite his claims of peace, he continued to draw attention. True crime documentaries, podcasts, and dramatizations have kept his name in the public eye for decades. His case is frequently cited in discussions of media-driven hysteria, mental illness in the criminal justice system, and the role of profiling in modern investigations.

The Son of Sam case also led to legal reforms. After Berkowitz's arrest, publishers rushed to offer book and movie deals. In response, New York passed the "Son of Sam" law in 1977, which prohibited criminals from profiting off the publicity of their crimes. The law was later overturned on First Amendment grounds but was revised and re-enacted in other forms in multiple states. The idea that a killer could become a celebrity sparked a national conversation about the ethics of media, profit, and public attention.

In many ways, David Berkowitz was not the most prolific or methodical serial killer. But the context of his crimes (the scale of the panic, the randomness of the attacks, the messages to the press, and the invocation of Satan) made him one of the most terrifying. He didn't kill for money or revenge.

He claimed he killed because something dark and ancient told him to. Whether one believes that claim or not, the impact was undeniable. He made an entire city feel hunted. He turned backseats into coffins and neighborhoods into killing fields.

His crimes revealed the vulnerability of modern urban life and the fear that anyone, anywhere, could become a target. They exposed cracks in the justice system, flaws in mental health intervention, and the dangers of media sensationalism. And they forced people to ask hard questions about the nature of evil, responsibility, and whether someone like David Berkowitz could ever be anything other than what he was when he held the gun.

As of when this is being written, David Berkowitz remains in prison. He is a relic of a time when horror walked the streets of New York and signed its name with blood and ink. He insists he has changed. The world, however, remembers who he was.

Edmund Kemper

Edmund Emil Kemper III was not what most people envisioned when they thought of a killer. At 6 feet 9 inches tall and weighing over 250 pounds, he towered over others, physically imposing but also soft-spoken, articulate, and eerily self-aware. Unlike many serial killers who eluded police through deception or luck, Kemper turned himself in. He had no interest in fleeing. He wanted to talk. And when he did, what emerged was a confession of stunning brutality, methodical planning, and a psychological depth that would both fascinate and horrify investigators and criminologists for decades.

Kemper was born on December 18, 1948, in Burbank, California. His childhood was marked by a volatile home environment. His parents, Clarnell and Edmund Jr., divorced when he was young. His mother was controlling and verbally abusive, frequently demeaning him and expressing resentment toward men in general. She reportedly locked him in the basement for long periods, fearing he would harm his two sisters. Even as a boy, Kemper showed signs of deep psychological disturbance. He decapitated his sister's dolls, fantasized about killing his mother, and once buried a pet cat alive. He later killed another cat with a knife and stored its remains in his closet. These early behaviors, hallmarks of severe conduct disorder, were warning signs few paid attention to at the time.

By age 15, Kemper had run away from home and made his way to his father's house, only to find his father had remarried and had no place for him. He was eventually sent to live with his paternal grandparents in rural North Fork, California. It was there, in 1964, that Kemper committed his first murders. During an argument, he shot his grandmother in the head and then stabbed her repeatedly after she was dead. He then killed his grandfather when he returned home, stating that he didn't want him to see what he had done to his wife. The calculated nature of the killings shocked even seasoned authorities.

Kemper was just 15 years old, but the crime was so brutal that he was diagnosed as a paranoid schizophrenic and committed to the Atascadero State Hospital, a maximum-security facility for the criminally insane. There, he underwent extensive psychological testing and therapy. Over the years, his diagnosis shifted. Doctors eventually concluded he was not psychotic but had a personality disorder marked by high intelligence, emotional detachment, and an obsessive need for control. He learned to manipulate staff, earning privileges and gaining access to sensitive psychological information. Ironically, Kemper assisted in administering tests to other inmates, absorbing clinical insight into how to appear rehabilitated.

At 21, he was released on parole, against the recommendations of several hospital staff members. Astonishingly, he was released into the custody of his mother, Clarnell Strandberg, the same person who had fueled much of his psychological instability.

The decision would prove disastrous. Though he seemed to lead a quiet life on the surface, working various jobs and attending community college, Kemper was unraveling internally. He purchased a car, which he fitted with police scanners, handcuffs, and weapons. He began picking up female hitchhikers, initially releasing them unharmed. But the fantasy of murder began to overtake him again.

Between May 1972 and April 1973, Kemper embarked on a killing spree that would leave at least six young women dead. His method was almost always the same: he would pick up college-aged hitchhikers along the highways near Santa Cruz, drive them to remote areas, and kill them, often by shooting, strangling, or bludgeoning.

He would then engage in post-mortem s**ual activity with their bodies, sometimes dismembering them and removing their heads. He disposed of the remains in ravines, wooded areas, or even outside police stations, in what he later described as a test of his cunning.

Kemper referred to these victims as "co-eds," a term he used clinically, stripping them of individuality. He admitted to driving around with their decapitated heads in his car and speaking to them, a grotesque attempt at achieving the intimacy he could not find with living people. Some heads he buried in his backyard, facing upward toward his mother's bedroom window, stating that he wanted his mother to be able to "look up to them."

Despite the horror of the crimes, no one suspected him. He was calm, cooperative with local law enforcement, and even frequented a bar called The Jury Room, where he socialized with police officers and discussed the ongoing investigation. He seemed to relish being close to the hunt.

In many ways, Kemper was playing a long game, testing the system that had once declared him rehabilitated. He kept track of media coverage and refined his methods based on what he read and heard.

The killings culminated in an act that Kemper later described as inevitable. On April 20, 1973, he bludgeoned his mother to death with a claw hammer while she slept. He then decapitated her, performed s**ual acts with the severed head, and placed it on a shelf. He stuffed her vocal cords into the garbage disposal, explaining that she had spent her life "screaming at him." Afterward, he invited one of his mother's friends to the house, killed her as well, and fled the state.

Three days later, while in Pueblo, Colorado, Kemper called police and confessed to the murders. At first, they didn't believe him. He had to call back multiple times before authorities finally took him seriously. When arrested, he was calm and cooperative. He provided detailed confessions, describing each crime with disturbing precision and emotional distance. He seemed less interested in denying guilt than in making sure he was fully understood.

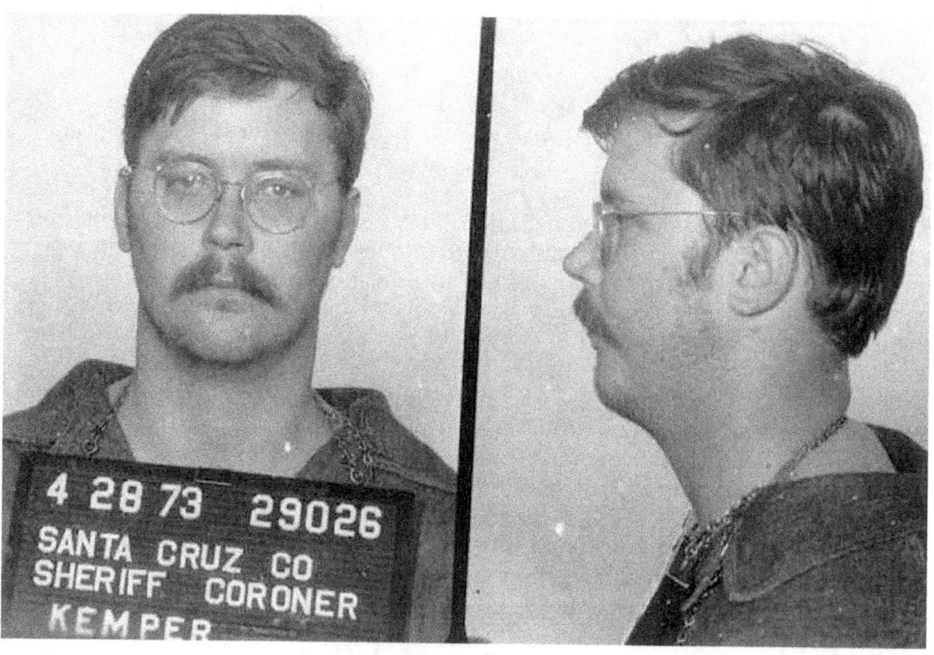

Kemper was indicted on eight counts of first-degree murder. He was found legally sane and pled guilty. In November 1973, he was sentenced to life imprisonment without the possibility of parole and was sent to California Medical Facility in Vacaville. There, he became a model prisoner. He read books onto tape for the blind, worked in the prison library, and granted interviews to psychologists, journalists, and criminologists. In many of these sessions, he discussed his crimes with chilling candor, providing insight into his motives, thought processes, and the roots of his violent fantasies.

What set Kemper apart was not only the brutality of his crimes but the way he analyzed them. He spoke in terms of control, inadequacy, and anger, particularly toward women and his mother. He described his killings as "possessions," moments when he could freeze time, silence criticism, and create a world where he was in command. His intelligence and introspection made him a prime case study for behavioral science.

FBI profilers, including those in the Behavioral Science Unit at Quantico, interviewed Kemper extensively to better understand serial homicide. He became a real-world example of what the FBI would later term an "organized killer," one who plans meticulously, charms victims, and leaves little trace.

Kemper's crimes coincided with a wave of serial killings in California in the early 1970s. At the same time he was active, the state was also contending with killers like Herbert Mullin and John Linley Frazier.

Santa Cruz, in particular, became known as the "murder capital of the world." But whereas Mullin was overtly psychotic and delusional, and Frazier believed he was acting under divine command, Kemper's killings were cold, rationalized, and deeply personal. He didn't kill out of ideology or hallucination. He killed to resolve rage and humiliation, especially the feelings projected onto his mother and the women he associated with her.

Though he has been eligible for parole several times, Kemper has consistently waived his right to a hearing. He has said he does not believe he should ever be released. His case continues to be studied in law enforcement and psychological circles, not only because of the scale and savagery of his crimes, but because of how lucidly he reflects on them. He is a serial killer who understands exactly what he is, and who has explained, in painful and clinical detail, how he came to be that way.

As of now, Edmund Kemper remains incarcerated in California. He is aging, physically weakened, and rarely makes public appearances or statements. Yet his influence endures. He has been featured in films, documentaries, and television shows, and his interviews have become required material in courses on abnormal psychology and criminal profiling.

In a grim sense, he has become a mirror, reflecting what happens when deep psychological wounds are left untreated, when early violence is ignored, and when a person chooses to respond to pain not with healing, but with destruction.

Albert DeSalvo

In the early 1960s, a series of murders cast a dark shadow over Boston. Women across the city were being found strangled in their apartments, often posed in disturbing ways, with signs of s**ual assault. There were no signs of forced entry, few patterns in victim type, and little forensic evidence to tie the scenes together. The killer's ability to move through the city undetected earned him a name that would haunt Boston for decades: the Boston Strangler.

For years, fear ruled the city. Police were overwhelmed. The public was desperate for answers. Then, in 1965, a man named Albert DeSalvo confessed to the crimes. But the case that seemed to be resolved only raised more questions.

Albert Henry DeSalvo was born on September 3, 1931, in Chelsea, Massachusetts, into a life already marked by violence. His father was an alcoholic who reportedly beat his wife and children with belts, fists, and broomsticks. By some accounts, DeSalvo watched his father break his mother's fingers one by one.

In other cases, he reportedly rented his wife out for s** while the children watched. This chaotic, abusive household shaped DeSalvo's view of women, power, and control from an early age.

As a child, DeSalvo showed classic signs of antisocial behavior. He tortured animals, stole, and became known as a chronic liar. He was first arrested at the age of 12 for theft. Over the next few years, he spent time in various juvenile facilities. Despite his early criminal activity, DeSalvo presented as personable and cooperative to authority figures. He seemed to crave approval, even as his actions became more disturbing. He enlisted in the U.S. Army in 1948 and served in Germany. While abroad, he married and started a family. Upon returning to the U.S., he attempted to lead a normal life, taking jobs as a factory worker and door-to-door salesman. But beneath the surface, DeSalvo's compulsions were escalating.

Before his name was connected to the Boston Strangler case, DeSalvo had already earned a disturbing reputation as the "Measuring Man." In the late 1950s, women in the Boston area reported being approached by a man claiming to work for a modeling agency. He would tell them they had the right body type for fashion work, then ask to take their measurements. Under the guise of professionalism, he would fondle their bodies and make s**ual remarks. Police eventually identified the perpetrator as DeSalvo, who admitted to hundreds of similar acts. He was arrested and served time but was released early for good behavior. This pattern, committing invasive, disturbing acts while appearing well-mannered and cooperative, would repeat in more chilling form just a few years later.

Between June 1962 and January 1964, at least 13 women between the ages of 19 and 85 were found murdered in the Boston area. Most had been s**ually assaulted and strangled, often with items of their own clothing. Some were stabbed. Others had been assaulted postmortem. The killer often left the bodies posed with legs spread and arms arranged, sometimes with decorative objects placed nearby. There were inconsistencies that puzzled investigators. Some women were elderly, others young. Some were white, others Black. Methods of killing varied. Yet there were also recurring elements: ligatures tied in complex knots, signs of s**ual sadism, and no signs of forced entry, suggesting the victims had willingly let the killer into their homes.

The press dubbed the killer "The Boston Strangler," and the name took hold. Panic swept the city. Women were afraid to answer the door. Lock sales surged. Self-defense classes filled up. The police had no solid leads, and their public appeals often revealed how little progress they were making. The lack of consistency between victims made it difficult to definitively link the crimes, but the fear of a serial killer gripped Boston and persisted long after the murders appeared to stop.

DeSalvo's eventual confession to being the Boston Strangler came almost by accident. In 1964, he was arrested for a series of violent s**ual assaults known as the "Green Man" rapes. These attacks had occurred throughout Massachusetts, often in daylight, with the offender gaining entry by posing as a maintenance worker or housing official. DeSalvo had used this ruse to assault dozens of women.

Once in custody, he confessed not only to these crimes but, surprisingly, to the Boston Strangler murders. His confession came during psychiatric interviews at Bridgewater State Hospital, where he was being evaluated for the Green Man assaults. He shared details of the murders that had not been made public (specific bindings, victim positions, apartment layouts) leading some investigators to believe he was the killer.

DeSalvo's descriptions of the crimes were chillingly accurate, but there were also inconsistencies. In some cases, his account of events didn't match the crime scene reports. He could not always identify the victims or remember specific dates. He gave details that were already public or that might have been inferred from newspaper coverage. Critics argued that DeSalvo was feeding off the notoriety, trying to secure fame through infamy. Supporters pointed to his knowledge of crime scene specifics and his tone of remorse. He didn't seem boastful; he seemed exhausted.

Regardless, there was a major complication: DeSalvo was never formally charged with any of the Boston Strangler murders. There was no physical evidence linking him to the crime scenes. Instead, he was convicted and sentenced to life in prison for the Green Man assaults.

His confessions were controversial from the start. Some law enforcement officials believed he was the killer. Others did not. The lack of physical evidence, the inconsistencies in his statements, and the different MOs used across the murders cast doubt. Multiple investigators suspected that more than one killer had been responsible for the crimes.

Some believed that DeSalvo had killed some, but not all, of the Strangler's victims. Others thought he had fabricated his involvement entirely, perhaps coached by fellow inmates or manipulated by his attorney. The question of whether Albert DeSalvo was the Boston Strangler became one of the most hotly debated issues in American criminal history.

DeSalvo's own behavior in prison only deepened the mystery. He recanted parts of his confession, then reaffirmed them. He expressed fear for his life and requested to be transferred to a different facility.

On November 25, 1973, he was found stabbed to death in his cell at Walpole State Prison. The killing was never solved. Some believed it was the result of a dispute with other inmates. Others speculated that he had been silenced. Without a trial or formal conviction for the murders, DeSalvo's death left the case in permanent limbo.

In 2013, decades after the murders, new DNA testing shed light on at least part of the mystery. Biological evidence from the 1964 murder of 19-year-old Mary Sullivan, long believed to be the last victim of the Boston Strangler, was tested using advanced forensic methods. The DNA found at the scene matched Albert DeSalvo's profile, confirmed by testing his exhumed remains.

For the first time, physical evidence tied DeSalvo directly to one of the victims. But even this confirmation raised questions. If he had killed Mary Sullivan, did that mean he had killed the others? Or was he a copycat who mirrored an earlier set of killings? The answer remains unsettled.

The legacy of the Boston Strangler case is one of fear, confusion, and ongoing controversy. It exposed the limitations of forensic science in the 1960s, the fragility of confessions as evidence, and the risk of rushing to closure in the face of public panic. Albert DeSalvo was a deeply disturbed man with a long history of s**ual violence and manipulation. His own statements (disjointed, often contradictory) suggested both a need to confess and a need to control the narrative. He wasn't insane in the legal sense, but his compulsions were extreme and violent, driven by a need to dominate and degrade.

To this day, some believe the Boston Strangler was not a single person, but a convenient label applied to a series of unrelated or loosely connected crimes. Others see DeSalvo's confession and subsequent DNA confirmation as proof that he was the man who terrorized Boston.

What is clear is that Albert DeSalvo was a dangerous s**ual predator who committed dozens of attacks and at least one murder with certainty. Whether he was the only killer behind the infamous string of strangulations remains one of the most enduring mysteries in American crime history.

H. H. Holmes

Long before the term "serial killer" entered the American lexicon, one man's crimes would set the template for a new breed of murderer, one who killed not in rage, but by design. His real name was Herman Webster Mudgett, but he is remembered by the name he gave himself: Dr. Henry Howard Holmes. Known simply as H. H. Holmes, he is widely regarded as America's first known serial killer. His name is forever linked to Chicago's 1893 World's Fair, a spectacle of innovation and wonder that stood in stark contrast to the horrors Holmes carried out just a few miles away. The so-called "Murder Castle" he designed and operated became the stuff of legend, filled with hidden passages, soundproof rooms, gas chambers, and incinerators. Fact and fiction have long blurred around Holmes, but what remains undeniable is his place at the origin of America's long fascination with the intelligent, manipulative, and lethal predator hiding in plain sight.

Born on May 16, 1861, in Gilmanton, New Hampshire, Herman Mudgett grew up in a strict and religious household. His father was a violent alcoholic who believed strongly in discipline and punishment. Holmes later claimed he had been bullied as a child and described an early fascination with skeletons and death. These stories, whether embellished or true, fit the pattern of later behavior that would blend cruelty, detachment, and a need for control. He was reportedly intelligent and studious, with a particular interest in medicine and anatomy. As a teenager, he was suspected of killing animals and once allegedly lured a friend into a trap to witness the dissection of a bird. The theme of manipulation followed him throughout his life.

Holmes attended medical school at the University of Michigan, where he honed both his knowledge of human anatomy and his skills as a con artist. While in school, he stole cadavers, disfigured them, and posed them as accident victims in insurance scams.

The schemes were relatively simple: take out a policy on a fictitious person, provide a mutilated corpse, collect the payout, and move on. This early blending of death and profit would become a hallmark of his life. He graduated in 1884 and moved frequently, always leaving behind suspicious debts, allegations, and rumors.

Eventually, he arrived in Chicago in 1886, now going by the name H. H. Holmes. He presented himself as a charming, well-educated doctor and soon secured work in a pharmacy on the city's South Side. Within a short time, he purchased the pharmacy, allegedly after the mysterious disappearance of the original owners, and began acquiring adjacent property.

Over the next several years, Holmes would construct what would later be known as the "Murder Castle," a three-story building filled with bizarre features: windowless rooms, trapdoors, hidden staircases, soundproof walls, gas lines controlled from secret panels, and a basement outfitted with surgical tables, vats of acid, and a crematorium.

Holmes claimed the building was intended to serve as a hotel for visitors to the upcoming 1893 World's Columbian Exposition. In reality, it was a labyrinth designed for concealment and control. Workers hired to build the castle were frequently dismissed and replaced so that no one had a full understanding of the structure. Rooms were built and rebuilt, hallways led to nowhere, and some doors opened into brick walls. Holmes's meticulous planning was such that no one could navigate the building except him.

During the lead-up to and during the World's Fair, Holmes lured numerous victims to his building under a variety of pretexts. Many were young women looking for work, lured in by advertisements offering lodging, jobs, or modeling opportunities. Others were his employees, often required to take out life insurance policies naming Holmes as the beneficiary. Once inside, they were isolated, incapacitated, and killed, through gassing, strangulation, or chemical poisoning. Some were dismembered. Others were burned in the basement incinerator. Still others were reduced to skeletons and sold to medical schools under false documentation. Holmes exploited every part of the human body for personal gain.

It is impossible to determine how many people Holmes killed. He confessed to 27 murders but later retracted some of the confessions. Historians believe the true number could be much higher, possibly over 100. Many of his victims simply

(The H.H. Holmes castle, demolished in 1938. The site was later redeveloped and eventually became a U.S. Post Office, which still occupies the location today.)

vanished, never seen again after answering an advertisement or moving into his hotel. The transient nature of life in late 19th-century America, combined with poor recordkeeping and Holmes's skill at fraud, allowed him to operate unchecked for years.

Holmes's downfall came not directly from his murders, but from his scams. After the Fair ended, he left Chicago and continued to defraud insurance companies, sell stolen goods, and swindle business partners.

One such scheme involved a man named Benjamin Pitezel, whom Holmes convinced to fake his own death in order to collect a life insurance policy. Holmes later killed Pitezel for real, likely to eliminate a witness, and then killed three of Pitezel's children as well. These murders, unlike his earlier ones, left a trail.

Authorities began to investigate. Detective Frank Geyer of the Philadelphia police followed Holmes's movements across several states, uncovering the remains of the Pitezel children in rented homes. The discovery shocked the public and finally led to Holmes's arrest in 1894 in Boston. As investigators went deeper into his background, they uncovered the horrors of the Chicago castle. Police found bones, clothing, and chemical vats filled with body parts in the building's basement. The media dubbed it a "house of horrors," and Holmes quickly became a national sensation. The idea that a man could construct a building specifically for the purpose of murdering strangers defied comprehension.

At trial, Holmes was calm, composed, and articulate. He represented himself in court and appeared to revel in the attention. He confessed to numerous murders, then recanted, then confessed again. His story changed with each retelling. He claimed he was possessed by the devil. He claimed he killed only out of necessity. He also claimed he was a victim of circumstance. His contradictory statements did little to help his case. He was convicted of the murder of Benjamin Pitezel and sentenced to death.

While awaiting execution, Holmes wrote an autobiography titled *Holmes' Own Story*, which was published and widely read. In it, he presented himself as a misunderstood genius, a wronged man, and a tragic figure. The book included portions of his confessions but painted them with ambiguity, further fueling public fascination. Even in captivity, Holmes manipulated the narrative. He wanted to be remembered not just as a killer, but as a man of intrigue, complexity, and criminal brilliance.

On May 7, 1896, Holmes was hanged at Moyamensing Prison in Philadelphia. His death was slow and gruesome; he did not die instantly, but instead strangled for over 15 minutes.

Before his execution, he requested that his body be buried in a coffin filled with cement and placed ten feet underground, fearing that grave robbers might steal his corpse for medical dissection, the same way he had profited from corpses. His request was granted.

Holmes's legacy is a tangle of myth, fear, and unresolved questions. While some historians have challenged the more extreme elements of his story (suggesting the number of victims may have been inflated, or the layout of the Murder Castle exaggerated) the core facts remain disturbing. He was a man who built a structure to facilitate murder, who preyed on the vulnerable, and who turned death into a business. He operated with confidence, intelligence, and an absence of empathy. Whether he killed dozens or hundreds, Holmes stands as a foundational figure in the study of serial crime.

The case also marked a turning point in American culture. Holmes represented the dark side of the American dream: a man who rose from obscurity, used charm and ingenuity to accumulate wealth, and left a trail of destruction in his wake. He was one of the first killers to be turned into a media spectacle, with newspapers printing his face, his stories, and his supposed genius alongside lurid descriptions of his crimes. He helped establish the trope of the sophisticated killer; the man who looks normal, even admirable, but hides monstrous urges beneath the surface.

For law enforcement, Holmes became a case study in the failure of fragmented policing. He committed crimes in multiple states, used false identities, and exploited the lack of communication between jurisdictions.

His fraud schemes were as dangerous as his murders, creating a network of deceit that protected him for years. In response, American law enforcement began to evolve, gradually adopting more centralized systems for tracking suspects and sharing information.

In the years since, the Murder Castle has become a fixture of true crime lore. The building was partially demolished after Holmes's arrest and later burned down under suspicious circumstances. No complete floor plan remains. Yet its image (a house with secret rooms, gas lines, and death traps) has become iconic. Whether every detail of the structure is accurate is less important than what it represents: the idea that someone could design a building as an instrument of murder and hide it in plain sight.

Today, H. H. Holmes is remembered as the archetype of the American serial killer. His life and crimes have been the subject of books, television series, and even speculative claims linking him to Jack the Ripper, a theory widely discredited but illustrative of his mythic stature.

He is a symbol of pre-modern horror, a man whose cruelty anticipated the cold rationality that would characterize so many killers of the 20th century. He killed for money, for power, and for the thrill of control. And he did so not in the shadows, but while running a business, making small talk, and shaking hands with the people who never suspected a thing.

Andrei Chikatilo

The collapse of the Soviet Union revealed many secrets: economic stagnation, political repression, widespread corruption. But perhaps none were as grotesque or deeply buried as the crimes of Andrei Romanovich Chikatilo, the man who came to be known as the "Butcher of Rostov." Over a span of twelve years, from 1978 to 1990, Chikatilo brutally murdered, mutilated, and in many cases cannibalized at least 52 victims across the Soviet Union. Men, women, and children fell prey to his compulsions.

His killing spree exposed not only the depths of human depravity but also the systemic failures of Soviet policing, secrecy, and forensic science. The case would go on to reshape criminal investigation in post-Soviet states and stands as one of the most disturbing chapters in the history of modern serial murder.

Chikatilo was born on October 16, 1936, in the Ukrainian village of Yabluchne, during a time of devastating famine caused by Stalin's forced collectivization policies. Known as the Holodomor, the famine killed millions and left lasting scars across the population. His early years were marked by starvation, trauma, and humiliation. Chikatilo claimed that his older brother had been kidnapped and cannibalized during the famine, though this was never confirmed. He grew up hearing constant stories of deprivation and terror, and his formative environment was saturated with paranoia and scarcity.

His father, a soldier in the Red Army, was later captured during World War II and labeled a traitor upon return, further stigmatizing the family. At school, Chikatilo was shy, thin, and nearsighted. He suffered from chronic bedwetting and was frequently bullied. He later described himself as a "mother's boy" who was mocked for his physical weakness and introversion. Compounding these issues was a condition he carried into adulthood: s**ual impotence. His first known s**ual experience, as a teenager, occurred when he ejaculated while struggling with a girl during a non-consensual encounter. The fusion of arousal, humiliation, and violence left a psychological imprint that would shape his entire life.

As an adult, Chikatilo attempted to live a respectable life. He joined the Communist Party, graduated with a degree in Russian literature, and worked as a teacher. He married and had children, though the marriage was reportedly unfulfilling and s**ually dysfunctional.

Despite his respectable exterior, problems soon emerged. Students accused him of inappropriate behavior, including fondling and voyeurism. He was eventually dismissed from several teaching jobs, but each time he managed to find new employment thanks to lax recordkeeping and his membership in the Party. He later took a job as a supply clerk for a construction firm in Shakhty, a mining town in the Rostov Oblast. It was here that his killing began.

His first known murder occurred in December 1978. The victim was a nine-year-old girl named Yelena Zakotnova. Chikatilo lured her to an abandoned house, where he attempted to s**ually assault her. When she resisted, he stabbed her repeatedly, deriving s**ual satisfaction from the act of killing. He later dumped her body in a river. A young man was arrested for the crime, confessed under intense pressure, and was executed. Chikatilo, meanwhile, went free, having learned that murder could both fulfill his desires and remain undetected.

Over the next several years, Chikatilo perfected his technique. He targeted runaways, vagrants, s** workers, and children, anyone who appeared vulnerable and who would not be missed.

His approach was consistent: he would lure victims near train stations or marketplaces with promises of food, money, or shelter. Once isolated, he would attack them: stabbing, bludgeoning, biting, and often mutilating their bodies. He frequently gouged out eyes, believing in an old superstition that victims' eyes retained the image of their killer. Some bodies were partially eaten. He would later admit to drinking the blood of several victims.

The brutality of his killings shocked even hardened investigators. Many victims were found with dozens of stab wounds, deep bite marks, and genitals mutilated. Yet the Soviet press reported almost nothing. The state denied the existence of serial killers, viewing them as a capitalist phenomenon. Officials were reluctant to admit that such evil could exist in a society built on socialist ideals. This ideological rigidity allowed Chikatilo to keep killing. He moved from town to town, targeting strangers, often using the Soviet railway system to cover great distances. He was careful not to return to the same locations too often, making it difficult for police to identify a pattern.

Despite the secrecy, a special task force was eventually formed to investigate the growing number of unexplained murders. Dubbed "Operation Forest Path," the unit worked under extreme limitations. There was no centralized DNA database, no computerized criminal profiles, and limited forensic resources.

Early on, the task force arrested a number of suspects. Several of them confessed under torture or duress. At least one was executed before Chikatilo was ever seriously considered.

In 1984, Chikatilo was briefly arrested after acting suspiciously near a Rostov train station. He was found with a knife and rope in his bag, and blood stains on his clothing. He was detained and tested, but the semen samples from the crime scenes did not match. Soviet testing procedures were flawed and outdated; at the time, investigators were unaware that Chikatilo's blood type and semen type did not match, a rare biological anomaly that allowed him to slip through their net.

He continued killing throughout the late 1980s. Victim after victim was found in wooded areas, near train lines, or in abandoned lots. The murders became more frequent, more frenzied. His confidence grew, even as the KGB and local police expanded their surveillance. Still, political pressure discouraged open acknowledgment of a serial killer operating in the region.

It wasn't until 1990 that Chikatilo was finally caught. After years of mounting pressure, improved coordination among agencies, and enhanced surveillance, investigators began focusing on frequent train travelers and known s** offenders. They placed undercover agents near train stations and wooded areas.

On November 6, 1990, Chikatilo was spotted acting suspiciously at a Rostov station. He was brought in for questioning. This time, investigators had better tools, more experienced profilers, and enough circumstantial evidence to hold him.

Chikatilo initially denied everything, but after several days of interrogation, he confessed. Over the course of multiple interviews, he admitted to killing 52 people. He described the murders in chilling detail, explaining his techniques, his fantasies, and his psychological compulsions. He said that killing made him feel powerful, s**ually alive, and in control. He told investigators that the act of stabbing and mutilating gave him the release he couldn't achieve through normal s**ual activity. He was not insane in the traditional sense, as he knew what he was doing was wrong, but he was driven by urges he could not suppress.

He was formally charged with 53 counts of murder, including one case where he later denied responsibility. His trial began in 1992 and quickly became a national spectacle. Chikatilo was placed in a steel cage during court proceedings, both for his own safety and to contain his behavior. He frequently interrupted the trial with outbursts, insults, and bizarre statements. He exposed himself, screamed at the judge, and declared that he was the victim of a vast conspiracy. Psychiatrists evaluated him and concluded that he suffered from borderline personality disorder with sadistic features, but that he was competent to stand trial.

The courtroom was packed with families of victims, reporters, and members of the public. Chikatilo showed little remorse. He often appeared smug, indifferent, or mocking. Witnesses wept as they described the loss of their loved ones. Prosecutors presented overwhelming forensic and testimonial evidence. In October 1992, he was found guilty on 52 counts of murder and sentenced to death. The courtroom erupted in applause.

Chikatilo spent the next two years on death row. He was executed by a single gunshot behind the right ear on February 14, 1994, at a prison in Novocherkassk. His death closed the case, but the horror he inflicted continues to reverberate. The scale of his crimes, the brutality of his methods, and the sheer length of time he operated make him one of the most lethal serial killers in modern history.

The Chikatilo case had far-reaching consequences. It exposed the systemic failures of Soviet policing; how ideology overruled practicality, how forensics were underdeveloped, and how innocent people were sacrificed to maintain the illusion of control. His case also led to significant reforms in criminal investigation, forensic science, and interagency cooperation in Russia and surrounding states.

From a psychological standpoint, Chikatilo remains a case study in complex pathology. He wasn't driven by trauma alone, though his early life was filled with it. He wasn't a sadist purely for pleasure, though he took immense satisfaction in violence. He was a man who found s**ual release only through the degradation and destruction of others, and who maintained the appearance of normalcy (family man, party member, teacher) while killing again and again. He is often described as an "organized-disorganized" hybrid: calculating in his planning, frenzied in execution.

Andrei Chikatilo was a product of repression: personal, political, and s**ual. He operated in the shadows of a society that denied the existence of people like him, and he used that denial to prolong his crimes. His name now sits beside the darkest in criminal history, not because of how he died, but because of how many suffered before anyone dared to believe that such a killer could exist.

Pedro López

Pedro Alonso López remains one of the most disturbing figures in the annals of criminal history. Dubbed the "Monster of the Andes," López confessed to murdering hundreds of young girls across Colombia, Ecuador, and Peru during the 1970s and early 1980s. Although exact numbers remain uncertain, authorities verified dozens of bodies buried where he directed them, lending credibility to his own claims of over 300 victims. His story is not only one of personal pathology but of institutional failure, social invisibility, and cross-border impunity. López exploited some of the most vulnerable populations in South America, often without detection, for years.

He was born on October 8, 1948, in Santa Isabel, a mountainous region in Colombia's Tolima department. The seventh of thirteen children, López came into the world under harsh conditions. His mother, a s** worker, struggled to provide stability. His father was reportedly killed in a civil conflict before López was born. From an early age, he experienced chronic neglect, poverty, and abuse. As a child, he reportedly witnessed violence in the home and was subjected to frequent beatings. By age eight, his mother expelled him from the home after she caught him in an inappropriate situation with his younger sister. Homeless and vulnerable, López became a street child in Bogotá, where survival was precarious and predation was common.

The experiences López had on the streets shaped his psychological development in profound ways. He later claimed that he was repeatedly assaulted by strangers and other homeless youth. These years of marginalization likely deepened his mistrust of authority and intensified a desire for control. By the time he was a teenager, López was already engaging in theft and petty crimes. At age 18, he was incarcerated for auto theft. While imprisoned, he reported being assaulted by other inmates. He later claimed to have killed several of them in retaliation, although this account remains unverified.

After his release, López began to drift through South America. The killings began in the early 1970s and escalated in frequency and brutality over the next decade. His victims were nearly always girls between the ages of eight and twelve. He specifically targeted children from impoverished, rural, or indigenous communities, individuals unlikely to be quickly missed or rigorously searched for. He often approached them in markets or near schools, sometimes pretending to be lost or offering candy, toys, or small jobs. Once alone with them, López would assault and kill them, typically by strangulation. He then disposed of their bodies in remote locations or shallow graves. The simplicity of his methods, combined with his mobility and the under-resourced law enforcement agencies in these countries, allowed him to avoid detection for years.

What is particularly disturbing is López's consistency. He was not erratic or disorganized. His pattern was deliberate and honed. He followed a geographic progression, moving from Colombia to Ecuador and then to Peru. In each place, he repeated the same process: seek out vulnerable communities, establish a temporary base, identify victims, and leave before suspicion could mount. His crimes remained largely invisible, in part because of the sociopolitical context.

These countries, during that era, faced internal conflict, weak forensic systems, and fragmented police coordination. Reports of missing children were frequent, but follow-through was limited. López understood this landscape and used it to his advantage.

The turning point came in 1980, in Ambato, Ecuador, when an attempted abduction failed. A young girl escaped, and angry locals apprehended López. He was turned over to police, and under questioning, he began to confess, first to a handful of murders, then to dozens, and eventually to more than 300. At first, investigators were skeptical. The scope seemed unbelievable.

But when López began guiding them to gravesites across multiple provinces, authorities uncovered dozens of remains. Many of the victims matched existing reports of missing girls. López provided details only the perpetrator could have known.

Ecuadorian authorities charged him with the confirmed murders of 57 girls, although he was suspected in many more. Under Ecuadorian law at the time, the maximum prison sentence, even for multiple murders, was 16 years. He was convicted and sent to prison in 1983. Throughout his incarceration, López maintained a calm and cooperative demeanor. He spoke to investigators and journalists alike with chilling composure, offering clinical descriptions of his crimes without remorse. In interviews, he referred to his victims in disturbingly detached language, expressing no empathy or guilt.

Psychological evaluations conducted during this period described López as exhibiting antisocial traits, manipulative behavior, and profound emotional detachment. Some examiners noted that his ability to speak eloquently about his crimes without showing affect suggested either psychopathy or severe dissociation. What remained striking was his self-justification. López portrayed himself as a victim of childhood abuse and societal neglect, and he claimed his violence was an act of retribution against a world that had hurt him. However, such narratives, while possibly reflective of internal delusion, did not align with any form of mental illness that would absolve him of criminal responsibility.

In 1994, López was released from prison after serving just 14 years, two years short of the maximum sentence, due to good behavior. He was declared rehabilitated by prison officials and transferred to Colombian authorities, where he faced additional charges. In Colombia, he was held briefly, evaluated for mental illness, and placed in a psychiatric facility.

After one year, he was declared sane and released on $50 bail. Despite Colombian prosecutors' efforts to reopen cases and detain him further, the legal framework at the time provided little recourse.

López's release was met with outrage across South America. Families of victims, journalists, and human rights organizations questioned how a man who had confessed to such an immense number of murders could be allowed to walk free. Ecuadorian law was later amended to allow longer sentences for serial murder, in part due to public reaction to López's case. Yet those changes came too late to affect his fate.

After 1998, López disappeared. His whereabouts remain unknown. Some reports claim he was re-arrested under a false identity. Others allege he may have resumed killing. However, no confirmed sightings or charges have emerged since. In official records, he remains at large.

The López case revealed deep systemic vulnerabilities. It exposed the fragility of international coordination in tracking violent offenders, particularly in developing nations with limited resources. It also illustrated how legal limitations, such as sentencing caps or lack of forensic databases, can hinder justice even when guilt is certain. Perhaps most sobering was the realization that a serial killer could exploit poverty and marginalization so effectively that hundreds of victims could vanish with minimal public notice.

López's victims, many of whom remain unidentified, came from communities where infrastructure was weak and attention to missing persons was sporadic. This silence was not just institutional but cultural. In rural regions of Ecuador, Colombia, and Peru, where distrust of government and police was common, families often did not report disappearances or lacked the means to do so. Girls were expected to be self-reliant from a young age, increasing their vulnerability to manipulation. López targeted this social blind spot precisely because it allowed him to act without detection.

In terms of criminology, López's case defied some established expectations. Unlike many serial killers who seek infamy or challenge law enforcement, López did not attempt to insert himself into investigations or play mind games with the public. He did not appear to be seeking recognition during the time he was active. His killing was compulsive and repetitive, focused entirely on gratification and control. He did not vary his methods significantly, nor did he escalate in sophistication. His killings were opportunistic, guided by routine rather than elaborate planning.

From a psychological standpoint, López fits within the category of organized serial predator, though his mobility and geographic scope were unusually broad. He selected victims based on predictable vulnerabilities, showed an ability to control his environment, and evaded law enforcement for years. However, his ability to rationalize his actions and his lack of emotional reaction to their consequences suggested a degree of moral disengagement that many experts found hard to categorize. His detached manner in interviews, his apparent comfort with recounting acts of violence, and his lack of internal conflict indicated someone who had long since normalized what he was doing.

Today, López is rarely mentioned alongside more publicized figures from North America or Europe, yet his case is arguably more chilling. It involved hundreds of children, widespread geographic activity, and institutional collapse at multiple levels.

His story is less about the individual pathology of a killer and more about the context that allowed him to operate. It forces a confrontation with uncomfortable realities, about inequality, oversight, and the way some lives are valued less than others.

The legacy of Pedro López isn't only found in forensic files or true crime documentaries, but in the legal reforms and awareness campaigns that followed his release. His crimes spurred international discussions about cross-border cooperation, data sharing, and the need for more robust systems to monitor s**ual and violent offenders. Perhaps most significantly, his case led to a renewed focus on the rights and safety of children in rural and underserved communities.

The mystery of his whereabouts continues to haunt those who study violent crime. Whether López is alive or dead, in hiding or once again preying on the vulnerable, the fact that so many of his crimes remain unresolved casts a long shadow. For the families of victims, there is little closure. Many never recovered the remains of their daughters or received formal confirmation of what happened. Their grief exists in the space between confession and proof, acknowledgment and justice.

Pedro López remains one of the darkest figures in modern criminal history. Not because of how he looked, or how he spoke, but because of what he was allowed to do, and how long it took for anyone to stop him.

Harold Shipman

Among modern serial killers, Harold Shipman presents a singularly disturbing case. Unlike others who stalked dark alleys or targeted vulnerable victims in remote locations, Shipman operated in plain sight, under the respected title of "Doctor." A practicing general practitioner in the United Kingdom, he used his medical credentials not only as a shield but as a weapon. His crimes shattered public trust in medical authority and raised existential questions about the systems designed to protect life. Shipman's victims weren't hidden in shallow graves or abducted from city streets; they were elderly patients, often found peacefully dead in their own homes, with a physician's signature on their death certificate.

Born on January 14, 1946, in Nottingham, England, Harold Frederick Shipman was the second of four children in a working-class family. His father, a lorry driver, and his mother, Vera, were known to be strict, particularly Vera, who played a dominant role in Shipman's early upbringing. She reportedly held high ambitions for her son and instilled in him a sense of superiority over others, which may have contributed to his aloof and authoritarian personality later in life. When Vera developed terminal cancer, Shipman, then a teenager, took on a caretaker role. He closely observed the administration of morphine, the same substance he would later use to end lives, and witnessed her slow decline. Her death in 1963 had a profound effect on him and is often cited as a psychological inflection point.

Shipman pursued medicine at Leeds School of Medicine, qualifying as a doctor in 1970. His early medical career was promising but marred by his first brush with scandal. In 1975, while working at a practice in Todmorden, West Yorkshire, Shipman was caught forging prescriptions for pethidine, a powerful opioid he had become addicted to. He was fined, briefly entered rehab, and avoided being struck off the medical register. The incident, though serious, faded into obscurity, and by 1977, he had re-established himself as a GP in the market town of Hyde, Greater Manchester. Here, over the next two decades, he would kill an estimated 215 to 250 patients, though the real total may be even higher.

Unlike many serial killers, Shipman didn't seek thrill or notoriety in the conventional sense. His murders were quiet, methodical, and almost clinically detached. He chose victims who were typically elderly women, though some men were also targeted. Most were alone when they died, and nearly all had one thing in common: trust in their doctor. Shipman visited patients at home or treated them in his practice, often administering a lethal dose of diamorphine, a medical-grade heroin, and then recording their deaths as natural causes. In some cases, he falsely claimed the patient had been terminally ill or suffering from cardiac conditions.

His ability to conceal these deaths for so long was due in large part to the systems that enabled him. Doctors in the UK had the legal authority to certify deaths without post-mortem examination, particularly for elderly patients with no obvious signs of foul play.

Shipman exploited this authority, and because his patients were often already frail or elderly, their deaths raised little suspicion. In fact, many families were grateful that their loved ones had died peacefully under medical care. Few questioned the circumstances.

Patterns, however, eventually began to emerge. Shipman's practice recorded an unusually high number of patient deaths compared to others in the area. Many patients died shortly after house visits, often within an hour. Several local undertakers began to notice the frequency with which they were called to pick up bodies from Shipman's patients. Some even discussed concerns among themselves, but their suspicions were slow to translate into formal complaints. Shipman's professional demeanor and reputation as a diligent doctor created a psychological barrier to suspicion.

The real unraveling began in 1998 with the death of Kathleen Grundy, an active, well-known former mayor of Hyde. She was found dead in her home after a visit from Shipman. Despite her good health, Shipman declared her death natural and without need for post-mortem.

However, Grundy's daughter, a lawyer, grew suspicious after discovering a will, typed and signed, that left her mother's entire estate to Shipman. This document raised immediate red flags. Kathleen Grundy had not been known to use a typewriter and had never mentioned such a will.

The family contacted the police. Grundy's body was exhumed and found to contain a fatal dose of diamorphine. A handwriting expert concluded the will was forged. Shipman was arrested in September 1998. What followed was one of the most extensive murder investigations in British history. Police began reviewing records of deaths associated with Shipman's patients. As they cross-referenced medical notes, witness accounts, and prescribing patterns, a picture emerged of a long, uninterrupted killing spree.

In total, Shipman was charged with the murders of 15 patients between 1995 and 1998. The prosecution focused on this narrow window, knowing that proving earlier cases, many of which lacked preserved bodies, would be difficult.

At trial, prosecutors presented evidence of forged documents, altered medical notes, and testimony from families who described unexpected or implausible deaths. Shipman denied all charges, maintaining that he was simply a conscientious doctor misunderstood by a system he had faithfully served.

The jury was unconvinced. On January 31, 2000, Shipman was found guilty on all 15 counts of murder and one count of forgery. He was sentenced to life imprisonment without the possibility of parole. The presiding judge recommended that Shipman never be released, and the public largely agreed. The case dominated headlines in the UK and led to a national reckoning about how deaths are monitored, how medical professionals are held accountable, and how much trust should be placed in individual practitioners.

Following the trial, a public inquiry chaired by Dame Janet Smith reviewed more than 500 deaths attributed to Shipman's care. The inquiry concluded that he was likely responsible for at least 215 murders, though the number could be as high as 250. Some cases were impossible to confirm due to cremation, poor records, or lack of physical evidence. The inquiry also examined the structural failings that had allowed the crimes to continue unchecked. Among the findings were recommendations for reforming death certification, introducing better oversight of controlled substances, and instituting stronger accountability mechanisms within the National Health Service.

One of the most unsettling aspects of Shipman's crimes was their apparent lack of clear motive. Financial gain had a role in some cases, such as the forged will of Kathleen Grundy, but most murders involved no obvious benefit to Shipman. He didn't kill for revenge, political ideology, or even overt cruelty. His demeanor suggested a quiet assertion of control, an expression of power over life and death carried out in an environment that offered little resistance. Psychologists and criminologists proposed various theories, ranging from narcissistic personality traits to compulsive disorder rooted in childhood trauma, but no single explanation proved satisfactory. Shipman's psychology was as opaque as it was calculated.

On January 13, 2004, Harold Shipman was found dead in his cell at Wakefield Prison. He had hanged himself using bed sheets, the day before his 58th birthday. His suicide sparked renewed public anger. Many families felt cheated out of answers, and prison authorities faced criticism for not preventing his death. Others argued that his suicide was a final act of control, choosing his own end, just as he had chosen the end for so many others.

The case of Harold Shipman stands apart in the annals of serial crime. It wasn't just the number of victims or the duration of his crimes, but the context. He was not an outsider, a drifter, or a fringe figure. He was a doctor, trusted, respected, and professionally licensed. His patients welcomed him into their homes. They asked for his help. Many died within minutes of receiving it.

The lessons of Shipman's crimes extend beyond true crime literature or forensic case studies. His actions led to systemic reforms in the UK's healthcare system, including the introduction of the Controlled Drugs (Supervision of Management and Use) Regulations, tighter controls over the cremation process, and the creation of the National Clinical Assessment Authority. His story became a catalyst for rethinking professional oversight, reminding both the public and institutions that vigilance must be constant, even in places long assumed to be safe.

Harold Shipman is remembered not only as Britain's most prolific serial killer but as a cautionary figure, an embodiment of how trust, when unchecked, can be manipulated with devastating consequences. His crimes shook the foundation of medical ethics, exposed blind spots in regulatory systems, and forced a reckoning with the darkest corners of human behavior hiding in plain sight.

Jack the Ripper

Jack the Ripper is the most iconic unidentified serial killer in history. More than a century after the brutal murders that terrorized London's Whitechapel district in 1888, the name still evokes fascination and dread. The crimes attributed to him, five savage killings of women over just a few months, would be shocking in any era. But what elevates the case to near-mythic status isn't just the violence, but the enduring mystery. Despite countless investigations, theories, books, and forensic reconstructions, the Ripper's identity has never been conclusively proven. He has become a symbol of anonymous evil, a ghost that haunts both historical inquiry and public imagination.

The killings began in late August 1888 and ended abruptly in November of the same year. The five victims officially recognized as the "canonical" Ripper victims were Mary Ann Nichols, Annie Chapman, Elizabeth Stride, Catherine Eddowes, and Mary Jane Kelly. All were women engaged in prostitution or s** work and were killed at night in or near the slums of Whitechapel.

The brutality of the murders, particularly the postmortem mutilation, suggested not only rage, but a distinct and deliberate signature. Each scene became more grotesque than the last, culminating in a final murder so horrific that police wouldn't release the full details to the public.

The first known victim, Mary Ann Nichols, was discovered on the morning of August 31, 1888. Her throat had been cut, and her abdomen had been slashed. The location, Buck's Row (now Durward Street), was dimly lit and poorly patrolled. Just over a week later, on September 8, Annie Chapman was found in a backyard off Hanbury Street with her throat cut and her uterus removed. Police began to suspect that these killings weren't isolated incidents, but the work of a repeat offender.

The fear grew with the so-called "double event" of September 30. Elizabeth Stride was found dead but without the extensive mutilation that marked earlier crimes, leading many to believe the killer had been interrupted. Less than an hour later, Catherine Eddowes was found in Mitre Square. Her throat had been slashed, her face mutilated, and her kidney removed. The sudden escalation in violence and precision suggested to investigators that the killer may have had anatomical knowledge or training. At the time, the idea that a surgeon or butcher could be responsible became a widespread, and frightening, belief.

The final canonical victim, Mary Jane Kelly, was found on November 9, murdered in her own room in Miller's Court. She was the only victim killed indoors, and her body had been extensively mutilated and dismembered. The carnage surpassed all previous attacks and left detectives shaken. Her remains were barely recognizable. This final act, carried out in relative privacy and without the risk of street discovery, showed how much more time the killer had taken and how intensely personal the act had become.

Despite growing public pressure, the Metropolitan Police were unable to solve the case. Multiple suspects were arrested, questioned, and released. The police, press, and public all floated theories, some more grounded than others, but no one was ever formally charged. Letters signed "Jack the Ripper" began arriving at newspaper offices and police stations. Some were later considered hoaxes, but one letter, known as the "Dear Boss" letter, is considered potentially authentic and marked the first known use of the name "Jack the Ripper." The moniker stuck, fueling headlines and public fascination.

The failure to catch the killer had multiple causes. Victorian London was a city of stark inequality and overpopulation, particularly in the East End, where the murders occurred. Whitechapel was rife with poverty, prostitution, alcoholism, and overcrowding. It was a chaotic district where law enforcement struggled to maintain order. The lack of forensic science, poor communication between divisions, and limited investigative tools all hampered efforts. Crime scenes weren't preserved as they would be today. There were no fingerprints, no DNA testing, and no effective criminal profiling. Investigators relied heavily on eyewitness accounts, many of which were contradictory or unreliable.

Moreover, the public pressure created a frenzied environment that made methodical police work nearly impossible. The press capitalized on every detail, often distorting facts and inserting speculation into coverage. Competing newspapers sought to outdo

(The "Dear Boss" letter)

each other, sometimes fabricating letters or inventing details. The case became not just a criminal investigation but a media spectacle.

Despite this, the investigation was thorough by the standards of the time. Detectives interviewed thousands of people, conducted hundreds of house-to-house inquiries, and distributed flyers across the East End. The case was led by several senior figures, including Chief Inspector Donald Swanson and Detective Inspector Frederick Abberline. They considered dozens of suspects (doctors, barbers, sailors, and lunatics). Many of these names would echo through decades of Ripper lore, including Montague John Druitt, a barrister who drowned himself shortly after the last murder; Aaron Kosminski, a Polish-Jewish barber confined to an asylum; and Michael Ostrog, a career criminal and con man.

Each theory had its merits and weaknesses. Druitt's suicide was suspiciously timed but lacked forensic connection. Kosminski was mentally unstable and lived in the area, but there was no direct evidence linking him to the crimes. Others, such as

Francis Tumblety, a quack doctor with misogynistic leanings, were suspected but never charged. In 2014, a book claimed that mitochondrial DNA from a shawl found near a victim connected Kosminski to the killings, but the methodology and provenance of the shawl were hotly debated by experts. As of today, no theory has achieved consensus.

What makes the Ripper case particularly chilling is the silence that followed. After Mary Jane Kelly's murder, the killings stopped. Whether this was due to the killer dying, being incarcerated for another crime, or fleeing London remains unknown. Unlike many serial killers who seek attention, the Ripper never taunted police directly in person, never reappeared, and left no confirmed trace after November 1888.

Jack the Ripper's legacy is profound. He wasn't the first serial killer in history, but he was the first to emerge in an urban, industrialized society with a mass media capable of amplifying his crimes. His case shaped the development of modern criminal profiling and forensic psychology. The pattern of targeting vulnerable individuals in a concentrated area became a recognized typology.

In fact, the Ripper murders helped formalize the idea of a "serial killer" decades before the term existed. Investigators began to look for behavioral patterns, victimology, and geographical mapping, laying the groundwork for future casework.

The social impact of the murders was equally significant. The East End, long ignored by London's elite, suddenly found itself under scrutiny. The killings exposed not just the savagery of the crimes but the squalor of life in places like Whitechapel. Public outcry led to debates in Parliament about policing, poverty, and social reform. Charitable organizations mobilized, and calls for urban renewal grew louder. Though little changed immediately, the Ripper murders revealed the hidden world of those left behind by Victorian prosperity.

Culturally, Jack the Ripper became an enduring figure of fascination. He appears in fiction, film, and popular culture in countless forms, from horror novels to conspiracy theories involving royalty and the Freemasons. Unlike other historical killers whose stories lose relevance, the Ripper endures because he was never caught. His anonymity invites projection, interpretation, and myth-making. He is a cipher upon whom society places its fears, of strangers, of institutions failing, of violence that can't be understood.

More than a century after the crimes, forensic experts, historians, and amateur sleuths continue to investigate the case. New technologies, including geographic profiling, digital reconstructions, and mitochondrial DNA analysis, have been applied to the available evidence. While some researchers remain hopeful that the Ripper's identity may one day be conclusively determined, others believe the case is unsolvable. Too much time has passed, records are incomplete, and forensic contamination too widespread. In that sense, Jack the Ripper is as much a mystery as he is a murderer.

The five canonical victims have, in recent years, become the focus of more empathetic historical study. Rather than merely being seen as props in a sensational narrative, they are now recognized as individuals, women with lives, struggles, and histories. Mary Ann Nichols, Annie Chapman, Elizabeth Stride, Catherine Eddowes, and Mary Jane Kelly weren't nameless casualties; they were mothers, daughters, workers, and members of a marginalized community. New efforts have emerged to memorialize them and shift attention away from the killer's legend and toward the human cost of his crimes.

In many ways, Jack the Ripper is a case study in the limits of detection and the dangers of mythologizing violence. His crimes shocked a society that believed itself civilized and safe. They exposed the fragility of social order, the dangers lurking in dark corners, and the illusion that evil always wears a recognizable face.

That he operated in one of the world's great cities, under gaslight and fog, with thousands of people nearby, and still vanished into history, makes him unique. Jack the Ripper remains not just an unsolved case, but a cultural shadow, a reminder that some crimes may never be solved and that mystery itself holds a kind of power.

Robert Hansen

In the wilderness beyond Anchorage, Alaska, Robert Hansen created a private hunting ground for his most brutal desires. Known later as "The Butcher Baker," Hansen was a soft-spoken bakery owner by day and a sadistic predator by night, responsible for the abduction, rape, and murder of at least 17 women, and suspected of far more.

From the 1970s through the early 1980s, he used Alaska's vast, unpatrolled terrain as his personal dumping ground, literally flying victims into the woods before giving them a running start and hunting them down like game. His crimes combined the primal with the calculated, and his ability to hide behind the façade of an ordinary life made him one of the most terrifying figures in American criminal history.

Robert Christian Hansen was born on February 15, 1939, in Estherville, Iowa. His upbringing was deeply shaped by a strict, often domineering father of Danish descent who owned a bakery and expected hard work from his son. Hansen grew up shy, awkward, and painfully introverted, suffering from a pronounced stutter and severe acne.

He was relentlessly bullied by his peers and rejected by girls, which bred deep resentment and a festering sense of inadequacy. Social rejection would become a recurring theme in his psychological profile and ultimately fuel his violent fantasies of control and revenge.

Though he later became known for extreme violence, Hansen's early criminal record was relatively mild. In 1960, at age 21, he was arrested for arson after burning down a school bus garage in revenge for perceived wrongs during high school. He served 20 months in prison and was diagnosed by psychiatrists as having an "infantile personality." This early diagnosis of emotional immaturity foreshadowed the compulsive, narcissistic need for domination that would define his crimes. After his release, he attempted to build a normal life. He married, had children, and eventually moved to Anchorage, Alaska, in the late 1960s. There, he opened a successful bakery and built a reputation as a quiet, hardworking family man.

Alaska offered Hansen something most predators never find, complete geographic insulation. The remote, sprawling wilderness combined with a transient population of young women, many of whom were s** workers or dancers, created an environment ripe for exploitation.

Between 1971 and 1983, Hansen began abducting women from the Anchorage area. His method was horrifyingly consistent: he would lure them with promises of money or jobs, sometimes at gunpoint, then take them to his home, where he would rape and torture them. Some victims were released, others were never seen again. Those he killed were flown, using his private bush plane, into remote wooded areas outside Anchorage, where he would release them and hunt them with a rifle.

The horror of Hansen's ritual cannot be overstated. Survivors reported being chained, beaten, and raped. Those who perished were stripped of dignity and reduced to prey. In some cases, he kept trophies (jewelry or other small items) from his victims. He also kept a map of the Alaskan wilderness with marks that would later be linked to body dump sites.

This mixture of methodical tracking and dehumanizing violence put him into a rare category of offender: the organized, cold-blooded serial predator who operated within a dual existence of social normalcy and hidden depravity.

For years, law enforcement struggled to understand what was happening. Victims disappeared, but many were marginalized women with few support systems, and police resources in Anchorage were stretched thin. Bodies occasionally turned up in the wilderness, but the vastness of the landscape made pattern recognition difficult. Some victims were assumed to have left town or overdosed. Others were buried under snow and silence.

The first major break in the case came in June 1983, when a 17-year-old girl named Cindy Paulson escaped. Hansen had abducted her and taken her to his home, where he chained her by the neck, assaulted her, and told her he would kill her. He eventually drove her to Merrill Field Airport, intending to fly her into the wilderness. As he loaded gear into his plane, Paulson saw an opportunity. She bolted and flagged down a passing truck. The driver, realizing something was wrong, took her to a nearby motel and called the police.

Paulson's account was detailed, credible, and horrifying. She described Hansen's house, his airplane, and even the inside of his car. But despite her testimony, Hansen initially denied everything and wasn't immediately arrested. His reputation as a "nice guy" and business owner led some in law enforcement to dismiss her story. Frustrated but not deterred, investigators from the Alaska State Troopers' Criminal Investigation Bureau decided to dig deeper.

Detective Glenn Flothe and others began re-examining missing persons cases from the past decade. They noted similarities between Paulson's story and earlier unsolved murders. With assistance from FBI criminal profilers, most notably John Douglas, they developed a behavioral profile of the killer. The profile matched Hansen closely: a quiet man with social difficulties, a need to dominate women, a background in hunting, and a history of minor offenses. They obtained a warrant to search Hansen's home.

What they found shattered any doubts. Hidden in a crawl space were weapons, jewelry from victims, a .223-caliber rifle, and an aviation map with X-marks across remote Alaskan wilderness. Many of the Xs corresponded to known body recovery sites. Others pointed to locations yet to be discovered.

Confronted with the evidence, Hansen confessed to killing at least 17 women, although he claimed he couldn't recall all the names or details. Some estimates put the number of victims closer to 21. He also admitted to s**ually assaulting many others who were never killed.

Hansen's trial was brief and procedural. In 1984, he was sentenced to 461 years in prison plus a life sentence without the possibility of parole. The sentence reflected the magnitude of his crimes and the community's need for closure. He was incarcerated at Spring Creek Correctional Center in Seward, Alaska, where he remained until his death from natural causes in 2014 at the age of 75.

The aftermath of Hansen's crimes reshaped how law enforcement approached serial violence, particularly in remote regions with transient populations. His case highlighted the need for better coordination between local, state, and federal agencies and for treating missing persons cases, especially those involving marginalized victims, with greater urgency. Many of the women Hansen targeted were dancers or s** workers, groups often dismissed or ignored in criminal investigations. His ability to prey on these women with minimal suspicion for years exposed painful truths about institutional blind spots.

Psychologically, Hansen's behavior fits the mold of a power-assertive serial killer. He didn't merely kill to eliminate witnesses; he killed to reinforce a fantasy of domination and retribution. His own words, recorded during interrogation, revealed that he saw his victims as lesser beings, women who had "cheated" or "used" men. He justified his crimes by convincing himself that these women deserved their fate. In his mind, the wilderness hunt was both punishment and purification.

The dichotomy of Hansen's life (successful business owner, husband, and father on one side, serial predator on the other) created a level of deception that stunned the public. He was active in his church, participated in local activities, and won awards for his hunting skills. He even held records for big-game trophies in Alaska. To neighbors and customers, he was a quiet, respectful man. To his victims, he was a monster cloaked in civility.

His duality echoes that of other notorious killers who operated within society's rules while violating its most sacred boundaries. Like Dennis Rader (BTK) or John Wayne Gacy, Hansen understood the value of appearing normal. That mask of normalcy allowed him to move undetected while continuing his spree.

In Alaska, Hansen's crimes became part of the state's dark lore. Murals were painted over, clubs where he found his victims were renamed, and the city tried to distance itself from the memory. But his story refuses to fade. In 2013, a film titled *The Frozen Ground* dramatized his crimes, starring Nicolas Cage as the detective and John

Cusack as Hansen. While fictionalized, the film brought renewed attention to the case and to the victims whose stories were too long ignored.

Ultimately, Robert Hansen's legacy is one of predatory calculation and human cruelty made possible by systemic failure. His crimes didn't happen in a vacuum; they were aided by indifference, institutional blind spots, and social stigma. His victims weren't high-profile or powerful, and that is precisely why he was able to target them for so long.

The story of Robert Hansen is a warning about what hides behind appearances and what can fester when society refuses to look too closely. It's also a reminder that beneath every victim's name is a life that deserved more protection, and a system that must do better.

Israel Keyes

When investigators first connected Israel Keyes to a kidnapping in Anchorage, Alaska in 2012, they had no idea they had stumbled upon one of the most methodical and elusive serial killers in American history. By the time Keyes took his own life in jail later that year, he had confessed to at least 11 murders and hinted at many more, spanning across the United States. What made Keyes terrifying wasn't just his crimes; it was the planning. Unlike most serial killers, who operate within a specific geography or follow impulsive patterns, Keyes designed his acts like military operations. He traveled thousands of miles, buried "kill kits" years in advance, and chose victims randomly to avoid detection. His anonymity was deliberate. His goal wasn't attention; it was control.

Born on January 7, 1978, in Richmond, Utah, Israel Keyes was raised in a strict, isolated household. His parents were fundamentalist Mormons who later became affiliated with white separatist Christian Identity beliefs. The family lived off-grid in rural Washington state without electricity or running water. The children were homeschooled and isolated from mainstream society. Keyes grew up hunting, often killing animals for sport, and showed early signs of cruelty. In later interviews, he would refer to himself as being fascinated by death from a young age.

In his teen years, Keyes rejected religion but kept his detached, solitary nature. He later served in the U.S. Army from 1998 to 2001, stationed at various bases in the U.S. and abroad. While there are no confirmed crimes during his military service, some believe he may have used the time to refine the discipline and mobility that defined his later crimes. He was described by peers as quiet and polite but aloof. After leaving the military, Keyes moved around frequently, eventually settling in Anchorage, Alaska, where he ran a small construction company.

What distinguishes Keyes from most known serial killers is how he actively avoided detection. He didn't have a "type" of victim. He didn't kill close to home. He didn't stalk individuals for extended periods. Instead, he chose victims based on opportunity. He would fly across the country, rent a car, drive hundreds of miles, and use tools he had buried months or years earlier to carry out his crimes. These "kill kits" contained guns, duct tape, rope, and Drano, among other things. After the murders, he would often drive or fly to another state, establish an alibi, and blend back into everyday life.

Keyes claimed to have committed his first murder in 2001 or 2002, but he was deliberately vague. He refused to name victims or locations. His motivation seemed to be rooted in personal control and an effort to keep investigators in the dark even after capture. In interviews, he said he admired Ted Bundy for his double life but criticized him for getting caught. Keyes took pride in remaining invisible.

The case that led to his capture began on February 1, 2012, when 18-year-old Samantha Koenig, a barista in Anchorage, was abducted from her coffee stand. Surveillance footage showed a masked man forcing her at gunpoint into a vehicle. What no one knew at the time was that Samantha was alive for several hours after the abduction. Keyes took her to a shed on his property, s**ually assaulted her, and eventually killed her. He then left her body in a freezer, took a cruise with his family in New Orleans, and returned to Alaska two weeks later.

Keyes attempted to collect ransom money from Samantha's family by texting them using her phone, making it appear she was still alive. He posed her corpse to look as if she were still living, using makeup and sewing her eyes open, then photographed her and sent the image to the family with a ransom demand. It was one of the most chilling acts of manipulation in modern criminal history.

The ransom drop led investigators to trace Keyes through ATM withdrawals he made using Koenig's debit card. He withdrew money in Arizona, New Mexico, and Texas.

On March 13, 2012, he was pulled over in Lufkin, Texas. In his vehicle, officers found Koenig's card, her phone, and other damning evidence. He was arrested and extradited back to Alaska.

Once in custody, Keyes began talking, but on his own terms. He confessed to killing Samantha and later led police to her remains, buried near a frozen lake. Then he began revealing details of other murders, many of which remain unsolved. He described flying to Chicago, renting a car, and driving to Vermont, where he abducted and killed Bill and Lorraine Currier in June 2011. Their home had been selected at random. He broke in during the night, bound them, and took them to an abandoned farmhouse, where he killed them. Their bodies were never recovered, and the farmhouse was later demolished.

Keyes also admitted to numerous burglaries, arsons, and bank robberies, all of which he used to fund his lifestyle and crimes. He was a textbook loner in some ways, but his behavior was anything but erratic. It was systematic. He was careful to never leave digital traces, bought tickets with cash, and turned off phones or used ones that couldn't be traced. His crimes weren't about rage or impulse; they were about control, secrecy, and the execution of a dark personal code.

Despite investigators' efforts, Keyes refused to provide full details about most of his crimes. He enjoyed the power imbalance, letting bits of information slip while keeping the broader picture hidden. When he was asked why he killed, he simply responded, "Why not?" He seemed to view his murders as a personal challenge, a demonstration of skill and discipline. The lack of a clear motive frustrated law enforcement and profilers.

Over time, he became increasingly difficult to manage in custody. On December 2, 2012, while awaiting trial, Israel Keyes was found dead in his jail cell from self-inflicted wounds. He had cut his wrist and strangled himself using a bedsheet. Near his body was a chilling 4-page note, described as an ode to murder filled with cryptic, poetic language. It named no victims and provided no useful leads. It was the final act of a man determined to keep control over his story, even in death.

After Keyes died, the FBI released portions of the investigation to the public, including a map found among his belongings. The map showed 12 red dots scattered across the United States, potential kill locations. To this day, many of those sites remain linked to no known victims. Authorities believe he may have killed more than 20 people.

Keyes's case has profoundly influenced how the FBI and other agencies think about serial killers. His profile defies conventional assumptions: no specific victim type, no emotional escalation, no compulsion to communicate with media or police. He was a hybrid predator; part methodical planner, part cold-blooded opportunist. His ability to mask his intentions and remain undetected for years has been studied as a worst-case scenario in criminal investigations.

Perhaps most disturbing is how ordinary Keyes seemed. He had a daughter. He had a business. He went on family vacations. His outward life was not only undistinguished, it was functional. That someone could live a double life with such precision and without suspicion is a reminder that danger doesn't always announce itself. Some predators work in silence.

Though Keyes never reached the public infamy of Bundy or Gacy, his story resonates with investigators and criminal psychologists for its implications.

He didn't want fame or recognition. He wanted control, privacy, and anonymity. He wanted to demonstrate that he could beat the system; and for a time, he did.

In the end, Israel Keyes left behind a legacy of questions. How many people did he actually kill? Were there accomplices? What signs, if any, did those around him miss? Could his military training or upbringing have shaped his worldview in a way that made human life expendable? The answers are likely buried with him, lost to his calculated silence.

Samuel Little

For decades, the most prolific serial killer in American history sat unnoticed in plain sight. His name was Samuel Little, and by the time he died in 2020, he had confessed to killing 93 people, almost all women, over a span of more than four decades. Authorities have verified over 60 of those confessions with corroborating evidence, an unprecedented number in American criminal history.

But what makes Little's story even more haunting is that, for most of his life, he was virtually invisible to the criminal justice system, drifting from town to town, leaving broken lives behind him. His victims were often on the margins of society: s** workers, drug users, or women of color, whose disappearances drew little media attention and even less law enforcement effort.

Samuel Little was born on June 7, 1940, in Reynolds, Georgia. His mother was reportedly a s** worker, and his early life was shaped by neglect, instability, and violence. He was raised mostly by his grandmother in Lorain, Ohio, and he struggled in school from an early age. He would later claim he had violent s**ual fantasies starting in childhood. As a teenager, he began engaging in petty theft, assault, and peeping tom behavior. These early offenses revealed a disturbing pattern of deviance and predation, but he slipped through the cracks of institutions that often saw him only as a petty criminal.

By the 1960s, Little was already a seasoned drifter. He never held a stable job, instead supporting himself through shoplifting, burglary, and odd labor gigs. He lived in cheap motels, drove beat-up cars, and frequently changed cities, traits that made him nearly impossible to track. He had an uncanny ability to blend into urban poverty while preying on the most vulnerable women. These were women whose lives were transient, who might not have family searching for them, who could vanish without a trace or a police investigation.

Between 1970 and 2005, Little claimed to have murdered 93 women across 19 states, including California, Texas, Florida, Ohio, Louisiana, Mississippi, and Arizona. Unlike many serial killers, he didn't have a single preferred method of operation that made his crimes easier to detect as a pattern.

However, one detail was remarkably consistent: strangulation. He rarely used weapons. Instead, he relied on his hands or improvised ligatures. This left little forensic evidence. Moreover, his victims were often found without signs of trauma that would raise suspicion, leading many coroners to list their deaths as overdoses or natural causes.

Despite the scope of his crimes, Little spent most of his adult life in and out of jail for non-homicidal offenses. He was arrested more than 100 times across multiple states for theft, assault, fraud, rape, and attempted murder. Yet he was convicted only once for a homicide, in 2014, long after his most active years.

It's difficult to overstate how many opportunities were missed to stop him. In the pre-DNA era, different jurisdictions rarely communicated, and marginalized victims didn't attract attention from media or law enforcement. These systemic weaknesses were exactly what Little relied on.

He avoided detection through careful targeting and transience. His victims were not picked at random, but they weren't stalked over time either. He selected women who were vulnerable in public spaces: at bars, on street corners, or walking alone at night. He would often offer them a ride, sometimes with the promise of drugs or alcohol. Once they were in his car, often a beat-up coupe with no interior handles, it was too late. He later described taking women to secluded areas, often near highways or behind buildings, where he would strangle them and leave their bodies in places where they would either go unnoticed or be mistaken for overdoses.

(Samuel Little mugshots)

In many ways, Little's predatory behavior was a perfect storm of low visibility and high mobility. He had no desire for attention. He didn't write letters to newspapers, call police, or taunt investigators like some killers. He operated in silence and with precision, always one step ahead of any suspicion. He was calculating enough to understand how systems failed. And he used that knowledge to stay free for decades.

The breakthrough came in 2012 when Little was arrested in Kentucky on a narcotics charge and extradited to California, where he was wanted for failing to appear in court for an earlier charge.

While in Los Angeles County jail, his DNA was collected and matched to three unsolved murders from 1987 and 1989, all involving women who had been beaten and strangled. The cases had gone cold for years. When confronted with the DNA evidence, Little showed no remorse. But over time, as the investigation deepened, he began to talk.

By 2018, Samuel Little was speaking with Texas Ranger James Holland, a skilled interrogator who gained his trust. Over hundreds of hours of interviews, Little began confessing to murder after murder, often recalling astonishing details: the victim's clothing, physical features, where he left the body, what the weather was like. Though his memory of dates was unreliable, his visual recall was uncannily sharp. He even drew dozens of portraits of his victims from memory, pastel sketches that eerily resembled real, long-missing women. Many of the portraits were matched with cold cases, validating his confessions.

Little's ability to recall specific details decades after the killings astonished investigators. In one case, he described a woman he killed in Arkansas in the mid-1990s. Though no records initially matched his account, his memory of a nearby landmark helped local law enforcement locate the area. When they found human remains buried in an unmarked grave, it confirmed what he had said. In another confession, he recalled killing a woman in Mississippi and dropping her body by a roadside sign. Investigators located skeletal remains in that exact area. These confirmations gave his confessions unprecedented credibility.

But why confess at all? By the time Little opened up, he was already serving multiple life sentences without the possibility of parole.

Some believe he confessed for attention, while others think it was about control, deciding when and how his crimes were finally revealed. Little himself said he wanted to "clear his conscience," though many found that statement hollow. His matter-of-fact tone in interviews showed no remorse. He smiled when describing the deaths. He showed no empathy, even when shown photos of the victims.

Little's legacy is now as much about systemic failure as it is about his own evil. The fact that a man could kill dozens of women across the country and evade capture for decades has become a case study in institutional neglect. His victims were disproportionately women of color, poor, or involved in s** work. In many cases, their deaths weren't even investigated as homicides. Coroners would declare heart attacks or overdoses without performing thorough autopsies. Police departments didn't connect the dots. Families were left without answers. Little thrived in that void.

The FBI took the unusual step of creating a public page for Samuel Little, listing sketches of unidentified victims and seeking help from the public to match names to faces. To date, dozens of these portraits remain unmatched, and the full number of his victims may never be known. Some of his confessions describe women in cities where records of missing persons are incomplete. In other cases, victims may have never been reported missing at all.

In 2019, the FBI declared Little the most prolific serial killer in U.S. history. That title, while horrifying, is a critical acknowledgment of the scale of violence he enacted. It also reflects a sobering fact: many of his victims had been forgotten long before he ever confessed. Their names were not etched into the public's memory. They were buried not only physically, but administratively, by bureaucracy, by apathy, by social judgment. Little's case forced agencies to revisit cold cases with renewed focus, and in many jurisdictions, it triggered major reforms in how missing persons and unexplained deaths are handled.

Samuel Little died on December 30, 2020, at the age of 80 in a California hospital. Official cause of death was heart disease and diabetes. He never expressed regret, and he never stood trial for most of the murders he confessed to. His story remains one of the most chilling in modern American history, not only because of what he did, but because of how long it took for anyone to fully grasp the extent of it.

What makes Little different from many serial killers isn't just his numbers, but his invisibility. He didn't seek media attention. He didn't keep trophies. He didn't live in isolation or in a fantasy world. He lived in the open, but carefully under the radar. He manipulated weakness, exploited institutional flaws, and targeted those least protected by society. He understood systems, and avoided them.

Samuel Little isn't just a story of evil. It is a story of who gets noticed and who doesn't, of which victims are seen as worthy of justice and which are forgotten. His crimes didn't happen only in dark alleys or back roads. They happened in the blind spots of a society that failed to see.

Herb Baumeister

To the outside world, Herb Baumeister was a successful businessman, a devoted husband, and a father of three. He ran a popular chain of thrift stores called Save-A-Lot in Indianapolis, and he lived in a sprawling estate called Fox Hollow Farm. Yet beneath that polished exterior lay a disturbing dual life. In reality, Baumeister was likely responsible for the deaths of at least eleven young men, whose skeletal remains were discovered in the woods behind his home. Many more may never be identified. What makes his case uniquely unsettling is the contrast between his family-man persona and the hidden horrors buried just steps from his back door.

Herbert Richard Baumeister was born in Indianapolis, Indiana, on April 7, 1947. From an early age, he showed signs of psychological instability. Classmates described him as odd and socially withdrawn. He was known for inappropriate behavior, such as urinating on a teacher's desk and bringing in dead animals to school. Though clearly troubled, his behavior was often dismissed as mere eccentricity. As he entered adolescence, the signs of deeper disturbance intensified, but his privileged background and supportive family shielded him from serious consequences.

In his early twenties, Baumeister was briefly institutionalized. He was diagnosed with schizophrenia and antisocial tendencies, yet he never followed through on treatment. Instead, he attempted to move on with his life.

He eventually married Juliana "Julie" Saiter in 1971, and the couple had three children. To all appearances, they were a typical middle-class family. Herb worked various low-level jobs before opening Save-A-Lot thrift stores in 1988. The business was profitable, giving the family a comfortable lifestyle and enabling them to purchase Fox Hollow Farm, a massive Tudor-style mansion on 18 wooded acres in the affluent suburb of Westfield, Indiana.

By the 1990s, Herb Baumeister was seen as a pillar of the community. Yet his marriage was deeply strained. Julie later stated they had s** only a handful of times over their two-decade relationship. Herb often retreated into himself, becoming more erratic and secretive. He spent increasing amounts of time away from home, especially during the night. His behavior was particularly bizarre during the summers, when his wife and children would go to their lake house for several months. Herb stayed behind, ostensibly to run the business. In truth, these were the periods when most of the murders are believed to have occurred.

The victims shared common traits: they were young men, mostly in their twenties, many of them gay, and several had last been seen at gay bars in downtown Indianapolis. At the time, missing persons reports involving gay men didn't receive the same urgency or media attention as other cases. Many of the disappearances went cold.

But one man, Tony Harris, refused to let the matter drop. After the disappearance of his friend, he went undercover at local bars to gather information. He eventually told authorities about a man named "Brian Smart," who had tried to strangle him during a s**ual encounter at what he described as a lavish estate with a pool and mannequins.

This lead might have gone nowhere if not for the efforts of Detective Mary Wilson of the Indianapolis Police Department and Detective Virgil Vandagriff, a private investigator working on the missing persons cases. In 1995, Harris saw "Brian Smart" again and got his license plate number. It traced back to Herb Baumeister. Investigators now had a name and a suspect. But without hard evidence, they couldn't secure a search warrant for Fox Hollow Farm.

At the same time, Baumeister's personal life was unraveling. His business was faltering, and he became increasingly paranoid. Julie, long suspicious of her husband's behavior, had grown concerned about what was happening on the property while she and the kids were away. In June 1996, when detectives approached her directly, she finally consented to a search of the estate. What followed was one of the most gruesome discoveries in Indiana history.

Behind the house, in a wooded area near the family's pool and carriage house, investigators found human remains: bones scattered, some burned, others buried shallowly. Over the next several weeks, authorities recovered over 5,500 bones and bone fragments, representing at least eleven individuals. Some were missing person cases that had languished for years. Most of the victims were never identified. The scene suggested that Baumeister had used his property as a personal dumping ground, possibly staging the bodies for days before disposing of them.

But by the time the search began in earnest, Herb Baumeister was gone. Fleeing the investigation, he drove to Canada. On July 3, 1996, his body was found at Pinery Provincial Park in Ontario. He had shot himself in the head.

Beside him was a note, but it made no mention of the murders. Instead, it focused on business troubles and the failure of his marriage. It was a final act of denial from a man who had spent his life compartmentalizing his darkest impulses.

The story, however, didn't end with his death. As investigators dug deeper, they began to link Baumeister to a series of murders along Interstate 70 between Indiana and Ohio. These were gay men who had disappeared in the early 1980s and early 1990s. Their bodies had been found dumped in rural fields or ditches, often strangled or showing signs of s**ual assault. While conclusive forensic evidence was never obtained, the FBI listed Baumeister as a prime suspect in at least nine of these

I-70 corridor slayings. The theory was that he had killed on the road before acquiring Fox Hollow Farm and transitioning to his private estate.

Baumeister's case revealed disturbing blind spots in how missing person cases, especially those involving LGBTQ+ individuals, were handled. His ability to avoid detection for so long stemmed in part from society's apathy toward his victims. Many of them were assumed to have left town voluntarily, to be "runaways," or drug users. Their families were left with no answers for years. Baumeister knew this and exploited it. He chose victims whose disappearances wouldn't provoke immediate action, whose lives could be erased with little inquiry.

There's also the psychological dimension. Baumeister didn't fit the mold of a deranged loner. He was functional in society. He ran a business, paid taxes, raised children, and made charitable donations. But behind closed doors, he lived in near-total isolation, consumed by fantasies of control, domination, and death. The mannequins he kept around his pool were described as arranged like guests at a party, silent, compliant, and motionless. They symbolized his desire for control, his retreat into a world where he could play god.

His ability to live a double life challenges assumptions about what serial killers look like. The dichotomy between the public-facing businessman and the private killer is what continues to fascinate criminal profilers and psychologists. Baumeister wasn't driven by rage or impulse in the traditional sense. His crimes were deliberate, ritualistic, and opportunistic. He showed little interest in fame or recognition. Like Israel Keyes or Dennis Rader, his satisfaction came from control and secrecy, not notoriety.

Today, Fox Hollow Farm still stands, though it has changed ownership multiple times. The property has even become the subject of paranormal investigations, though those accounts are, of course, speculative. What's not in doubt is the legacy of horror that Baumeister left behind. The land itself became a silent witness to acts of unspeakable cruelty.

Herb Baumeister's crimes shocked the Midwest and permanently altered how law enforcement treats patterns in missing persons cases. His story is a case study in how dangerous people can hide in plain sight, how silence and social stigma allow predators to operate, and how systems must evolve to protect the vulnerable. He never stood trial. He never confessed. He left behind more questions than answers. But for the families of his victims, and for those trying to make sense of what he did, the truth that emerged was clear: the monster lived next door.

Joel Rifkin

Joel Rifkin never looked like someone who would become one of New York's most prolific serial killers. He was awkward, soft-spoken, and reclusive. He wasn't charming like Bundy or calculating in the same way as Gacy. He faded into the background, unnoticed and underestimated. But between 1989 and 1993, he killed at least 17 women, most of them s** workers, in and around New York City. Rifkin operated quietly, methodically, and with chilling indifference. What finally brought him down wasn't an investigation or a tip; it was a simple traffic stop for a missing license plate that revealed a body in the back of his pickup truck.

Born on January 20, 1959, in New York City, Joel Rifkin was adopted as an infant by a well-off couple from Long Island. His father, Bernard, was an engineer; his mother, Jeanne, a schoolteacher. By all outward appearances, Rifkin grew up in a stable and supportive home. But from early on, he showed signs of deep social anxiety and low self-esteem. He struggled academically and was relentlessly bullied by peers for his awkward demeanor and poor athletic performance. Even in his teen years, Rifkin remained withdrawn, fantasizing about revenge and violence, though no one seemed to notice the internal world he was building.

Despite a high IQ, Rifkin dropped out of college after several failed attempts at academic success. He drifted between odd jobs, unable to hold steady employment. At home, he grew increasingly isolated. He began frequenting s** workers and obsessively consuming violent p***ography. These fantasies gradually evolved into homicidal ideation. He later admitted that Jack the Ripper was a personal obsession and even studied books about dismemberment and criminal investigation techniques. For Rifkin, murder wasn't about s**ual gratification in a conventional sense; it was about dominance and control. His victims were disposable in his eyes, and he saw himself as intellectually superior to those trying to catch him.

His first known murder occurred in 1989. Rifkin picked up a woman named Heidi Balch in Manhattan and brought her back to his mother's home in East Meadow, Long Island, where he lived at the time. After having intercourse, he bludgeoned and strangled her. He then dismembered her body in the basement and scattered the remains in different parts of New York and New Jersey. Some were placed in the East River. Other body parts were deposited near the New Jersey Turnpike. He kept her head in a paint can, which he later disposed of in the woods. It would be decades before her identity was confirmed. For years, she was known only as "Jane Doe."

After that first kill, Rifkin waited more than a year before murdering again. But once he resumed, the frequency accelerated. By 1991, he had developed a grim routine: pick up s** workers from the streets of Manhattan, drive them to his mother's house, kill them during or after s**, and dispose of their bodies. Sometimes he dumped them in rivers. Other times he left them in alleys or on highways. Occasionally he dismembered them, but often he just left the bodies intact in garbage bags or wrapped in tarps. In a few cases, he even slept next to their corpses for days before removing them.

Rifkin's mother was often away visiting relatives during the time of these murders, giving him both the space and the time to carry out his crimes. What's especially disturbing is how easily he was able to avoid detection despite the growing number of victims. Law enforcement agencies across boroughs and counties didn't always coordinate, and many of the women he killed weren't immediately reported missing. Rifkin knew this and deliberately targeted those on the margins: addicted, transient, economically vulnerable. Their disappearances rarely made headlines.

By 1993, Rifkin had killed at least 17 women, though some investigators believe the number may be higher. He kept no trophies and made no attempt to taunt police.

His motivations remain ambiguous, even after years of interviews and psychological profiling. He claimed to feel remorse and disgust but also described his crimes with clinical detachment.

For him, murder was a compulsion that he didn't fully understand but couldn't resist. Some experts believe his killings were driven more by repressed rage and powerlessness than s**ual desire.

His downfall came on June 28, 1993, in a way that was almost absurdly mundane. Rifkin had recently killed a woman named Tiffany Bresciani, a 22-year-old s** worker and aspiring actress. He placed her body in the back of his 1984 Mazda pickup truck and drove around for days with it under a tarp, hoping to find a secluded place to dump it. But he never got the chance. At about 4 a.m., New York State Troopers noticed that his truck was missing a rear license plate and pulled him over on the Southern State Parkway in Nassau County. As they approached the vehicle, they smelled a foul odor. When they looked in the back, they found the decomposing corpse of Bresciani.

Rifkin was arrested on the spot. During initial questioning, he tried to deflect but quickly gave in and confessed not only to the murder of Bresciani, but to sixteen others. Over the following weeks, he led police to the sites where he had dumped several victims, some of whose remains had never been identified. In total, he was linked to 17 murders spanning a four-year period. Authorities were stunned. Rifkin had never been a suspect. He had no prior arrests for violent crime, and his name was not in any investigative databases connected to the killings.

The trial was quick and highly publicized. In 1994, Rifkin was convicted of nine counts of murder and sentenced to 203 years to life in prison. He would later receive additional sentences for the other killings. Today, he is incarcerated at the Clinton Correctional Facility in upstate New York. His earliest possible parole date is in the 2190s, effectively guaranteeing he will die in prison.

In interviews conducted after his conviction, Rifkin expressed what appeared to be genuine regret, though it was often undercut by an unsettling emotional distance. He admitted that he didn't really understand why he killed. He said he felt an uncontrollable urge, and that each murder provided only temporary relief before the compulsion returned. Some psychologists have speculated that Rifkin may have suffered from a combination of antisocial personality disorder and depressive tendencies, with a deeply impaired ability to form normal emotional attachments. He wasn't delusional. He knew right from wrong. But he lacked empathy and viewed his victims as objects rather than people.

What sets Rifkin apart from other serial killers is not just the number of his victims, but how long he went undetected despite a clear pattern. There were no elaborate disguises, no fake names, no international travel. He operated within a 50-mile radius, killed in the same house repeatedly, and left bodies in public spaces. The fact that he was never seriously investigated until he was caught by accident is a sobering reminder of how easily serial predators can operate when their victims are marginalized. Rifkin was acutely aware of this dynamic. He once told police, "They were throwaways. That's what made it easy."

The media frenzy surrounding his arrest and trial led to renewed scrutiny of how law enforcement handled missing persons cases, especially those involving s** workers. It also highlighted the failures of social systems to protect people at the margins. Many of Rifkin's victims had struggled with homelessness, addiction, or mental illness. They had fallen through the cracks long before they crossed paths with him. In this sense, Rifkin wasn't just a lone predator, but a symptom of broader systemic neglect.

The public fascination with Rifkin continues in part because of his apparent normalcy. He wasn't charismatic or theatrical. He didn't seek out attention or try to manipulate the media. He lived quietly in the suburbs, mowed his lawn, and took care of his elderly mother. He read true crime books and watched detective shows. He was the kind of man who might live down the street from you, and that's what makes him so terrifying.

Joel Rifkin's case endures as a chilling example of how deeply buried rage and isolation can erupt into violence. His ability to evade detection for years, despite such a consistent pattern, exposed significant blind spots in law enforcement coordination. His selection of victims (young, poor, female, and often nonwhite) revealed societal prejudices about who gets searched for and who is forgotten. Rifkin's life and crimes have become a grim reference point in criminology and victimology. He is a reminder that evil doesn't always roar. Sometimes, it whispers and hides in silence until it is far too late.

Leonard Lake

Leonard Lake didn't begin his descent into depravity overnight. His life was a slow burn of paranoia, violent fantasy, and control obsession. What makes his case especially disturbing is not just the number of people he and his accomplice, Charles Ng, are believed to have murdered (at least 11 confirmed victims, possibly up to 25) but the way in which Lake turned torture, captivity, and complete domination into a dark ideology. He wasn't simply a killer. He was a man on a mission to build his own twisted world, where human lives were nothing more than tools for gratification or obstacles to eliminate.

Born in San Francisco on October 29, 1945, Leonard Thomas Lake experienced a childhood that set the stage for his later cruelty. After his parents separated, Lake was sent to live with his grandparents. By his own account, he began taking nude photos of his sisters at a young age, allegedly encouraged by his grandfather. This early exposure to inappropriate s**ual boundaries blurred his understanding of control, consent, and power. His fascination with domination, photography, and apocalyptic thinking took root early and never left.

Lake joined the U.S. Marine Corps during the Vietnam War. Though he never saw direct combat, his time in the military deepened his survivalist mentality. He developed a fear of global collapse and nuclear war, believing that society was teetering on the brink of total destruction. After being diagnosed with schizoid personality disorder, he was discharged and briefly institutionalized. Once back in civilian life, Lake bounced between failed relationships, fringe ideologies, and extremist survivalist groups.

Throughout the late 1970s and early 1980s, Lake's worldview grew darker. He immersed himself in dystopian literature and survivalist propaganda, stockpiling weapons and fantasizing about life after civilization's collapse.

But unlike other doomsday preppers, Lake didn't just want to survive; he wanted to rule. He began formulating plans for a fortified bunker, dubbed "the Miranda Project," named after a fictional character he invented to represent the ideal submissive woman. The bunker would become the setting for unspeakable crimes.

Lake's fantasies would have likely remained confined to journals and delusions if he hadn't crossed paths with Charles Ng in the early 1980s. Ng, a Hong Kong-born former Marine with his own history of theft and violence, was drawn to Lake's charisma and ideology. The two men bonded over shared interests in weapons, torture fantasies, and an absolute disdain for societal rules. Ng was impulsive and volatile. Lake was methodical and manipulative. Together, they formed a uniquely dangerous partnership.

The pair eventually set up residence in a remote cabin near Wilseyville, California, on a rural property owned by Lake's ex-wife. Here, Lake constructed a concrete bunker, a two-room structure built into the earth, reinforced with thick walls and soundproofed doors. Inside, he kept recording equipment, restraints, drugs, and survival gear. His vision of a post-apocalyptic sanctuary was now a functioning dungeon.

Their crimes followed a grim pattern. Most of their victims were lured under false pretenses; some were men responding to ads for work or trades, others were entire families. Once captured, the men were often killed quickly. Lake saw them as threats or obstacles. The women, however, were frequently kept alive for longer, raped, filmed, and tortured. Some were forced to watch recordings of previous victims. Lake kept meticulous notes and videos. In his mind, he was documenting an experiment in absolute control.

Among the most chilling pieces of evidence recovered after their arrest were videotapes showing Lake speaking to the camera about his philosophy. In one, he calmly explains his belief that women exist to serve men, particularly men like him, who are "prepared for the collapse of civilization."

He details how he wants to enslave women to serve domestic and s**ual needs in his post-apocalyptic compound. These videos are emotionless, methodical, and delivered with the composure of someone who believes in the righteousness of their actions.

The victims came from various walks of life. Donald and Brenda Dubs, along with their baby son, were among those abducted. Brenda was later found on one of Lake's videotapes, visibly distressed and being forced to comply with his demands. The child was never found, and it is assumed he was murdered soon after the abduction. Another couple, Lonnie Bond and his girlfriend, along with their infant, were similarly targeted and disappeared. Some victims were acquaintances. Others were complete strangers. Lake showed no preference for age or background, only that the victim could be controlled or silenced.

It was a mistake that finally ended their spree. In June 1985, Ng was caught shoplifting a vise from a hardware store in South San Francisco. While fleeing the scene, he left behind the getaway vehicle, registered to one of their victims. The police traced the car back to Leonard Lake. When they arrived to question him, Lake calmly handed over identification. But within moments, he asked to retrieve a glass of water. Inside the bathroom, hidden from view, he swallowed a cyanide pill he had kept in his clothing. He collapsed and died a few days later in custody, leaving behind a trail of unanswered questions and a co-conspirator still at large.

Charles Ng fled the country, initiating one of the most complex international manhunts of the era. He made it to Canada, where he was eventually arrested for shoplifting and attempted murder after shooting a security guard during his capture. The legal battle to extradite Ng to the United States dragged on for years, delayed by appeals and human rights challenges. He was finally returned to California in 1991 to stand trial for the murders.

Ng's trial was one of the most expensive in California history, lasting over six years and costing taxpayers more than $20 million. He was convicted in 1999 of 11 murders and sentenced to death. Unlike Lake, who embraced death to avoid accountability, Ng has remained alive on death row at San Quentin State Prison, continuing to file appeals and denying key elements of the case.

The scale of the horror found at the Wilseyville property shocked even seasoned investigators. Over 40 pounds of charred bone fragments were discovered, representing at least 11 individuals. Diaries, videotapes, and personal items confirmed the identity of several victims, but many remains couldn't be conclusively matched.

The tapes showed both men taking part in the abuse, but Lake was clearly the dominant figure, the architect of the crimes. Ng may have participated enthusiastically, but the philosophy, bunker, and vision were Lake's.

The psychological portrait of Leonard Lake is one of extreme narcissism layered over a foundation of paranoia and control obsession. He envisioned himself as a pioneer of a new order, one that could only rise after the world collapsed. In that imagined world, Lake would no longer be an outsider or a failure. He would be king. His crimes weren't impulsive but premeditated. They were ritualistic and symbolic, affirming his belief in his own superiority and entitlement to dominate others.

Lake's story also became a warning about the convergence of ideology and pathology. His crimes weren't random; they were systematized, goal-oriented, and driven by a belief structure. He believed in what he was doing. That's what makes him so dangerous in retrospect. While many serial killers act out of compulsion, rage, or fantasy, Lake acted out of conviction. That conviction turned deadly when paired with another willing accomplice and a secluded place to carry it out.

Public reaction to the Lake and Ng case was intense. The rural landscape of Northern California seemed forever tainted by the events at Wilseyville. The story was covered in every major newspaper, and the recovered videotapes became part of

FBI training material on organized serial killing and sadism. It was one of the earliest American cases that resembled what later would be known as "team killers" or "coercive pairings," where one dominant personality draws in a willing or submissive accomplice.

In the years since Lake's death and Ng's conviction, the Miranda bunker has become a dark point of fascination for true crime enthusiasts. The site was eventually razed, but the myth of what happened there remains. The combination of planning, ideology, and brutality continues to baffle experts. Many believe there are still victims who have never been found – people whose names were never known, whose families never got answers.

Leonard Lake left behind more than victims. He left behind a case study in how violent belief systems can incubate unnoticed, how predators can operate in plain sight, and how partnership can amplify cruelty.

He was the calm voice in front of the camera, speaking about obedience and apocalypse. And behind that calmness was a man who had turned murder into purpose.

Charles Ng

Charles Ng's story cannot be told without Leonard Lake, but he was not merely a follower in a larger man's fantasy. Ng brought his own darkness into the equation, one that, while less methodical, was no less cruel. Their partnership was one of the most disturbing collaborations in the history of American serial crime. But even among co-offending killers, Ng stands out for his volatility, self-absorption, and chilling lack of remorse.

Born in British-controlled Hong Kong on December 24, 1960, Ng was the son of a wealthy, authoritarian businessman. He grew up in a household steeped in control and corporal punishment. His father, by many accounts, was physically and emotionally abusive. Ng developed into a defiant child, expelled from multiple schools and sent to the United States as a teenager to live with relatives. But relocation did nothing to curb his behavior. He committed petty theft and was arrested multiple times. Eventually, he falsified documents to join the U.S. Marine Corps, an audacious act that would mark the beginning of his contact with Leonard Lake.

During his time in the military, Ng stole weapons and was soon arrested. He escaped custody and fled to California, where he crossed paths with Lake. By this point, Lake had already begun constructing his plan for an underground bunker designed to survive societal collapse.

But what he truly wanted was power over others. Ng's arrival gave him something more, an accomplice who could share the labor, enable the fantasy, and inflict pain without hesitation.

To understand Charles Ng is to examine the psychological dynamic of dominance and submission that often characterizes co-offending duos. Ng was not the planner. He was impulsive, unstable, and disorganized. But he wasn't coerced. Video recordings of their victims, recovered from the Wilseyville bunker, show Ng actively participating in s**ual assault, physical torture, and degradation. He often mocked the victims and displayed a sadistic streak that suggested more than just complicity; he derived enjoyment from the suffering.

What made Ng especially dangerous was his lack of boundaries. While Lake maintained a disturbing rationale behind his "project," Ng acted with raw cruelty. During interactions with victims, he oscillated between forced politeness and overt menace. One survivor described him as having a "childlike cruelty" – an erratic, almost playful viciousness that made him impossible to predict. This unpredictability was part of what gave the pair their lethal efficiency. Victims couldn't reason with them because there was no logic to appeal to.

The crimes committed at the Wilseyville compound were methodical on Lake's part, but Ng introduced chaos. Lake wanted control. Ng wanted chaos and gratification. Where Lake kept journals and wrote manifestos, Ng left behind destruction. Where Lake viewed his crimes as part of a grand, delusional scheme, Ng operated like a storm: sudden, brutal, and indiscriminate.

After the two men fled following a botched shoplifting attempt in 1985, Lake was quickly apprehended and died by suicide. Ng, however, fled to Canada, where he was eventually arrested for shooting a security guard during another theft attempt. What followed was one of the longest and most expensive extradition battles in U.S. legal history. Canadian authorities, facing political pressure from anti-death penalty groups, resisted returning Ng to a country where he would face capital punishment. Ng, ever manipulative, exploited every legal avenue, filing countless appeals and delaying the process for nearly six years.

When Ng finally stood trial in California, the case stretched on for years, costing taxpayers over $20 million. His defense portrayed him as a passive participant, someone under the psychological control of the older, dominant Lake. But the evidence, particularly the videotapes, undermined that narrative. He wasn't a bystander. He was a full participant. The trial resulted in 11 murder convictions and a death sentence in 1999.

Despite the verdict, Ng remains on death row at San Quentin State Prison. His appeals have continued, some based on alleged misconduct during the trial, others on procedural technicalities. Ng has never expressed remorse. Interviews and court transcripts reveal a man more concerned with legal gamesmanship than accountability. His courtroom behavior was erratic and manipulative. He often appeared to relish the attention, contradicting any portrayal of him as a man ashamed of his actions.

Psychologists who've studied Ng often describe him in terms of narcissistic personality disorder and antisocial traits. He is a man with a high need for stimulation, low empathy, and a distorted self-image. Where Lake was a controlling ideologue, Ng was a mirror that reflected and amplified cruelty. He brought spontaneity and aggression to their crimes. The combination proved lethal.

Perhaps the most troubling aspect of Ng's case is how quickly he adapted to Lake's worldview. It didn't take years of indoctrination. It didn't require threats or coercion. Ng stepped into the role of torturer and killer with apparent ease. His criminal record before meeting Lake already included violence and theft. Lake simply provided a structure, and a physical location, where Ng could act without consequences.

Ng's role in the Wilseyville murders also invites questions about the nature of criminal partnership. Why did two men from such different backgrounds coalesce into such a destructive force? What made them trust each other with such disturbing secrets?

The answer likely lies in shared pathology. Both men were drawn to domination, control, and the dehumanization of others. They weren't equals in intellect or planning, but they were equals in cruelty. And once enabled, Ng showed no hesitation in carrying out the worst of Lake's vision.

Today, Charles Ng remains a cautionary figure in criminal psychology and law enforcement circles. His case is used in forensic studies on co-offending, sadism, and manipulation. He is remembered not just as a killer, but as a man who actively prolonged suffering, who denied closure for years through legal stalling, and who had a key role in one of the most sadistic serial murder cases in U.S. history.

While Leonard Lake took the ideology to his grave, Charles Ng continues to exist within the system he once tried to defy. He is a reminder that evil need not always present itself as methodical or rational. Sometimes, it's chaotic, gleeful, and opportunistic, and just as deadly.

Arthur Shawcross

Arthur Shawcross is one of the most disturbing case studies in modern American criminal history; not only because of the crimes he committed, but because of the system's failure to stop him sooner.

Known as the "Genesee River Killer," Shawcross was convicted of murdering 11 women between 1988 and 1989 in upstate New York. But his killing career had already begun long before that. In 1972, he was convicted of killing two children in Watertown, New York. He served just 15 years before being released, only to go on a second spree, this time with even more victims. The failure to anticipate his recidivism would later ignite controversy across the justice and mental health systems.

Born on June 6, 1945, in Kittery, Maine, Arthur John Shawcross grew up in a troubled household in Watertown. His early life was reportedly marked by physical and s**ual abuse, including disturbing claims that his mother and aunt molested him. While some of these accounts remain unverified and came later in interviews, they shaped how Shawcross would explain his own behavior. Teachers described him as a poor student with limited impulse control. He had a documented low IQ and struggled to keep up academically. As he grew older, his behavior became increasingly erratic and violent.

Shawcross was often involved in fights and petty crimes. He dropped out of school in the ninth grade and enlisted in the Army, eventually serving in Vietnam. There, he claimed to have committed atrocities, including cannibalism and murder.

But military records don't support these claims. Whether they were real or fabricated, these stories became part of the mythology he constructed around himself, one where violence and dominance were central themes. What is more certain is that after returning home, he continued exhibiting aggressive behavior, often directed at the vulnerable.

In 1972, Shawcross lured a 10-year-old boy named Jack Blake into the woods in Watertown and murdered him. Just weeks later, he raped and killed 8-year-old Karen Ann Hill. The brutality of these crimes was shocking, and Shawcross was quickly arrested. To the bewilderment of many, he was allowed to plead guilty to a reduced charge of manslaughter and received a 25-year sentence. He served just 15 years before being released in 1987. The parole board cited good behavior and psychological evaluations that deemed him no longer a threat. That decision would have deadly consequences.

After his release, Shawcross was relocated multiple times due to community outrage and fear. Eventually, he settled in Rochester, New York, where he took a job as a food delivery driver and began a new relationship. For a brief period, he appeared to be reintegrating into society. But behind the scenes, Shawcross was hunting again, this time with a more refined method and a broader target pool.

Between March 1988 and January 1990, the bodies of 11 women, most of them s** workers, were found dumped near the Genesee River, often mutilated and exposed to the elements. Some had been strangled, others bludgeoned, and a few were left in grotesque positions. The killer showed knowledge of the terrain, returning to the same dump sites more than once. Police were initially slow to connect the murders due to jurisdictional overlaps and the marginalized status of many victims. But eventually, a task force was formed, and patterns began to emerge.

Shawcross had developed a formula. He would drive around Rochester's red-light districts, picking up women under the pretense of paying for s**. Once in his vehicle, he would take them to isolated areas, typically near rivers, bridges, or wooded zones, where he would murder them. Afterward, he sometimes returned to the bodies, a detail that indicated a ritualistic or psychological attachment to the crime scenes. In one instance, police observed him eating lunch near one of the victim's remains, an act that reinforced the grotesque intimacy he seemed to seek with death.

What made Shawcross particularly dangerous was his ability to operate undetected for so long. He maintained an ordinary appearance: a blue-collar job, a live-in girlfriend, and no overt signs of mental instability to casual observers. This normalcy gave him cover and allowed him to exploit gaps in the system.

By the time investigators began zeroing in on him, nine women were already dead. His downfall came after aerial surveillance caught his vehicle near a crime scene.

Ballistics and forensic evidence soon followed, along with a confession that stunned investigators.

Shawcross admitted to the murders in graphic detail, showing little remorse. He spoke about his victims in dismissive or utilitarian terms. He described how they "annoyed" him or made demands, and in his mind, that justified their deaths.

Psychological evaluations painted a complex picture. Some experts diagnosed him with antisocial personality disorder, while others argued he had dissociative tendencies rooted in childhood trauma. He was manipulative, articulate, and eerily calm. The most unsettling quality wasn't rage; it was control. Shawcross did not lose his temper. He made decisions. Cold, calculated ones.

During his 1990 trial, Shawcross's attorneys attempted an insanity defense, citing PTSD from Vietnam and a history of abuse. The prosecution countered with evidence of planning, concealment, and the repeated nature of the killings. The jury wasn't swayed by the psychological arguments. Shawcross was convicted of 10 counts of second-degree murder (one charge was dropped due to insufficient evidence) and sentenced to 250 years in prison. He would never be eligible for parole again.

In the years following his conviction, Shawcross became a figure of macabre curiosity. He granted interviews to psychiatrists, journalists, and documentary filmmakers, often offering conflicting narratives. At times, he claimed regret. Other times, he deflected blame or hinted at forces beyond his control. He remained a puzzle, one that many professionals studied to better understand the anatomy of repeat offenders. His case became part of criminal justice reform debates, particularly around parole policy for violent offenders.

One of the most lasting impacts of Shawcross's crimes was the public outrage surrounding his release in 1987. Victims' rights groups and law enforcement agencies pointed to his case as a glaring example of system failure. How could someone who murdered children ever be released? Why were red flags ignored?

The case spurred changes in New York State's parole practices, including stricter risk assessments and more oversight for high-profile releases. In this way, Shawcross reshaped policy, not through design, but through horror.

He also left a mark on the understanding of serial killers as complex and adaptive. Shawcross was not the archetype of a genius killer. He was a man of average intelligence, limited education, and no sophisticated plan. But he knew how to exploit those more vulnerable than himself. He knew how to hide behind routine.

And he understood, perhaps better than most, how to leverage invisibility in plain sight. His calm demeanor, unremarkable job, and unassuming appearance gave him cover. He wasn't a shadowy figure stalking in the dark. He was the man delivering your groceries.

Shawcross died in 2008 at the age of 63, after being transported from prison to an Albany hospital due to cardiac arrest. His death closed the chapter on one of New York's most notorious serial murder cases, but the questions he raised still linger. He represented not just an individual pathology, but a challenge to institutions meant to predict and contain human danger. His crimes forced an entire state to reconsider what it means to assess risk and protect the public.

More than thirty years later, Arthur Shawcross remains a reminder that evil doesn't always wear a monster's face. Sometimes it looks like a neighbor, a coworker, or the , but the camouflage.

Paul Bernardo

Paul Bernardo is one of Canada's most infamous convicted criminals, known for a series of violent assaults and the murders of two teenage girls that shocked the nation during the late 1980s and early 1990s. His crimes, committed in partnership with Karla Homolka, triggered widespread debate over parole policies, plea bargains, and psychological profiling.

Bernardo's ability to present a polished public image while concealing a darker reality contributed to his notoriety. His case is now studied extensively in both criminology and forensic psychology as a complex example of predatory behavior carried out in plain sight.

Born on August 27, 1964, in Scarborough, Ontario, Paul Bernardo was raised in a family that, despite financial stability, struggled with internal dysfunction. His father was later convicted of offenses against minors, and his mother became increasingly withdrawn as the years went on. Although these early factors didn't immediately signal the future severity of Bernardo's actions, his adolescence began revealing concerning traits. He was described by peers as charismatic but manipulative, and he maintained a carefully crafted image of success and composure.

Bernardo attended the University of Toronto's Scarborough campus, studying accounting. During these years, he cultivated a controlled and outwardly respectable demeanor. At the same time, however, he developed an interest in controlling and demeaning others, particularly women. By the late 1980s, a pattern of s**ual violence had emerged in the Scarborough area. A string of assaults occurred near public transportation stops and residential neighborhoods, all targeting young women. The perpetrator, dubbed the "Scarborough Rapist" by local media, operated with stealth and precision, and the attacks began to instill fear across the community.

Bernardo was later confirmed to be responsible for many of these assaults. He had been questioned by police and even submitted a DNA sample in 1990, but due to backlog and procedural delays, the sample wasn't tested until years later. This delay would prove costly. Between the time of his DNA submission and his eventual arrest, Bernardo escalated to even more serious crimes.

In 1987, Paul Bernardo met Karla Homolka, then a teenager, at a hotel convention. Their relationship developed quickly, and they moved in together soon after. Friends and family initially saw their partnership as loving, but beneath the surface, it was marked by control, coercion, and a shared disregard for moral boundaries. Homolka, rather than distancing herself from Bernardo's troubling behavior, enabled and at times actively participated in it. The psychological dynamic between them later became a subject of academic inquiry into co-offending relationships.

Bernardo and Homolka married in 1991, but by then, they had already committed multiple serious offenses. Their crimes were characterized by abduction, confinement, and violence. Two victims, Leslie Mahaffy and Kristen French, both teenagers, were abducted, held for extended periods, and ultimately murdered. The deaths of these two young women led to national media attention, major police investigations, and public mourning.

The police investigation eventually caught up with Bernardo in early 1993, when advances in forensic analysis linked his earlier DNA sample to several unsolved s**ual assault cases. Around the same time, Homolka sought legal counsel after their relationship deteriorated, citing domestic abuse. She offered testimony against Bernardo in exchange for a reduced sentence. This plea deal, later dubbed by the media as the "Deal with the Devil," sparked public outrage when it was revealed that Homolka had played a more active role in the crimes than initially disclosed.

In 1995, Bernardo stood trial in one of the most high-profile criminal cases in Canadian history. The evidence included testimony from Homolka and other witnesses, as well as recovered videotapes that had been hidden by the couple and later turned over to police. These tapes showed not only Bernardo's culpability but also contradicted Homolka's portrayal of herself as a passive victim. The jury found Bernardo guilty of multiple charges, including two counts of first-degree murder, and he was sentenced to life in prison without the possibility of parole.

The Bernardo case prompted intense public debate about how violent offenders are monitored, how plea bargains are negotiated, and how psychological evaluations are interpreted in court.

The delay in processing DNA evidence, in particular, led to reforms in forensic protocol in Ontario and other provinces. It also highlighted the importance of interagency cooperation, victim advocacy, and risk assessment in managing repeat offenders.

Psychologically, Bernardo fits the profile of a narcissistic and highly manipulative individual. Evaluations noted traits commonly associated with psychopathy, including lack of empathy, superficial charm, and a tendency to exploit others. His self-image was inflated, and he often expressed a belief that he was intellectually and socially superior. During post-trial assessments, he showed minimal remorse and continued to rationalize his behavior. His ability to compartmentalize his public and private personas made him particularly difficult to detect early on.

One of the most chilling aspects of Bernardo's crimes was the degree to which he operated within everyday society. He held a steady job, maintained a home, and interacted with others without raising suspicion. This duality, presenting as normal while secretly committing extreme acts, has become a key focus in criminology studies about high-functioning offenders. It challenges traditional assumptions about what danger looks like and reinforces the need for better behavioral and forensic screening.

Today, Bernardo remains incarcerated in Canada under a dangerous offender designation, which effectively ensures permanent detention. He is periodically the subject of parole reviews, but due to the nature and scope of his crimes, his release remains highly unlikely. The legal classification prevents him from being transferred to less secure facilities, and his movements and communications are tightly controlled. He remains one of the most reviled figures in Canadian criminal history.

In recent years, public interest in Bernardo has reignited during periodic parole hearings and discussions around Homolka's release and reintegration. Although Homolka served her sentence and has resumed life under a new identity, public scrutiny and moral outrage persist. Their case has been the subject of books, documentaries, and academic research, but it remains one of the most controversial in Canada's modern legal record.

Bernardo's crimes also had lasting consequences for the families of the victims, who have continued to advocate for changes in victim rights, parole transparency, and public safety measures.

The deaths of Leslie Mahaffy and Kristen French remain powerful reminders of the cost of criminal oversight and the importance of listening to early warning signs. Their legacy is reflected in changes to how cases are investigated, how evidence is prioritized, and how the system responds to claims of domestic violence and coercive control.

Paul Bernardo's legacy is not just one of violence, but of systemic failure and subsequent reform. His case forced Canada to confront uncomfortable truths about crime, justice, and accountability. It showed how easily danger can be hidden behind a polished exterior, and how criminal partnerships can function when individual pathology is reinforced by enablers. For all the damage he caused, Bernardo's name now serves as a cautionary example, one that continues to inform how societies detect, investigate, and prosecute predatory crimes.

Karla Homolka

Karla Homolka's name is synonymous with controversy in Canadian criminal history. Her involvement in a series of crimes committed alongside her then-husband, Paul Bernardo, generated widespread outrage and debate, not only due to the brutality of the acts themselves, but also because of how the legal system handled her cooperation with authorities. Homolka was a central figure in a case that revealed disturbing psychological dynamics, systemic oversights, and long-lasting questions about justice and culpability. Her story is not just one of criminal participation, but of legal ambiguity, public betrayal, and national soul-searching.

Born on May 4, 1970, in Port Credit, Ontario, Homolka grew up in what appeared to be a stable, middle-class environment. She was the eldest of three daughters and generally regarded as intelligent, outgoing, and responsible. Friends, teachers, and coworkers described her as friendly and ambitious. As a teenager, she held jobs at pet stores and aspired to work in veterinary care. There were no overt signs in her early life that hinted at what would later unfold, a fact that makes her case all the more unsettling.

In October 1987, Homolka met Paul Bernardo at a hotel conference in Scarborough. She was 17, he was 23. The attraction was immediate, and their relationship became serious within weeks.

What began as a passionate romance soon revealed darker undercurrents. Bernardo, who had already begun committing a series of s**ual assaults across Toronto's eastern suburbs, started expressing violent fantasies. Rather than distancing herself, Homolka appeared to accept and later participate in those behaviors. Their relationship evolved into something far more disturbing than anyone around them suspected.

The first known incident tied directly to both Homolka and Bernardo occurred on December 23, 1990, when Homolka's younger sister, Tammy, died at the family home. That night, Karla and Paul had given her a combination of sedatives and alcohol. Tammy passed out and never regained consciousness. Although the death was ruled accidental at the time, later evidence raised serious questions about what had occurred. This incident would eventually be viewed as the starting point of a descent into violence that would claim multiple lives. Crucially, it also showed that Homolka had crossed a moral threshold, choosing complicity over resistance.

Over the next two years, Homolka and Bernardo abducted and killed two teenage girls: Leslie Mahaffy in June 1991, and Kristen French in April 1992. The details of these crimes, while documented extensively in court records, remain difficult to discuss due to their extreme nature. What became clear, however, was that Homolka's role extended far beyond passive observation.

She assisted in luring the girls, took part in their captivity, and participated in their abuse. Video evidence later recovered by investigators revealed her active involvement, contradicting earlier statements that had portrayed her as coerced and dominated.

These tapes, discovered only after Homolka had struck a plea deal with prosecutors, would become the focal point of a national controversy. Facing mounting pressure to convict Bernardo, who was already suspected in several rapes and murders, the Crown agreed to a twelve-year sentence for Homolka in exchange for her testimony. At the time, authorities believed she was a battered woman who had acted out of fear. Once the tapes were reviewed and revealed her direct participation, the public's view shifted dramatically. The media dubbed the plea bargain "The Deal with the Devil," and faith in the justice system was deeply shaken.

The question of Karla Homolka's true level of responsibility has remained a topic of legal and psychological debate. Some experts have argued that she exhibited characteristics of dependent personality disorder, a condition marked by extreme submissiveness and a fear of abandonment. From this perspective, her behavior could be interpreted as the result of psychological manipulation by an abusive partner. Others contend that she demonstrated planning, control, and emotional detachment inconsistent with such a diagnosis. Her demeanor during court appearances (calm, articulate, and emotionally reserved) only fueled suspicions that she had skillfully manipulated both investigators and the legal process.

Public reaction to her sentencing and eventual release was intense and sustained. After serving her twelve-year sentence, Homolka was released from prison in July 2005. Although she had technically completed her punishment under the law, many Canadians felt that justice had not been served. Community groups protested her release, journalists tracked her movements, and legal scholars continued to question whether the plea deal should have been renegotiated in light of new evidence. For years after her release, she remained a polarizing figure, often vilified, occasionally defended, but never forgotten.

Homolka's attempts to reintegrate into society were met with mixed results. She changed her name, moved to Quebec, and later lived in the Caribbean before returning to Canada. She married the brother of her former attorney and started a family.

Despite her efforts to maintain a low profile, media outlets occasionally revealed her whereabouts, especially when she was spotted near schools or public areas. Each time, public concern reignited, forcing authorities to respond and monitor the situation closely.

In the years following her release, Homolka granted no formal interviews and made few public statements. Her silence has been interpreted in different ways, by some as a refusal to take responsibility, and by others as an attempt to avoid further harm to the victims' families. Whether she feels genuine remorse or has merely sought to escape public scrutiny remains unknown. What is certain is that her life after prison has never fully escaped the shadow of her past.

The legal and cultural legacy of Karla Homolka's case is significant. It exposed serious flaws in how plea bargains are negotiated, especially in cases involving co-offenders. It also highlighted the dangers of forming conclusions before all evidence is available. Most importantly, it forced Canada to reconsider how it views complicity, especially among women in violent crimes. While male serial killers are often the focus of public fear and legal attention, Homolka's case showed that female offenders can play active, even leadership, roles in criminal partnerships.

The aftermath of her crimes also spurred reforms in victim advocacy, media access to court evidence, and parole transparency. Victims' rights groups pushed for greater inclusion in judicial processes, especially in cases involving early release or plea agreements. Lawmakers debated new restrictions for high-risk offenders, including publication bans and post-release monitoring.

For scholars of criminal justice and psychology, Homolka's case continues to be a subject of study. It challenges assumptions about gender, victimhood, and responsibility. Was she a victim of coercive control, or a willing architect of suffering? Can two truths exist in one case: that she was abused, and that she also committed abuse? These questions offer no easy answers, but they are central to understanding how justice is applied in complex, high-stakes situations.

Homolka's life and actions remain a painful part of Canada's collective memory. The names of the victims (Leslie Mahaffy and Kristen French) are honored through scholarships, memorials, and community initiatives. Their families, along with advocacy organizations, have worked to ensure that their stories are not overshadowed by the notoriety of those who harmed them.

While Karla Homolka has faded from the headlines in recent years, the impact of her actions, and the legal consequences that followed, continue to shape how Canadians think about crime, punishment, and accountability.

Her story is ultimately one of dissonance: a seemingly ordinary young woman who crossed moral lines most people never approach, and a legal system that struggled to balance urgency with justice.

In the end, Karla Homolka's place in history is a reminder that criminal behavior isn't always easy to categorize, and that justice is not always perfectly served, even when the law is followed to the letter.

Peter Sutcliffe

Peter Sutcliffe, later known as the "Yorkshire Ripper," committed a string of murders and attacks in northern England that gripped the UK in terror from the mid-1970s until his arrest in 1981. His crimes were brutal and targeted, and his capture raised a host of disturbing questions about law enforcement's investigative methods, societal biases, and the dangers of underestimating certain types of offenders. Sutcliffe's name remains etched in British criminal history not only because of the body count, but because of the national trauma and institutional failures his actions exposed.

Born in Bingley, West Yorkshire, in 1946, Peter Sutcliffe's early life didn't mark him immediately as someone destined for infamy. He was one of six children in a working-class Roman Catholic family. Friends and family members described him as quiet, withdrawn, and somewhat awkward. He left school at fifteen, taking on a variety of low-skill jobs, including as a gravedigger, truck driver, and factory worker. There were hints of dark behavior, such as morbid jokes at the cemetery and an unusual fixation on s** workers, but little to suggest what would follow.

Sutcliffe married Sonia Szurma in 1974, and outwardly appeared to live a relatively normal life. Behind that façade, however, his worldview was warping. He developed an intense hatred toward s** workers, whom he believed were corrupting society. At one point, he would claim to have heard voices (he believed from God) telling him to rid the streets of immoral women. Whether this was delusion or a convenient excuse remains debated. His murders, which began shortly after his marriage, were violent, frenzied, and consistent in method. His targets were usually women, many of them s** workers or women he perceived as such, whom he bludgeoned with a hammer before stabbing them.

The first known victim was Wilma McCann, a mother of four, killed in October 1975. Her murder went unsolved for years. Sutcliffe struck again in January 1976, murdering 42-year-old Emily Jackson. The nature of the attacks began to show a pattern: sudden violence, repeated blows to the head, and post-mortem stabbing. Yet police failed to connect the dots early on. As his spree continued, more women were killed or seriously injured. Sutcliffe varied his targets just enough to confuse investigators; some were s** workers, others were not. Some were attacked late at night on city streets, others in more domestic or secluded settings.

By the late 1970s, the public was in a state of fear. Women in northern cities like Leeds and Bradford began altering their routines. Feminist groups held marches, urging people to understand that all women were at risk, not just those in the s** trade.

Law enforcement, under growing pressure, launched what became one of the most expensive and extensive manhunts in British history. Over 250 officers were involved, more than a million documents were collected, and countless interviews were conducted.

But the investigation was marred by systemic failures. The task force was overwhelmed by paperwork, lacked technological tools like databases or DNA matching, and struggled to manage leads effectively. The case was further derailed by a hoax that arrived in the form of cassette tapes and letters from someone calling himself "Wearside Jack." The sender claimed responsibility for the killings, and his accent misled police into looking for a suspect from the Sunderland area, pulling resources away from leads closer to Sutcliffe's actual location in West Yorkshire. The voice on the tape was later confirmed to be a hoax, but at the time, police treated it as authentic and disregarded suspects who didn't match the dialect. Sutcliffe himself was interviewed multiple times by police (at least nine) yet was never thoroughly investigated or connected to the crimes due to administrative errors and tunnel vision caused by the misleading audio recordings.

The body count climbed. In total, Sutcliffe murdered thirteen women and attempted to kill seven others. His final victim, Jacqueline Hill, was a 20-year-old university student murdered in November 1980. By this time, the public was enraged by the lack of progress in the investigation, and trust in the authorities was beginning to erode. It wasn't police detective work that brought Sutcliffe down; it was a routine traffic stop.

In January 1981, Sutcliffe was pulled over in Sheffield with a woman who turned out to be a s** worker. Officers became suspicious, and after a background check revealed inconsistencies and prior arrests for solicitation-related offenses, they took him in. While in custody, Sutcliffe attempted to hide incriminating evidence, including a knife and rope. The items were later recovered. When questioned further, he eventually confessed, not only to the crime at hand, but to the long string of unsolved murders.

At his trial, Sutcliffe pleaded not guilty to murder but guilty to manslaughter on grounds of diminished responsibility. He claimed he was suffering from paranoid schizophrenia. The court rejected this, and in May 1981 he was convicted of thirteen murders and seven attempted murders. He was sentenced to life imprisonment, with a recommendation that he never be released. He was later transferred to Broadmoor Hospital, a high-security psychiatric facility, where he remained for decades before being returned to a regular prison. He died in 2020 from complications related to COVID-19 while incarcerated.

Sutcliffe's case remains one of the most heavily analyzed in British legal and forensic circles. One major point of discussion centers on the police response. Investigators were accused of bias, both in how they dismissed survivors who weren't s** workers and in their general treatment of victims. Many survivors later stated that their testimonies weren't taken seriously, especially those who survived but were dismissed because they didn't "fit the profile" police had created. The fact that Sutcliffe was allowed to slip through the net despite repeated interviews is viewed as one of the great investigative failures in modern British history.

Another focal point has been the media's handling of the case. The press often sensationalized the story, referring to Sutcliffe as the "Yorkshire Ripper" to evoke echoes of Jack the Ripper. Tabloid headlines, graphic crime scene descriptions, and blame placed on victims added layers of distortion to public understanding. Over time, more thoughtful documentaries and academic studies have aimed to re-center the narrative on the victims themselves, rather than glorifying the perpetrator.

The psychological profile of Peter Sutcliffe is still debated. While some psychiatrists believed he met the criteria for paranoid schizophrenia, others viewed him as a cold, calculating predator who knew exactly what he was doing. There was no single trigger for his crimes; rather, they appeared to be the result of a blend of misogynistic hatred, suppressed rage, and a growing desire to exert control and cause pain. His work life and marriage appeared unremarkable during much of his killing spree, highlighting how well he compartmentalized his crimes.

Sutcliffe's trial and the years that followed led to significant introspection within British policing. There were reforms in how serial cases were handled, improvements in data management, and greater attention to the treatment of female victims and survivors.

New systems were eventually developed for managing large volumes of evidence, and new procedures were established for reviewing cases involving violence against women. However, many argue that it took too long for these changes to be implemented, and that if a more modern approach had been used earlier, lives might have been saved.

The cultural imprint of Sutcliffe's crimes is deep and persistent. His story has been the subject of numerous documentaries, books, and dramatizations, though these are often met with mixed responses. Survivors and victims' families have expressed concerns that sensationalized portrayals continue to place attention on the killer rather than those he harmed. This tension underscores the ongoing struggle in true crime media between informing the public and respecting the dignity of victims.

Perhaps the most haunting aspect of Peter Sutcliffe's crimes is how preventable many of them were. Not only was he known to law enforcement, but his behavior had repeatedly drawn attention. The failure to act decisively, exacerbated by miscommunication, false leads, and institutional blind spots, meant that a man responsible for a dozen murders was able to continue for years while police remained focused on the wrong profile. In the years since, the Sutcliffe case has been taught as a cautionary tale in criminal justice programs around the world.

Even decades after his arrest and death, the case evokes powerful emotions. The women he targeted were often marginalized, dismissed, or stigmatized, both in life and in death. His crimes forced British society to confront not just the existence of serial murder, but the deeper social failures that allowed it to continue. For many, Peter Sutcliffe is remembered not just as a brutal killer, but as a symbol of what happens when systems meant to protect the public fall short.

Robert Pickton

Robert William Pickton's story begins on the muddy, rural outskirts of British Columbia and ends in one of the most horrific criminal investigations in Canadian history.

The so-called "Pig Farm Killer" became infamous not just for the depravity of his actions, but for how long he operated unnoticed, even as women vanished from Vancouver's poorest neighborhoods. His case would reveal major lapses in policing, systemic disregard for vulnerable populations, and a disturbing portrait of a man who used his unassuming lifestyle and surroundings as camouflage for cruelty.

Born in October 1949 in Port Coquitlam, Pickton was raised on a pig farm alongside his brother and sister. His childhood was marked by isolation, hardship, and a lack of formal emotional development. His parents were known to be strict and eccentric; his mother, in particular, was feared by the children and reportedly cared more for the pigs than for people. From an early age, Robert was withdrawn, underperforming in school and eventually dropping out to work full time on the farm. He wasn't sociable, but he wasn't outwardly threatening either; he was considered strange, but mostly harmless by those who interacted with him casually.

In adulthood, Pickton and his siblings inherited the family farm after their parents passed. The property was vast, unkempt, and full of dilapidated machinery, scattered tools, and, of course, pigs. Over time, the land became not only a home but a dumping ground, a party venue, and a makeshift scrapyard. Pickton and his brother eventually registered a nonprofit charity called the "Piggy Palace Good Times Society," claiming it was intended to organize social events to raise money for local causes. In practice, these events turned into raucous parties, often featuring heavy drinking, drugs, and s** workers, many of whom would never be seen again.

Beginning in the late 1980s and escalating into the 1990s, women began to disappear from Vancouver's Downtown Eastside, a notoriously impoverished and marginalized part of the city. Most of the missing were Indigenous women or struggling with homelessness, mental illness, or addiction. Families and advocacy groups raised alarms repeatedly, but police and city officials were slow to act. For years, disappearances were treated as isolated incidents or dismissed entirely, under the assumption that many of these women had simply moved or left town. This attitude would later be criticized as deeply rooted in racism, classism, and systemic neglect.

By the mid-1990s, rumors began circulating about Pickton. Stories of women going to the farm and never returning, of weapons and restraints on the property, of disturbing behavior. In 1997, Pickton was actually arrested after a woman escaped from his trailer with serious injuries. She had fought him off and made it to safety, covered in blood, and told police she had been handcuffed and stabbed.

Pickton was charged with attempted murder, but the case was dropped because the woman, also from a vulnerable background, was deemed an unreliable witness. Despite this, police failed to follow up thoroughly, and Pickton returned to his quiet, filthy routine. Years later, investigators would discover that at the time of this arrest, remains of several victims were already on the property.

It wasn't until 2002 that police, acting on a weapons warrant, searched Pickton's farm again. This time, they uncovered human remains and personal belongings that linked him to several missing women. The property became the site of one of the largest and most expensive crime scenes in Canadian history. Forensic teams worked for months to excavate the land, sift through pig remains, and identify body parts.

It became clear that Pickton had been killing women for years, possibly decades, and disposing of their remains in the most grotesque ways imaginable. Some bodies had been butchered and fed to pigs. Others had been ground up and discarded. The sheer scale of what he had done stunned even seasoned investigators.

Pickton was eventually charged with the murders of 26 women, though evidence suggested he may have killed many more. At one point, he casually bragged to an undercover officer that he had killed 49 women and wanted to make it an even 50. He said he had been "sloppy" and "got caught because he was being careless."

The number itself became part of the mythology surrounding his crimes, though the true toll may never be known due to the advanced decomposition and destruction of evidence. Many of the remains found on the farm were fragmentary (bone chips, teeth, or DNA traces) and some victims were never conclusively identified.

His trial began in 2007 and focused on six of the murder charges. The prosecution chose to limit the initial case to those with the most complete evidence, fearing that presenting too many charges at once could overwhelm the jury or risk mistrial. The courtroom was filled with a sense of dread and grief. Families of the missing listened in horror as forensic details were read aloud and as prosecutors laid out how the women had been lured, killed, and discarded like garbage. The defense portrayed Pickton as simple-minded and incapable of such crimes alone, but the evidence was damning. After lengthy deliberations, the jury found him guilty on all six counts of second-degree murder. He was sentenced to life in prison with no possibility of parole for 25 years, the maximum penalty under Canadian law.

The aftermath of Pickton's conviction was not one of closure but of national reckoning. Public outrage exploded. Indigenous organizations and advocacy groups demanded answers about why warnings had gone unheeded for so long. The Royal Canadian Mounted Police and Vancouver Police Department were heavily criticized for their handling of the disappearances. A public inquiry, known as the Missing Women Commission of Inquiry, was launched and released a scathing report detailing years of missed opportunities, systemic discrimination, and institutional indifference. It concluded that bias against s** workers and Indigenous women had had a major role in the failure to catch Pickton earlier.

The inquiry also produced over 60 recommendations to improve police training, community outreach, and investigative coordination. However, implementation of those reforms has been uneven, and the families of many victims remain frustrated. Some of the recommendations called for better tracking of missing persons, trauma-informed policing, and cultural sensitivity training to avoid further marginalizing the most vulnerable. To this day, the Pickton case serves as a grim symbol of how deeply embedded prejudices can allow atrocities to go unchecked.

One of the more haunting elements of the case is Pickton himself. He never expressed remorse, never gave clear reasons for his actions, and seemed detached from the horror he had caused. In interviews and statements, he often rambled or downplayed his role, as if incapable of fully grasping the magnitude of what he had done.

Psychological evaluations suggested he was of average intelligence but socially underdeveloped. He wasn't a criminal mastermind. His success as a killer came not from cleverness, but from the silence and invisibility of his victims in a society that largely ignored them.

Since his incarceration, Pickton has remained largely out of public view. He's been the subject of documentaries, books, and academic studies, though all are treated with extreme caution given the sensitivities surrounding the case. He was reportedly attacked by other inmates in prison and has been moved for his own safety. There have been attempts to ban him from communicating publicly or writing about his crimes, especially after it was discovered he had worked with a ghostwriter to produce a short book that was briefly available online before being pulled.

To this day, the pig farm no longer stands, but the land is forever tainted. For many families, the farm remains a symbolic graveyard. Vigils and memorials have been held on the site, and community efforts continue to honor the women who were lost. Some victims' identities were confirmed only through tiny bone fragments or DNA traces recovered from pig waste or soil. The emotional weight of that reality is hard to overstate.

Robert Pickton's case isn't just a story of monstrous violence, but a story of societal failure. A man with no special intelligence or resources murdered dozens of women over years, while authorities failed to act on clear warning signs. He used the most basic tools available to him and was protected by a cloak of indifference that came not from genius, but from public apathy toward the poor, the addicted, and the Indigenous. His crimes demand remembrance not only for their brutality, but for the deep injustices that allowed them to happen.

Dean Corll

Dean Arnold Corll is one of the most chilling figures in American criminal history, yet for years his name remained overshadowed by more publicized killers. Known posthumously as the "Candy Man" because of his family's candy business and the way he used sweets to lure victims, Corll orchestrated a reign of terror in Houston, Texas, that left at least 28 boys and young men dead between 1970 and 1973.

His story is made all the more disturbing by the fact that his crimes only came to light when he was killed by one of his own accomplices, an explosive end to a case that exposed an underground world of manipulation, cruelty, and institutional blind spots.

Corll was born in 1939 in Fort Wayne, Indiana, and moved to Houston with his family during childhood. His upbringing was relatively unremarkable on the surface. He played musical instruments, was described as polite, and helped his mother run a candy company called Pecan Prince. Despite his courteous reputation, Dean was also reserved and had difficulty forming close relationships. After serving briefly in the military, Corll returned to the family business and lived in a modest home in the Houston Heights neighborhood. He was well-liked by neighbors, who remembered

(Corll in the 1960s)

him handing out free candy to local children and allowing kids to congregate at his house. Beneath this image of kindness, however, something much darker was brewing.

It was in the early 1970s that Corll's pattern of predation began in earnest. He formed close relationships with two teenage boys, David Owen Brooks and Elmer Wayne Henley, whom he manipulated into becoming his accomplices. Corll gained their trust with money, gifts, and the promise of inclusion. Both boys came from troubled backgrounds and lacked parental supervision. Corll positioned himself as a father figure and benefactor, but what he wanted in return was horrifying: help finding and subduing young male victims.

Corll's method followed a disturbing routine. With Brooks and Henley as lures, they would offer boys rides, drugs, or alcohol and bring them to Corll's home. Once inside, the victims were overpowered and tied to a plywood torture board that Corll had built specifically for this purpose. He would then torture and kill them in prolonged episodes of abuse. The bodies were either buried in a rented boat shed, in a shallow grave near Lake Sam Rayburn, or covered in lime and placed in various locations across southeast Texas. Despite the growing number of disappearances in the area, no serious investigation connected the cases. Police often classified the missing teens as runaways, and their families' pleas were dismissed or ignored.

What made Corll particularly terrifying wasn't only the violence of his actions, but the calculated way he built a system around them. He normalized the horror for his accomplices, turning them from vulnerable teenagers into active participants. David Brooks reportedly received a car and other rewards, while Elmer Henley later claimed he was originally led to believe they were involved in some kind of vigilante justice, punishing "bad kids" or runaways.

That illusion quickly crumbled. Henley eventually became deeply involved in the murders, assisting in the kidnapping, restraint, and disposal of victims. His own participation marked one of the darkest aspects of the case: the way Corll warped the morality and perception of his teenage recruits to such an extent that they not only obeyed him, but helped execute his crimes.

The murder spree might have continued even longer were it not for a moment of sudden reversal. On August 8, 1973, Henley brought two friends, a girl named Rhonda Williams and a boy named Timothy Kerley, to Corll's house. Corll was furious that Henley had brought a girl and accused him of ruining everything. He eventually tied all three teenagers up.

But Henley, sensing the end was near and fearing for his life, convinced Corll to let him go by claiming he would kill the other two himself. Corll relented. But instead of complying, Henley turned the gun on Corll and shot him multiple times, killing him on the spot. Then he called the police.

What followed was a confession that stunned law enforcement. Henley led detectives to the rented boat shed on Silver Bell Street, where they began recovering body after body in varying states of decomposition. Forensic teams worked for weeks to exhume the remains, and the nation watched in horror as the scope of the crimes came into view. Most of the victims were teenagers or young men, many of them known to the local community. Some had been missing for years. The recovery process was so extensive that some burial sites remained undiscovered until years later.

Corll had never been arrested or even seriously questioned in relation to any of the disappearances during his life. Despite his proximity to victims, despite rumors, despite signs that something was terribly wrong, he remained untouched by suspicion. In hindsight, many in the community, particularly the families of the victims, criticized law enforcement and city officials for their lack of urgency and their failure to properly investigate.

There were allegations of apathy due to the victims' social status and perceived lack of importance. Many were from poor families, had spotty school attendance, or had brushes with petty crime. Their disappearances were often chalked up to teen rebellion rather than foul play.

In total, 28 confirmed victims were linked to Dean Corll, making him one of the most prolific serial killers in American history at the time of discovery. Some believe the true number could be higher. Identification of the remains was a painstaking process, and to this day, a few victims remain unidentified. Advances in DNA analysis have helped solve some of these mysteries in recent years, bringing delayed closure to families who had waited decades for answers.

The two accomplices, David Brooks and Elmer Henley, were both arrested and charged with multiple counts of murder. Henley was ultimately convicted on six counts and sentenced to six consecutive life terms. Brooks was convicted on one count of murder and received a life sentence as well.

Their roles in the case have been debated, whether they were victims of manipulation or fully culpable collaborators, but the courts deemed them active participants. Henley remains incarcerated to this day and has given interviews from prison, in which he alternately expresses regret and tries to shift blame back onto Corll. Brooks died in prison in 2020.

The case left deep scars in the Houston community and reshaped public attitudes toward missing persons. It highlighted the need for better systems to track disappearances, greater sensitivity toward the families of victims, and a reevaluation of how law enforcement handles marginalized youth. In the years that followed, Houston authorities faced increasing pressure to reform their practices, particularly around runaway reports and youth crime.

Dean Corll's crimes also altered the psychological literature on serial killers. He didn't fit the classic lone predator archetype. He created a network of complicity, using the weaknesses and insecurities of others to construct a system of horror that functioned almost like a cult.

His charm was minimal, his intelligence average, and yet he was extraordinarily successful at evading detection because of how thoroughly he blended into his environment. He didn't seek fame or media attention. He worked in the shadows, relying on a facade of normalcy and the silence of others to continue his pattern.

For all the evil associated with his name, Dean Corll is ultimately remembered as a man who operated unchecked because society allowed him to. He didn't hide in the wilderness or prey in distant cities. He lived among his neighbors, offered them candy, and smiled as he walked through a community that never saw the predator within. His story is a warning about complacency, about trusting appearances, and about what can happen when certain lives are viewed as disposable.

Wayne Williams

Between 1979 and 1981, the city of Atlanta was paralyzed by fear. Children, teenagers, and young men, most of them Black, were disappearing at an alarming rate, only to be found dead days or weeks later. The victims ranged in age from seven to twenty-seven, and the methods of murder varied, but the pattern was unmistakable. The community demanded answers. Parents were afraid to let their children play outside.

Law enforcement, both local and federal, scrambled to coordinate a response. The media labeled the crisis the "Atlanta Child Murders," and over the course of two years, more than two dozen lives were lost.

In May 1981, after years of stalled investigations, Wayne Bertram Williams became the prime suspect. At the time, Williams was a 23-year-old Atlanta native, a freelance photographer and aspiring music producer. He had no serious criminal record, came from a relatively stable family, and had once dreamed of working in radio broadcasting. Nothing about him seemed to suggest he was capable of murder.

And yet, following a stakeout of bridges over the Chattahoochee River, where several victims had been dumped, officers heard a splash in the early morning hours and pulled over a car leaving the scene. That car was driven by Wayne Williams.

The incident that night led police to launch an intensive investigation into Williams. His alibi didn't hold up. Dog hairs found on the bodies of several victims were later matched to the German shepherds owned by his family. Carpet fibers found on the victims also matched the carpeting in his home and vehicle. Over time, investigators accumulated an array of circumstantial evidence tying Williams to multiple murders, even though they never caught him in the act and lacked a direct eyewitness to any killing.

The public case against Williams was built slowly, and with considerable debate. In June 1981, two days after the bridge incident, the body of Nathaniel Cater, a 27-year-old man, was found downstream. Another man, Jimmy Ray Payne, had gone missing earlier and would later be linked to the same pattern. In 1982, Wayne Williams was arrested and charged with the murders of Cater and Payne. Prosecutors elected to try him only for these two killings, hoping to secure a conviction based on the strongest available forensic links and avoid the risk of overextending the case.

The trial was highly publicized and lasted nine weeks. The prosecution introduced a fiber comparison analysis that, at the time, was considered cutting-edge forensic science. Fibers from Williams' car, bedspread, bathroom, and dog were all presented as consistent with those found on the bodies of Cater and Payne. Witnesses testified to hearing screams near Williams' home. Others claimed they saw him with young males shortly before those individuals went missing. The defense argued that the fiber evidence was unreliable, that the police were under immense political pressure to find a suspect, and that Williams had been scapegoated. But the jury ultimately returned a guilty verdict on both counts. He was sentenced to two consecutive life terms in prison.

What made the Wayne Williams case particularly controversial, and why it continues to provoke debate decades later, was the decision to link him to a total of 23 other killings after his conviction, without charging or trying him for them. Law enforcement officials, particularly from the FBI, maintained that the pattern of murders stopped abruptly after Williams' arrest, suggesting his guilt in the wider series. They publicly attributed many of the unsolved child murders to him, effectively closing the cases administratively. But no trials were held, and families of the victims were left with official conclusions but no courtroom justice.

Critics of the investigation, both then and now, have raised several concerns. One major point of contention is the question of whether all the murders were committed by a single individual. The victims varied significantly in age, ranging from elementary school children to adult men. The methods of murder included strangulation, bludgeoning, and asphyxiation. Some victims had been s**ually assaulted, others had not. Some were found in rivers, others in the woods or behind buildings.

To skeptics, the sheer diversity of the cases suggested multiple perpetrators or motives. They argued that the city, under political pressure and intense public scrutiny, needed to restore order and faith in law enforcement; and Williams, with his odd behavior, ambition, and proximity to the victims, became the perfect suspect.

In the years since his conviction, Wayne Williams has consistently maintained his innocence. He has granted numerous interviews from prison, insisting that he was framed and that the fiber evidence was misrepresented or misinterpreted. He has claimed the investigation ignored alternative suspects, and that authorities used him to close difficult, politically sensitive cases. A number of journalists, researchers, and civil rights activists have also questioned the thoroughness and fairness of the investigation, especially in a racially charged climate.

Some supporters point to the lack of physical evidence beyond fibers and dog hairs, neither of which is considered conclusive by today's forensic standards. Others emphasize the rapid decision to close dozens of cases after Williams' conviction, suggesting it was more about public relations than investigative certainty. Over time, doubts about the case have only grown, especially as cold case review units began reinvestigating other unsolved homicides in Georgia and beyond.

In 2019, responding to continued public outcry and demands from families of victims, Atlanta Mayor Keisha Lance Bottoms and Police Chief Erika Shields announced that several of the Atlanta Child Murder cases would be reopened using modern DNA technology. They acknowledged that while Wayne Williams remained the prime suspect, advances in forensic science could offer greater clarity, or possibly reveal errors in past conclusions. The renewed investigation was seen as a step toward transparency and accountability. However, as of early 2026, no definitive new evidence has been made public.

Williams' story, whether as a calculating predator or as a scapegoated misfit, remains one of the most polarizing in American criminal history. Unlike many serial killers who confessed or sought notoriety, Williams has remained defiant, casting himself as the victim of a flawed system.

Yet his behavior during the investigation and trial raised serious suspicions. He failed multiple polygraph tests, contradicted himself in interviews, and was described by some acquaintances as manipulative and controlling.

Investigators noted that he had a deep need for recognition, often inserting himself into conversations about missing children and claiming to have knowledge of the case. That need for validation, they argued, helped explain his ability to lure and dominate vulnerable victims.

Even his personal ambitions, particularly his efforts to break into the music industry, played into the case. Some victims were said to be aspiring performers or had been promised music connections by Williams. These alleged offers gave him access to individuals who trusted him, particularly in a community with limited opportunities and few outlets for creative expression. His perceived authority, coupled with his persuasive personality, allowed him to operate under the radar, even as the city fell deeper into fear.

To this day, Wayne Williams remains incarcerated in Georgia. He has filed multiple appeals, all of which have been denied. Yet the cultural legacy of the Atlanta Child Murders endures. It has inspired books, documentaries, podcasts, and dramatized series, most notably in the second season of Netflix's "Mindhunter." The victims are increasingly remembered not as entries in a crime database, but as individuals with lives and families and dreams. Murals have been painted, memorials held, and their names read aloud in ceremonies meant to honor lives lost far too soon.

The Wayne Williams case continues to serve as a grim mirror for society. It reflects the dangers of rushed justice and political pressure, but also the real horrors that unfolded in Atlanta over those dark years. Whether Williams acted alone, was part of a broader pattern, or was wrongly accused, the case remains a haunting chapter in American history, a story about race, trauma, and the desperate need for answers in the face of unbearable grief.

Henry Lee Lucas

Henry Lee Lucas is one of the most perplexing and polarizing figures in the history of American criminal justice. For a time, he was believed to be one of the most prolific serial killers the world had ever seen, claiming responsibility for hundreds of murders across dozens of states. Law enforcement agencies closed over 200 cold cases based on his confessions. But the deeper investigators looked, the more the story began to unravel. In the end, Lucas's case became a cautionary tale; not just about violence, but about deception, desperation, institutional failure, and the dangerous hunger for easy answers in the face of hard truths.

Born on August 23, 1936, in a rural part of Blacksburg, Virginia, Henry Lee Lucas grew up in what can only be described as a nightmare. His home life was violent, impoverished, and devoid of nurturing. His mother, Viola Lucas, was reportedly physically and emotionally abusive, a s** worker who openly despised her son. His father, Anderson Lucas, had lost both legs in a railroad accident and died of hypothermia after collapsing drunk outside their shack.

From an early age, Henry was subjected to extreme neglect and cruelty. By his own account, he was beaten, dressed as a girl, denied education, and exposed to s**ual abuse. Whether all of his stories were true remains unclear, but what is undeniable is that his early years were shaped by trauma and dysfunction.

Lucas dropped out of school in sixth grade, began committing petty crimes, and spent time in juvenile detention. His first known act of serious violence occurred in 1960 when, after a confrontation, he murdered his mother during an argument. Lucas claimed she was attacking him for planning to marry, and in a fit of rage, he struck her with a broom and stabbed her. He fled but was quickly captured.

Sentenced to 20–40 years, Lucas served only ten and was released in 1970 due to prison overcrowding. The fact that he was paroled after a matricide, with no psychological treatment or oversight, remains one of the early institutional failures that shaped what followed.

After his release, Lucas drifted across the southern United States, working odd jobs and moving frequently. He eventually met Ottis Toole, another drifter with a troubled past and suspected violent tendencies. Their relationship was both criminal and, by Lucas's claims, romantic.

Together, they became central figures in a terrifying narrative that would soon spiral far beyond their real crimes. Lucas and Toole were transient, jobless, and largely invisible to the systems that might have tracked them. They exploited this invisibility, moving from town to town, often sleeping in abandoned buildings or cheap motels.

The case that would propel Lucas to national infamy began in 1983, when he was arrested for illegal possession of a firearm in Texas. Once in custody, he began confessing, at first to a few murders, then to dozens, and eventually to hundreds. The sheer volume of confessions was staggering. He told police he had killed hitchhikers, children, s** workers, elderly women, and strangers across over 20 states. His accounts were detailed and often accompanied by sketches, names, dates, and supposed motives. Law enforcement, reeling from unsolved cases and under pressure from grieving families, took him at his word. Lucas became a phenomenon. Dubbed the "Confession Killer," he seemed to know details about crimes that had baffled detectives for years.

The Texas Rangers set up a task force, the "Lucas Task Force," which facilitated interviews between Lucas and investigators from across the country. In a surreal scene, officers from different states lined up to speak with him. Lucas was cooperative, charming in his own odd way, and always ready to talk. He became something of a celebrity within law enforcement circles, praised for bringing resolution to long-dormant cases. The problem was that few asked whether his confessions were actually plausible.

Lucas was never a particularly bright man. He was semi-literate, with low intelligence and a long history of mental illness. But he was a skilled manipulator, able to read his audience and tailor his responses. Investigators often fed him case details, sometimes intentionally, sometimes not, and he repeated them back as if they were memories. He received favorable treatment for cooperating: better meals, access to television, field trips to crime scenes. His sudden importance gave him a purpose he had never known. And in return, police departments began closing files. Closure was convenient. Whether it was accurate seemed secondary.

As the body count attributed to Lucas rose, some began to question the narrative. Journalists from the *Dallas Times Herald* and *The Dallas Morning News* noticed glaring inconsistencies. The timelines of the crimes didn't match his documented whereabouts. Gas receipts, time-stamped work logs, and arrest records showed that Lucas couldn't have physically been in multiple states on the dates he claimed to have killed. In one case, he claimed to have murdered a woman in Florida on the same day he was clocked in at a job in Maryland. When pressed, Lucas would often change or walk back his story.

Eventually, the house of cards collapsed. By the late 1980s, most of the cases Lucas had "solved" through his confessions were re-evaluated. Many were reclassified as unsolved. Some were conclusively linked to other perpetrators. Others were found to have no known connection to Lucas at all.

While he had almost certainly committed some murders beyond that of his mother (most likely the killing of an elderly woman named Kate Rich, and perhaps a few others) the majority of his confessions were false or unverified. Ottis Toole, his alleged partner in many of the killings, also proved to be a serial fabricator. Their combined stories collapsed under scrutiny.

Lucas was ultimately convicted of eleven homicides, including that of an unidentified woman known for years as "Orange Socks," whose body was found in 1979 in Texas. He was sentenced to death for that crime, but growing doubts about the case led then-Governor George W. Bush to commute the sentence to life in 1998, the only such commutation Bush granted during his term. Lucas would die in prison in 2001, still claiming to have committed hundreds of murders, still insisting that he had been telling the truth all along.

The real horror of Henry Lee Lucas's story lies not only in the crimes he may have committed, but in the systemic breakdowns that allowed him to mislead the country on such a massive scale. Dozens of law enforcement agencies, desperate for resolution, took shortcuts. The media inflated the narrative. A man of questionable reliability, with a proven record of manipulation and deceit, became the answer to hundreds of cases. The consequences were profound. Real killers may have gone free. Victims' families were given false closure. The justice system, in its eagerness to close cases, traded certainty for convenience.

In the years since, the Lucas debacle has become a case study in investigative failure. It exposed the risks of relying too heavily on confessions, especially when they aren't corroborated by physical evidence. It prompted changes in how interagency cooperation is managed and led to reforms in investigative training. It also contributed to a growing skepticism toward the cult of the "serial killer profile" that dominated criminal psychology in the 1980s. Lucas didn't fit any profile. He wasn't a highly organized predator or a methodical monster. He was impulsive, erratic, and often incapable of long-term planning. His manipulation didn't require sophistication, just a keen understanding of what people wanted to hear.

In retrospect, the Henry Lee Lucas saga is as much about the system that empowered him as it is about the man himself. His lies filled a vacuum created by fear, inefficiency, and bureaucratic desperation.

The sheer scale of his deception should have collapsed under its own weight much sooner. That it didn't, and that it took nearly a decade for the truth to emerge, speaks volumes about how crime, memory, and public trust interact.

While the full scope of Lucas's true crimes may never be known, one thing is certain: his name remains etched in history not just as a killer, but as a mirror held up to law enforcement at its most vulnerable.

He's a reminder of the dangers of tunnel vision, the seduction of easy answers, and the devastating cost of believing what we want to believe rather than what can be proven.

Ottis Toole

Ottis Elwood Toole's life was a spiral of trauma, violence, and confusion that eventually intersected with one of the strangest chapters in American criminal history. Long remembered as the less intelligent and more volatile counterpart to Henry Lee Lucas, Toole has often been relegated to the role of sidekick. But his life and crimes demand independent examination.

He wasn't simply an accessory to Lucas. He was a deeply disturbed individual whose own actions, confessions, and contradictions contributed to one of the most chaotic criminal narratives ever recorded.

Born on March 5, 1947, in Jacksonville, Florida, Ottis Toole entered the world into the kind of home environment that often preludes tragedy. His father was an alcoholic who abandoned the family early. His mother was reportedly abusive, religiously fanatical, and emotionally erratic. According to Toole's accounts, some of which were later challenged for reliability, he suffered s**ual abuse as a child, including from a neighbor and possibly a relative. He also claimed that his mother dressed him in girls' clothing and mocked him publicly, contributing to a fractured sense of identity and escalating behavioral issues. Toole's early years were also marked by significant cognitive challenges. He was diagnosed with intellectual disabilities and later assessed as having antisocial personality traits. His education was limited, and he dropped out of school in early adolescence.

Toole's criminal activity began young. He was arrested as a teenager for theft and loitering, and by his twenties, his record included arson and burglary. He was a drifter, often homeless, surviving through petty crime and hustling. He moved frequently and lived on the fringes of society, occasionally engaging in s** work. His self-described obsession with fire was a constant feature of his behavior; he admitted to setting fires purely to watch them burn, a compulsion that placed him on the radar of local law enforcement multiple times.

In the late 1970s, Toole met Henry Lee Lucas at a soup kitchen in Florida. Their encounter was the beginning of a toxic and unpredictable partnership. Lucas, older and somewhat more articulate, quickly developed a rapport with Toole, and the two began traveling together.

According to both men, their relationship became intimate, and they fed off each other's dysfunction. Whether they truly committed murders together is still debated, but their shared confessions in the years that followed suggested a terrifying alliance.

What propelled Toole into national headlines were the confessions he made following his arrest in 1983. Initially detained for an unrelated arson case, Toole began claiming responsibility for numerous murders, often in coordination with Lucas's own statements. He alleged that they had killed scores of people while hitchhiking or drifting through various states. The methods of murder varied, as did the supposed victims.

In some cases, Toole provided specific details. In others, his accounts were inconsistent, confused, or entirely fabricated. Despite the contradictions, law enforcement agencies eager to clear open cases began linking Toole to dozens of unsolved homicides.

One of the most infamous confessions came when Toole claimed responsibility for the abduction and murder of six-year-old Adam Walsh in 1981. The case had gripped the nation. Adam, the son of future *America's Most Wanted* host John Walsh, was kidnapped from a Sears department store in Hollywood, Florida, and later found decapitated. The case remained unsolved for years. In 1983, Toole confessed to the crime, providing a chilling account of how he had lured the boy into his car and murdered him. He later recanted, then confessed again. Police found no physical evidence linking him to the crime, no DNA, no fingerprints, no witnesses. Still, in 2008, after reviewing the case and examining decades-old leads, the Hollywood Police Department officially closed the Adam Walsh case, naming Ottis Toole as the likely killer.

That declaration did little to settle the matter in the public eye. Toole's shifting stories had long undermined his credibility. He confessed to crimes he couldn't have committed based on physical evidence or timeline. He sometimes contradicted himself in the same interview. He also had a habit of tailoring his confessions to please his interrogators or to gain attention.

Like Lucas, Toole seemed to relish the spotlight. He enjoyed being interviewed, praised, feared. He gave interviews to the press, often adding new details to his supposed murder spree with each retelling. And like Lucas, he received favorable treatment in exchange for his cooperation, with better meals, cigarettes, and relative comfort inside prison walls.

Despite the uncertainty around the number of murders he committed, Ottis Toole was convicted of six homicides during his lifetime. One of those convictions was later overturned on appeal, but he remained incarcerated. His most substantiated crime was the 1982 murder of George Sonnenberg, a 64-year-old man who had taken Toole in as a roommate. Toole burned Sonnenberg's house down with him inside. It was a cruel and deliberate act, fueled by rage and his compulsive attraction to fire.

In court, Toole appeared disengaged, almost amused by the proceedings. Mental health professionals described him as profoundly disturbed and emotionally detached from the reality of his crimes.

As his notoriety grew, so did the number of cases investigators attempted to link to him. But over time, most of those links fell apart. Forensic evidence didn't support his claims. Other suspects emerged. Alibis, receipts, and timelines showed that Toole couldn't have committed many of the murders he confessed to. His stories became more and more exaggerated, often borrowing details from newspaper accounts. It eventually became clear that Ottis Toole had built a false legend; perhaps not intentionally at first, but one that snowballed as police rewarded him for "helpful" information and the media turned him into a caricature of evil.

By the 1990s, public interest in Toole had waned, and the damage of his false confessions was becoming fully understood. Dozens of cold cases were left in limbo, closed too quickly based on unreliable confessions, then reopened years later with little progress. Families who had once believed they had closure were forced to reckon with the possibility that the wrong man had been blamed.

Meanwhile, Toole's health declined. He suffered from cirrhosis of the liver and other complications, and in September 1996, he died in prison at the age of 49.

Ottis Toole's legacy is inseparable from the broader failures of the criminal justice system during the height of the serial killer panic in the 1980s. He remains a symbol of what can happen when institutions prioritize resolution over truth, when confessions are accepted without evidence, and when emotionally disturbed individuals are treated as credible sources without adequate scrutiny. His partnership with Lucas became the subject of documentaries and journalistic investigations, many of which concluded that neither man was responsible for even a fraction of the crimes they claimed.

What's most disturbing about Toole is not the uncertainty of his body count, but the nature of his mind. He was unstable, prone to fantasy, and capable of real violence. He killed people, there's no doubt of that, but he also seemed to lose track of what was real and what was invented. He lived in a blur of attention-seeking behavior, genuine pathology, and the desire to matter in a world that had discarded him from the start. That blur confused the public and law enforcement alike and left behind a trail of unfinished stories, fractured investigations, and broken families.

Toole's story is not about the scale of his crimes, but about the way trauma, mental illness, and a craving for significance can converge into chaos. It's about how systems fail; not just in preventing crime, but in understanding it, responding to it, and learning from it. His name lives on not as a singular force of evil, but as a tragic figure caught between fact and fiction, surrounded by people who should have known better but didn't want to look too closely.

Belle Gunness

In the early 20th century, few figures inspired such confusion, speculation, and morbid fascination as Belle Gunness. Dubbed the "Black Widow of the Midwest," her crimes combined deception, greed, and violence in a manner that blurred the line between domestic life and death.

Born Brynhild Paulsdatter Størseth in Selbu, Norway, in 1859, Belle emigrated to the United States in her early twenties. She would eventually settle in La Porte, Indiana, where she cultivated an outward image of industrious respectability while secretly orchestrating one of the most chilling murder schemes in American history.

Belle Gunness didn't fit the popular image of a killer. She was large and imposing, reportedly standing over six feet tall and weighing more than 200 pounds, with a stoic expression and a thick Norwegian accent. Those around her described her as serious, hardworking, and focused on providing for her children. But underneath that exterior was a calculating opportunist who saw people not as companions, but as tools. She was methodical, cold, and, most disturbingly, exceptionally successful in hiding her crimes for years.

Her trail of death began in Chicago, where she married Mads Ditlev Anton Sorenson in 1884. The couple ran a candy store that mysteriously burned down. Not long afterward, their house also caught fire.

In both cases, Belle collected insurance money. Sorenson died under suspicious circumstances in 1900, reportedly after suffering a cerebral hemorrhage, coincidentally on the one day when two overlapping life insurance policies were both active. Belle collected the payout without incident. The pattern was beginning to take shape, but at the time, few suspected foul play.

After her husband's death, Belle moved to La Porte and purchased a farmhouse. There she remarried, this time to a man named Peter Gunness. His life ended soon after the wedding when, according to Belle, a meat grinder fell off a high shelf and struck him in the head. Once again, the death was ruled accidental, and Belle collected on the insurance. One of Peter's daughters from a previous marriage, who had been living in the house, vanished around this time. No explanation was ever given. With multiple dead husbands, unexplained disappearances, and burned properties already behind her, Belle still remained free from suspicion.

What truly set her apart, and what would later reveal the depth of her crimes, was the method by which she lured future victims. Belle placed ads in Scandinavian-language newspapers across the Midwest, describing herself as a wealthy widow with a large farm seeking a "steady and honest man" for companionship, possibly marriage. Dozens of men responded. Many of them traveled long distances, bringing with them savings, jewelry, and tools, expecting to start a new life. Instead, they were never heard from again.

Neighbors saw the men arrive at the Gunness farm and never leave. When asked, Belle would offer plausible excuses. They had gone to find work elsewhere. They had grown homesick. They had wronged her and she'd thrown them out. In a time before centralized records or background checks, it was easy for transient laborers and immigrants to vanish unnoticed. She exploited that fact ruthlessly.

To maintain the illusion of respectability, Belle continued raising her children, attending church, and operating her farm. But underneath the surface, her activities were unraveling. One of the men who had corresponded with her, a Norwegian named Andrew Helgelien, grew suspicious after his brother disappeared while visiting Belle. Andrew traveled to La Porte and pressed her for answers. Not long afterward, he too vanished. That disappearance would ultimately lead to Belle's undoing.

In April 1908, the Gunness farmhouse was engulfed in flames. When the fire was extinguished, authorities found four bodies in the basement: three children and one adult woman missing her head. The assumption was immediate: Belle Gunness had been murdered in her own home, her killer perhaps one of the many men she had rejected or defrauded. But investigators quickly noticed irregularities. The body attributed to Belle was much smaller than expected. Dental records were inconclusive. Rumors swirled that the fire had been staged, and that Belle had faked her death.

Those suspicions were confirmed when a search of the farm grounds turned into one of the most gruesome excavations in American history. As workers dug through the soft soil of the hog pen and garden, they uncovered body after body. Some were dismembered and stuffed into burlap sacks. Others had lime thrown on them to hasten decomposition.

In total, more than a dozen bodies were recovered; some estimated the final count to be over forty. Most had been killed with a blow to the head, likely from a hammer. All of them had disappeared after corresponding with Belle or visiting her farm.

The public reaction was one of horror and disbelief. Newspapers across the country published sensational stories about the "female Bluebeard" who killed for money and buried the evidence on her own land.

Forensic science in 1908 was limited, but the methodical nature of the murders was clear. Belle had likely drugged or poisoned her victims before striking them and disposing of the bodies. The ease with which she carried out these murders, while maintaining a home, raising children, and handling the daily operations of a farm, was staggering.

One man was arrested in connection with the fire: Ray Lamphere, a farmhand who had worked for Belle and harbored romantic feelings toward her. He admitted to helping her cover up some of the previous crimes but denied involvement in the murders themselves. Lamphere claimed that Belle had planned the fire and faked her death, escaping under the cover of chaos. He died in prison a year later, but not before giving a deathbed confession that added more intrigue to the story.

What happened to Belle Gunness after the fire remains one of the great unsolved mysteries in American crime history. Numerous sightings were reported in the years that followed, some as far away as California, but none were ever confirmed. Some investigators believed she had assumed a new identity and continued her crimes elsewhere. Others thought she had perished in the fire, and the body was misidentified due to the intense heat and trauma. With no definitive DNA analysis possible at the time, the truth was lost.

What makes Belle Gunness so disturbing is not just the number of victims, but the calculated nature of her actions. She preyed on loneliness and hope, presenting herself as a maternal figure, a businesswoman, and a potential wife.

In reality, she viewed human lives as expendable assets, interchangeable and disposable. Her crimes took place not in dark alleys or distant woods, but in the heart of rural America, in a home where children played and neighbors dropped by with baskets of food.

She upended expectations of who could be a serial killer and how they might operate. While many serial murderers act out of compulsion or psychological fixation, Belle appeared to kill primarily for financial gain. Her motives were practical, not sadistic, though the brutality of her methods suggested a chilling lack of empathy. She was organized, manipulative, and utterly without remorse.

In historical context, Belle Gunness represents a unique anomaly. Female serial killers are rare, and those who operate on such a scale, with such premeditation, are rarer still. She exploited the vulnerabilities of a highly mobile, poorly tracked population of men at a time when America was still grappling with the effects of industrialization, migration, and social change. Her farm became a killing ground, her ads the bait, her charm the trap.

More than a century later, Belle Gunness continues to fascinate historians, criminologists, and true crime enthusiasts. She remains a haunting figure; not only because of what she did, but because of what she represents: a reminder that evil can wear any face, live behind any door, and flourish in the spaces where no one is looking too closely.

Nannie Doss

Nannie Doss smiled through most of her life, and she smiled through most of her murders. The woman who would later become known as "The Giggling Granny" didn't fit the archetype of a serial killer. She wore floral print dresses, baked pies, and had a fondness for romantic magazines. But beneath the cheerful exterior was a woman capable of calculated, repeated murder, often of the people closest to her. Over the course of three decades, Nannie quietly poisoned husbands, children, grandchildren, and relatives, slipping under the radar with ease. She wasn't driven by rage or sadism. Her motive was often simpler and more chilling: she just didn't want them around anymore.

Born as Nancy Hazel on November 4, 1905, in Blue Mountain, Alabama, she was raised in a household marked by strict rules and emotional coldness. Her father, a domineering man, reportedly restricted access to formal education, forcing his children to work on the farm instead.

Nannie had little escape from the tedium of rural life, except for the fantasy worlds she created through love stories and confession magazines. These pulp serials promised passion, revenge, and freedom from dull lives. They became a blueprint for the relationships Nannie would pursue, and, eventually, destroy.

Her first brush with trauma came young. At age seven, she suffered a head injury in a train accident, which she later blamed for the headaches, blackouts, and mood swings that followed her throughout life. Though there's no confirmed link between the injury and her later crimes, head trauma is a recurring factor in the backgrounds of many serial killers. Whether it was the accident, her childhood, or something deeper, a seed was planted early on.

Nannie married for the first time at sixteen. Her husband, Charley Braggs, was a coworker at a linen factory and the only man she had ever dated. They had four children together in rapid succession, but the marriage soured quickly. Charley later claimed he was terrified of her mood swings and temper. Family pets died mysteriously. Two of their daughters died suddenly, though no one could prove anything at the time. The cause of death was attributed to food poisoning. Charley left her in 1927, taking one surviving daughter with him and leaving the other behind. When asked later about the separation, he simply said he was afraid of ending up dead.

Nannie moved on quickly. Her second marriage, to Frank Harrelson in 1929, started with romantic letters and promises. But behind the flowery words was a man with a drinking problem and a violent streak. The union lasted for sixteen years, despite physical abuse and infidelity.

During this period, several family members began to die mysteriously. Her own mother passed away after a sudden illness, followed by two sisters. Nannie's grandson died under suspicious circumstances as well, supposedly from asphyxiation while in her care. No charges were filed.

After World War II, Nannie began writing to lonely hearts columns again. She corresponded with men across the country, often seducing them with letters full of affection and flattery. One of these was Arlie Lanning, a man from North Carolina whom she married in 1952. As before, the marriage was marked by domestic dysfunction, and as before, the husband died soon after, reportedly of heart failure. Not long afterward, Arlie's mother died, and his house burned to the ground. Nannie collected the insurance money. She played the role of grieving widow flawlessly, attending church and caring for neighbors. Few suspected her of any wrongdoing.

Her trail continued to Kansas, where she married Richard Morton, a man who, like the others, had responded to one of her romantic ads. He, too, died within months of the wedding. During the same period, one of Nannie's daughters died unexpectedly, and her infant grandson passed away just after Nannie paid a visit. Patterns were beginning to emerge, but with deaths spread across multiple states and explanations that always seemed just plausible enough, law enforcement didn't yet see the full picture.

Her final husband was Samuel Doss of Tulsa, Oklahoma. Unlike the others, he wasn't abusive or unfaithful. He was simply controlling; he restricted her from reading romance novels and insisted on early bedtimes. For Nannie, that was enough. After a brief hospital stay for a "mysterious illness," Samuel died in October 1954. The attending doctor found the circumstances suspicious and requested an autopsy. High levels of arsenic were found in his system.

For the first time, a death linked to Nannie was not dismissed or buried. She was arrested and questioned, and eventually confessed; not just to Samuel's murder, but to killing multiple husbands, family members, and children.

Her confessions were delivered with a shocking lack of remorse. She giggled during questioning and reportedly told investigators that she was "looking for the perfect mate." If a man disappointed her, she moved on, but not by divorce. Her preferred method was pie laced with poison, or coffee mixed with rat killer. When asked why she killed, she never spoke of money, revenge, or mental illness. Her reasons were often disturbingly mundane. They snored. They drank. They bossed her around. In her own words, they just got on her nerves.

Public reaction to the case was a mix of horror and fascination. The idea of a grandmotherly figure calmly killing her loved ones over the course of decades shattered cultural expectations about gender and violence. Female serial killers are uncommon, and those who use poison as a weapon often escape suspicion longer than their more overtly violent male counterparts. Nannie took full advantage of this. She used charm, humor, and domestic skills to mask her true nature. She baked pies, cared for children, and smiled her way through funerals.

Psychiatrists who examined her debated her mental state. Some believed she was sane and calculating; others thought she had deep psychopathic tendencies masked by a genial demeanor.

Unlike many serial killers, she didn't seem to derive sadistic pleasure from the act of killing. Instead, it was transactional, almost bureaucratic. If someone in her life became inconvenient, she removed them. Her motives were often lazily rationalized; she thought she deserved better. She didn't like being controlled. She was tired of their habits. This chillingly casual logic made her all the more unsettling.

In 1955, Nannie Doss pleaded guilty to one count of murder and was sentenced to life in prison. She was never tried for the other deaths, though she remained a suspect in at least a dozen. She was incarcerated at the Oklahoma State Penitentiary, where she remained until her death in 1965 from leukemia. Even in prison, she maintained her cheerful persona, earning the nickname "the Giggling Granny" from guards and inmates. She gardened, read romance stories, and made jokes about her past. One guard said it was impossible to imagine she had done what she confessed to, until you remembered how many bodies she'd left behind.

Her case left a lasting imprint on American criminal history. It forced authorities to reevaluate how they investigate domestic deaths, especially those involving women. It also highlighted the dangers of romantic ads and pen-pal scams, which at the time were largely unregulated and widely trusted. The idea that someone could weaponize love, and that a grandmother could kill her own family, was deeply unsettling to a society still reeling from postwar idealism and rigid gender roles.

Nannie Doss wasn't a killer in the shadows. She lived openly, laughed often, and carried death with her like a purse. She killed not out of compulsion, but convenience. Her poison was patience. Her smile was a trap. And behind every friendly letter and every slice of pie was a woman who believed she deserved more than what life, and the people around her, had given her.

Elizabeth Báthory

In the shadowed corridors of European history, few names are as soaked in blood and legend as that of Countess Elizabeth Báthory. Born into one of the most powerful aristocratic families in Hungary in the late 16th century, Báthory held immense wealth, influence, and privilege. Yet her legacy would not be built on political power or noble deeds.

Instead, it would rest on accusations of unspeakable cruelty, whispered tales of torture, and one of the highest body counts attributed to a single figure in pre-modern Europe. Her story, steeped in myth, horror, and a distorted mirror of power, has endured for centuries, equal parts true crime and gothic nightmare.

Elizabeth Báthory was born on August 7, 1560, at Nyírbátor in the Kingdom of Hungary, into a family that wielded authority across the region. Her uncle was the king of Poland; her cousins included cardinals and other high-ranking officials. From a young age, she was exposed to court politics, military affairs, and the ruthless pragmatism of noble life. She was educated, multilingual, and highly intelligent. But she was also said to suffer from epileptic fits, mood swings, and violent outbursts. Some sources suggest early signs of cruelty, though this may have been exaggerated by later historians hungry for scandal.

At the age of fifteen, Elizabeth married Ferenc Nádasdy, a Hungarian nobleman and warrior renowned for his role in the wars against the Ottoman Empire. Their union merged two powerful dynasties and granted Elizabeth control of multiple estates, including the infamous Cachtice Castle, which would later become the site of her alleged crimes. While Ferenc was often away at war, Elizabeth managed the estate, administered justice over the peasantry, and supervised the domestic staff. Over time, she became known not just for her efficiency, but for the fear she instilled.

It was after her husband's death in 1604 that stories began to darken. With Ferenc gone, Elizabeth assumed even greater authority. Servants began disappearing. Village girls who entered the castle walls were never seen again. Rumors circulated of young women being abducted from nearby villages to serve in the household, only to meet horrifying fates. By the time formal complaints reached the ears of King Matthias II, it was already believed that dozens (perhaps hundreds) of women had died at the hands of the countess and her inner circle.

Testimonies collected during the investigation painted a picture of sadistic cruelty. Servants described young women being stripped, whipped, burned, starved, frozen, stabbed with needles, or mutilated. One recurring story told of a servant girl being forced to strip naked and stand outside in the snow while Elizabeth poured cold water over her until she froze to death. Another account alleged that Elizabeth bit chunks of flesh from her victims' faces and shoulders. Several claimed that she bathed in the blood of virgins, believing it would preserve her youth. This detail, perhaps more than any other, cemented her place in folklore as the "Blood Countess," a woman whose vanity knew no moral bounds.

The veracity of these accounts remains a subject of debate among historians. At the time, evidence relied heavily on hearsay, confessions extracted under torture, and politically motivated accusations.

Over 300 witnesses were interviewed. Some gave graphic accounts of the countess's cruelty; others had only second-hand information. The number of victims also remains uncertain. Estimates ranged from 36 to over 600, with one servant claiming to have seen a ledger listing the names of 650 girls. That ledger was never produced in court, and the extremes of the count raise questions about exaggeration. Yet even if the truth lies at the lower end of the scale, the deaths attributed to Elizabeth Báthory represent one of the most prolific cases of serial killing ever recorded.

In 1610, a group led by György Thurzó, the Palatine of Hungary, raided Cachtice Castle. What they found reportedly confirmed the worst. According to their report, bodies were found in the dungeons, some still warm. One girl was said to be found dying, her body covered in wounds. Though Elizabeth was arrested, she was never tried in a court of law. Her noble status protected her from public prosecution, and executing a member of the aristocracy would have triggered political repercussions. Instead, she was confined to her castle, walled into a set of rooms where she remained for the last four years of her life until her death in 1614.

Her accomplices, however, were not so lucky. Several servants were put on trial, tortured, and executed for their roles in the killings. Their testimonies helped shape the public narrative about Elizabeth's actions, yet it's unclear whether their confessions were coerced or genuine.

Over time, the line between fact and myth began to blur. The legend of the blood baths became central to her image, despite its dubious sourcing. In the centuries that followed, she was portrayed as a vampire-like figure, a proto-Dracula consumed by vanity and sustained by innocent blood.

Modern scholarship has attempted to reinterpret Báthory's case in light of political, cultural, and gender dynamics of the time. Some historians argue that she may have been the victim of a conspiracy, targeted by powerful families who wanted to seize her land and wealth. Her vast estates made her one of the most powerful women in Central Europe, and her independence posed a threat to male-dominated structures of governance. There is some precedent for powerful women in history being accused of witchcraft, sadism, or unnatural cruelty in order to justify their removal. However, this theory can't erase the significant number of testimonies and the consistent patterns in the accusations against her.

Regardless of motive, the image of Elizabeth Báthory remains enduring. She exists in the cultural imagination as a symbol of decadence, power gone unchecked, and the collision between nobility and horror. The fact that she operated within the walls of a castle, among velvet drapes and stone corridors, only enhances the contrast between her social rank and the brutality she is said to have committed. Unlike many serial killers who kill from the shadows, Elizabeth lived in the light of nobility, carrying out her alleged crimes while entertaining guests and attending Mass.

Her legacy has inspired countless works of fiction, from gothic novels to horror films, each exaggerating or reinterpreting her story. She is frequently compared to figures like Vlad the Impaler and Gilles de Rais, aristocrats accused of monstrous behavior whose lives became legends. Yet her story carries a distinctly gendered twist. While male historical killers are often portrayed as madmen or warriors, Elizabeth's tale revolves around vanity, beauty, and youth. The blood bath myth, in particular, plays on fears of female aging and power, turning her into a cautionary figure about the dangers of feminine ambition.

What remains chilling about Elizabeth Báthory is not just what she may have done, but how long she may have gotten away with it. For years, girls vanished under her watch, and yet she maintained her social standing, continued to collect rents, and hosted members of the nobility. Her crimes, if true, weren't hidden, but institutionalized. Servants assisted her. Officials looked the other way. Justice only arrived when political conditions made it convenient. This systemic failure, more than any individual act, speaks volumes about the nature of power in her era.

Elizabeth Báthory died on August 21, 1614, reportedly in her sleep, alone and sealed within her castle walls. No final confession was ever made. No apology was issued. She left behind estates, legends, and a void of certainty that historians have tried to fill ever since.

Whether viewed as a bloodthirsty killer, a victim of political ambition, or a monstrous anomaly of her time, her name continues to resonate. She is remembered not simply for what she did, but for what she came to represent: a woman whose story was written in blood, shadow, and silence.

John Bunting

In the barren outskirts of South Australia, a series of gruesome crimes unfolded in the 1990s that would shake the country's collective psyche and redefine the term "serial killer." The name at the center of it all was John Bunting, a man whose charismatic presence and twisted ideology drew others into a web of torture, control, and murder.

Known as the ringleader of what became known as the Snowtown murders, Bunting was no lone wolf. He operated as the orchestrator of a small cult-like circle, one that targeted individuals he deemed unworthy of life. The killings were brutal, premeditated, and terrifyingly personal. By the time authorities uncovered the full scope of what had occurred, twelve people were confirmed dead, several of them tortured for days, their remains discovered in acid-filled barrels inside an abandoned bank vault.

John Justin Bunting was born on September 4, 1966, in Inala, a working-class suburb of Brisbane, Queensland. His early life was marked by instability and alleged trauma. He later claimed he was abused as a child, and though much of his past remains cloaked in partial records and conflicting accounts, it's clear that violence and hatred took root in him early. By the time he reached adulthood, Bunting had developed a seething disdain for people he labeled as p***philes, homos**uals, or "weak." Whether this contempt was the result of personal experiences, social conditioning, or psychopathy remains a matter of debate, but it formed the ideological foundation for his crimes.

By the 1990s, Bunting had moved to the suburb of Salisbury North in Adelaide. He was perceived by neighbors as somewhat ordinary, helpful, charismatic, and even likable. But behind closed doors, he began building a network of followers drawn to his mix of confidence, paranoia, and vitriol. Two key figures entered his orbit: Robert Wagner and James Vlassakis. Wagner, a violent man with a similarly dark disposition, became Bunting's most loyal accomplice. Vlassakis, a vulnerable teenager, was slowly manipulated and later coerced into participating in several of the murders. Together, this group operated not as a gang of thrill-seeking killers, but as a self-righteous tribunal, executing those they claimed were threats to society. In truth, the selection of victims was often opportunistic, guided by access, grudges, and money.

Their methods were horrifying in detail and execution. Victims were abducted and brought to homes where they were restrained, beaten, electrocuted, and tortured for days. The killers recorded their screams, forced them to confess to fictitious crimes, and, in some cases, coerced them into reading scripted messages on tape, messages that were later used to explain their disappearances. These weren't impulsive crimes.

They were orchestrated and methodically carried out with the help of others in the group. In some cases, the killers used victims' social security cards to withdraw government payments after their deaths, effectively profiting from their murders.

The first confirmed murder occurred in August 1992, when Bunting killed Clinton Trezise, a 22-year-old man he accused of being a p***phile. The body was buried in a shallow grave and remained undiscovered for two years. Bunting called it his "practice run."

Over the next several years, the killings continued, each one marked by a chilling combination of moral justification and raw cruelty. Victims included acquaintances, friends of friends, and even family members of the co-conspirators.

One of the most disturbing aspects of the case was the internal logic Bunting imposed; he convinced his accomplices that they were doing necessary work, cleansing society of predators and parasites. But in truth, some of the murdered had no known criminal history at all. The labels Bunting assigned were often arbitrary, shaped by suspicion, personal vendettas, or convenience.

Bunting's ability to manipulate others was central to his reign of terror. He preyed on vulnerable people (those with low intelligence, troubled pasts, or social isolation) and pulled them into his world. He created an environment where dissent was dangerous, loyalty was expected, and violence was normalized. He positioned himself as a leader, a protector, and a moral crusader, even as he orchestrated unimaginable suffering. Those who followed him became complicit, sometimes out of fear, sometimes out of a warped sense of purpose, and sometimes out of their own sadistic tendencies.

The crimes might have remained hidden for years longer if not for the eventual unraveling of the group from within. James Vlassakis, still a teenager at the time of several murders, became increasingly disturbed by what he had been part of. His conscience began to fracture under the weight of the killings, and in time, he confessed to his role in the crimes and provided details to police. His cooperation was the key that unlocked the entire case.

In May 1999, police raided an old, disused bank in the small town of Snowtown, where the group had recently relocated several bodies stored in large barrels. The discovery shocked the nation. The smell was overwhelming, and the reality of what had occurred was far worse than anything initially imagined. Authorities found eight dismembered corpses submerged in acid, with forensic analysis confirming the remains belonged to people previously reported missing. This moment marked one of the most gruesome crime scenes in Australian history.

The trial that followed was one of the longest and most expensive in the nation's legal records. Bunting was charged with eleven counts of murder and found guilty on all. In 2003, he was sentenced to life imprisonment without the possibility of parole.

Wagner received the same sentence. Vlassakis, who had testified against the others, was given a reduced sentence but remains imprisoned for his direct involvement in four of the murders. Another accomplice, Mark Haydon, was convicted for assisting with the disposal of bodies but not of murder. His relatively light sentence, in comparison, sparked criticism, but it also illustrated the complexity of the web Bunting had spun; some were active killers, others enablers.

What separates Bunting from many other serial killers in history is the degree to which he operated as a leader of a group, effectively forming a death cult under the guise of moral purification. His killings weren't driven solely by personal gratification, though sadism was clearly present. He framed them as a form of justice, using false confessions, carefully staged disappearances, and the complicity of others to construct a distorted narrative of social cleansing. This created a level of premeditation and deception that is both rare and uniquely chilling.

There was no single psychological diagnosis that could easily explain Bunting's actions. He wasn't legally insane. He understood right from wrong. He was aware of what he was doing and worked to avoid detection. Some experts described him as a controlling narcissist with sadistic tendencies and an intense need for domination.

But his ability to build a network around himself, to create a world where others were not just passive observers but active participants, speaks to something more insidious than pathology. It reveals the terrifying potential of ideology, manipulation, and misplaced loyalty when combined with unchecked brutality.

The Snowtown murders also sparked widespread reflection in Australia about how systems could fail so catastrophically. Many of the victims were people on the fringes of society: poor, disabled, isolated, or struggling with addiction. Some had minimal family support. Their disappearances went uninvestigated for years, and in several cases, Bunting and his accomplices were able to collect their government benefits without raising alarms. This led to criticism of social services, law enforcement, and the bureaucratic indifference that allowed such killings to continue undetected. The victims weren't just killed; they were erased.

In the years since the case, Snowtown has become synonymous with horror in the Australian public imagination. The town itself was largely innocent of the crimes beyond housing the final crime scene, but the name stuck. A film was later made about the murders, further cementing their place in the national consciousness. Yet beyond the media and morbid fascination lies the brutal truth: John Bunting orchestrated a series of murders rooted in ideology, power, and calculated cruelty. He wasn't insane. He wasn't out of control. He was deliberate.

John Bunting remains incarcerated in a maximum-security prison in South Australia. He has never expressed remorse, nor has he admitted that his actions were unjustified. In his mind, he likely still believes he was delivering justice. That belief, wrapped in charisma and reinforced through violence, was enough to turn a handful of followers into a killing machine. In the end, the story of John Bunting isn't just about a murderer; it's about how one man, driven by hatred and convinced of his moral superiority, can create a world in which killing becomes normalized, and evil is justified as virtue.

Fred and Rose West

Few criminal cases in modern British history have unsettled the public as deeply as the crimes of Fred and Rose West. Their story isn't only about murder. It's about deception, domestic secrecy, manipulation, and the terrifying reality that violence can be hidden inside what appears to be an ordinary family home.

For years, the couple lived at 25 Cromwell Street in Gloucester, raising children, taking in lodgers, and interacting with neighbors. Behind that façade, a pattern of exploitation, abuse, and killing unfolded over decades.

Frederick Walter Stephen West was born on September 29, 1941, in Much Marcle, Herefordshire. He grew up in a rural farming family marked by strict discipline and instability. Later in life, Fred claimed he had experienced s**ual abuse within his family, though some details remain disputed.

What is more certain is that he left school at fifteen with limited education and soon developed a reputation for dishonesty, manipulation, and inappropriate behavior toward women and girls. Early criminal offenses included theft and assault, setting a pattern of disregard for the law.

In his late teens, Fred suffered serious head injuries, including a motorcycle accident that left him in a coma. Some criminologists later speculated that these injuries may have worsened impulsivity and reduced empathy, though they don't explain the deliberate and prolonged nature of his later crimes. By his early twenties, Fred had entered into a relationship with Rena Costello. The relationship was volatile and abusive. Rena already had a child, and together they had another daughter. During this period, Fred began exhibiting increasingly disturbing behavior, including controlling tendencies and s**ual exploitation of vulnerable women.

In 1967, Rena's friend Anna McFall disappeared. Years later, her remains would be linked to Fred. This early case suggested that long before his partnership with Rose, Fred had already crossed into calculated violence. After Rena left him, Fred drifted, moving frequently and engaging in unstable relationships. In 1969, he met Rosemary Letts, a fifteen-year-old girl who would become both his wife and his criminal partner.

Rosemary Pauline Letts was born on November 29, 1953, in Devon. Her childhood was troubled. Her father struggled with mental health issues, and the household was unstable. Rose was described as rebellious, often difficult, and prone to aggressive behavior. By her teenage years, she was already displaying patterns of defiance and volatility. When she met Fred, she was still a child by modern standards, and he was nearly twice her age. Despite concerns from her family, the relationship quickly intensified.

Rose moved in with Fred and became pregnant soon afterward. The dynamic between them blended control, secrecy, and shared deviance. Fred had already demonstrated coercive behavior in previous relationships, but with Rose he found someone who did not simply tolerate his actions. Over time, she became an active participant.

The couple eventually settled at 25 Cromwell Street in Gloucester. The house appeared ordinary from the outside. Inside, it was chaotic but unremarkable to neighbors. Children lived there. Lodgers came and went. Visitors passed through. Fred worked laboring jobs and performed renovations around the house. Rose managed much of the household. To outsiders, they were unconventional but not extraordinary.

Behind closed doors, however, the environment was one of fear and control. Over the years, several young women connected to the household disappeared. Some were lodgers. Some were acquaintances. Some were connected through social networks. Many were vulnerable, lacking stable housing or strong support systems. The Wests often offered accommodation or help, creating a sense of trust that masked darker intentions.

Fred's role in the crimes included luring victims, exercising physical dominance, and concealing bodies within the property. Rose's involvement went beyond passive awareness. Evidence later demonstrated her participation in abuse, intimidation, and in several cases, direct involvement in murder.

Survivors and family members described a regime of strict control inside the house. Children were isolated, monitored, and subjected to severe discipline. Fear prevented many from speaking out.

The structure of Cromwell Street itself became part of the concealment. Fred carried out renovations that included digging in the cellar and garden. Over time, remains were buried beneath floors and in shallow graves on the property. The duality of daily family life continuing above while crimes were hidden below created one of the most disturbing aspects of the case. It demonstrated not only cruelty, but an extraordinary capacity for compartmentalization.

For years, suspicions were limited and fragmented. Some individuals raised concerns, but no single report triggered a full investigation. It was the disappearance of Heather West, the couple's daughter, that eventually drew serious attention. Heather had not been seen since 1987, and the explanations offered by Fred and Rose were inconsistent. In 1994, police began a focused investigation.

When officers searched 25 Cromwell Street, they uncovered human remains buried on the property. The discovery horrified the nation. Forensic teams conducted careful excavations over weeks. Multiple victims were identified, with additional remains linked to other locations associated with Fred. The full scope of the crimes extended back decades.

Fred was arrested and charged with multiple counts of murder. During questioning, he confessed to several killings, at times attempting to take sole responsibility. His statements were inconsistent and appeared motivated by a desire to control the narrative. Before his trial could begin, Fred died by suicide in prison in January 1995. His death prevented a full public trial and left many questions unanswered.

Rose West, however, stood trial. The evidence against her included forensic findings, witness testimony, and accounts from surviving family members. Prosecutors argued that she was not merely an accessory, but a participant. The trial revealed a pattern of shared cruelty and mutual reinforcement between the two. In 1995, Rose was convicted of ten counts of murder and sentenced to life imprisonment with no possibility of parole.

The case forced the public to confront uncomfortable realities. The crimes had taken place within a family home, over many years, in a quiet residential street. The idea that such sustained violence could remain hidden for so long shook assumptions about safety and normalcy.

It also highlighted institutional failures. Earlier complaints and warning signs had not been fully pursued. Vulnerable victims had not received adequate protection.

The partnership between Fred and Rose added another layer of complexity. Criminal couples are rare, and cases in which both partners actively participate in multiple murders are even rarer. Criminologists have debated the dynamics of their relationship. Some suggest that Fred initiated the pattern and Rose gradually became entrenched. Others argue that Rose displayed independent cruelty and agency. The evidence presented at trial supported the conclusion that she was a willing participant in key acts.

Gender assumptions played a role in public reaction. Many struggled to accept that a mother could commit such crimes. Rose's involvement challenged stereotypes about nurturing and caregiving. Her refusal to admit guilt after conviction further deepened public anger and fascination.

After the case concluded, 25 Cromwell Street was demolished. Authorities determined that the property could not remain standing. The site became an empty lot, serving as a quiet reminder of what had occurred. For the families of victims, the demolition marked both an ending and a painful acknowledgment of loss.

The legacy of Fred and Rose West extends beyond the individual crimes. Their case influenced investigative procedures, particularly in handling missing persons and domestic abuse reports. It also underscored the importance of listening to children and vulnerable individuals who report fear or mistreatment. The prolonged secrecy within the household demonstrated how intimidation and isolation can silence victims.

In examining Fred and Rose together, what emerges is a portrait of shared pathology reinforced by mutual control. Fred displayed long standing patterns of manipulation, s**ual aggression, and violence before meeting Rose. Rose, however, did not remain a passive follower. Over time, she became embedded in the same system of cruelty. Their partnership amplified risk rather than restraining it.

Their story stands as one of the darkest chapters in British criminal history. It is a reminder that danger can be concealed within domestic walls, that ordinary appearances can mask extraordinary harm, and that vigilance and accountability are essential in protecting the vulnerable.

The crimes of Fred and Rose West were not sudden or chaotic. They were prolonged, deliberate, and hidden in plain sight. Understanding their case isn't about sensationalism. It is about recognizing how patterns develop, how control can escalate, and how silence can allow harm to continue.

Their names remain linked, not simply because they were married, but because together they created an environment in which violence became routine. And it's that shared responsibility that guarantees their place in history as one of the most notorious criminal partnerships ever uncovered.

Juana Barraza

Juana Barraza occupies a unique place in the history of serial crime. Her case, unfolding in early 21st-century Mexico, stunned the public not only for the nature of her crimes but for the unexpected intersection of her identity as a former professional wrestler, a single mother, and a convicted serial killer. Her story challenges many of the assumptions traditionally held about serial offenders, especially in regard to gender, motive, and social background. Dubbed "La Mataviejitas" (the "Little Old Lady Killer") by the media, Barraza's crimes forced Mexican law enforcement and the public to confront systemic failures in crime detection and the way marginalized victims are treated by society.

Born on December 27, 1957, in Epazoyucan, Hidalgo, Barraza's early life was shaped by poverty and trauma. Raised in a rural setting, she experienced neglect and abuse that would leave a psychological imprint lasting well into adulthood.

According to later reports, her mother was an alcoholic who allegedly traded her to a man in exchange for alcohol. Barraza would claim she was subjected to s**ual violence and suffered long-term consequences from these experiences. The betrayal and abandonment by her mother created a deep reservoir of anger and mistrust, particularly toward older women, an emotional wound that some criminologists believe played a formative role in her later crimes.

Barraza eventually moved to Mexico City, where she tried to make a living through various means, including selling popcorn at events and working odd jobs. She married and had children, though her relationships were reportedly troubled and abusive. Over time, she became known in certain circles as a participant in *lucha libre*, the flamboyant world of Mexican wrestling. Under the ring name "La Dama del Silencio" (The Silent Lady), Barraza performed in small venues wearing a pink mask and costume, often cast as the villain in staged matches. While not widely famous in the wrestling world, she was known well enough to cultivate a double life, one as a public entertainer and another as a predator operating in anonymity.

Her victims were almost exclusively elderly women, many of them living alone. This victim profile was especially shocking in Mexican culture, where older women are often seen as maternal figures deserving of respect and care.

The murders, which spanned from the late 1990s to her capture in 2006, generated fear in neighborhoods across Mexico City. Residents began changing locks, installing new security devices, and warning their aging relatives to be cautious. But despite widespread panic and dozens of deaths, the case remained unsolved for years.

Investigators initially struggled to make progress. Part of the difficulty stemmed from the fact that many of the victims were dismissed as dying of natural causes or domestic accidents. Several crime scenes were poorly processed or misclassified. It wasn't until forensic patterns began emerging (signs of asphyxiation, specific ligature marks, and consistent targeting of women over 60) that authorities began to suspect a serial offender. The growing number of unexplained deaths eventually forced law enforcement to publicly acknowledge the possibility that a single killer might be responsible.

Police formed a task force and began assembling a profile. They believed the killer posed as a social worker, healthcare provider, or government official to gain access to homes. Witness descriptions varied, but some recalled seeing a muscular woman fleeing crime scenes.

This detail led to initial confusion, as police believed the killer might be a man dressed as a woman. Investigators even mistakenly detained several trans women and marginalized individuals in a misguided dragnet that led to public criticism and delayed progress. The misdirection underscored weaknesses in forensic training and investigative strategy.

The breakthrough came on January 25, 2006, when Barraza was caught leaving the home of her latest victim, an elderly woman named Ana María de los Reyes. Witnesses saw her fleeing the scene, and she was promptly apprehended. At the time of her arrest, she had identification papers on her and was carrying items stolen from the apartment. The murder weapon, a stethoscope used to strangle the victim, was also found in her possession. Her capture marked the end of a years-long manhunt and the beginning of a court case that would dominate headlines across Mexico.

What surprised many was how ordinary she appeared. Barraza did not fit the stereotypical image of a serial killer. She was soft-spoken, stocky, and middle-aged. Yet as investigators dug into her background, they uncovered a consistent modus operandi: she would approach elderly women living alone, often under the pretense of offering help or government assistance. Once inside, she would assault them and take personal belongings. Many of her crimes showed signs of premeditation, but her choice of victims and method of killing suggested a deep-seated emotional component; not just opportunism, but resentment.

During her trial, prosecutors presented evidence linking her to at least eleven murders, though she was suspected of involvement in as many as forty-seven. DNA and fingerprint evidence connected her to multiple crime scenes, and stolen items were recovered from her home. Her wrestling career, once a source of theatrical strength, was now used to illustrate her physical capability to overpower victims. The prosecution argued that Barraza acted out of a combination of rage rooted in childhood trauma and financial desperation. The jury found her guilty, and in 2008, she was sentenced to 759 years in prison.

Her conviction made her one of the few confirmed female serial killers in Latin American history. It also reignited discussions around how gender biases may cloud criminal investigations. Many officials had simply not believed a woman could be responsible for so many brutal murders, especially not of elderly women. This assumption delayed her capture and allowed the crimes to continue. After her arrest, criminologists began studying her case more deeply to understand the psychological and sociological dynamics at play.

Barraza's actions challenged existing frameworks in both law enforcement and psychology. While female killers are generally categorized as acting out of revenge, profit, or psychological breaks, Barraza demonstrated a more complex profile. She combined instrumental motives, such as theft, with personal ones. Her resentment toward older women may have stemmed from her fraught relationship with her mother, but her continued offenses indicated more than emotional reaction. Her behavior was systematic and, to an extent, strategic. She targeted women who were unlikely to resist, unlikely to report suspicious activity, and often ignored by society.

Though she denied full responsibility during trial proceedings, Barraza's later interviews revealed a mix of denial, justification, and emotion. At times she expressed sympathy for her victims, at others she deflected blame. These contradictions added another layer to her psychological profile.

Some observers argued that she exhibited narcissistic traits, projecting an image of herself as misunderstood, even victimized by circumstance. Others pointed to the normalization of violence in her early life and the societal neglect faced by impoverished women in Mexico as contributing factors.

Her legacy in criminal history is complicated. On one hand, her crimes are emblematic of serial predation in urban environments – carefully chosen victims, repeated method, and evasion of capture. On the other, she represents how social structures can fail both perpetrators and victims.

Many of the women she killed were isolated, lacking strong community support, and overlooked by authorities. Barraza, too, was shaped by years of trauma and societal indifference. In a different context, perhaps her life would have taken a different trajectory. But in the world she inhabited, violence became both a shield and a weapon.

Juana Barraza remains incarcerated in Mexico, serving her sentence in a women's prison where she has maintained a low profile. Occasionally, she is the subject of documentaries and psychological studies.

Her story continues to provoke debate, not only because of the nature of her crimes, but because of what they reveal about social neglect, investigative bias, and the limits of public imagination when it comes to understanding women who kill.

Yang Xinhai

In the early 2000s, a name emerged from the shadows of rural China that would shake the country to its core. Yang Xinhai, later referred to in national headlines as one of the deadliest serial killers in Chinese history, became the subject of intense scrutiny and public fear following his arrest in 2003.

His crimes, committed across multiple provinces over a span of four years, revealed a pattern that was both calculated and deeply disquieting. What stood out was not just the number of lives he took, but the chilling detachment and apparent randomness of his actions.

Yang was born on July 29, 1968, in a small village in Henan Province. He was the youngest of several children in a family marked by economic hardship and limited opportunity. The household, like many in rural China at the time, relied heavily on agricultural work, and formal education was minimal. Despite early signs of intelligence, Yang dropped out of school before completing middle school. He was described by locals as quiet and reserved, though not particularly troublesome in his youth. There were no immediate warning signs, no records of juvenile delinquency, no early displays of violence that would foreshadow what he would later become.

As he entered adulthood, Yang drifted from place to place. He held a series of low-paying, itinerant jobs, mostly in construction or day labor. China during this period was undergoing rapid urbanization, and men like Yang (young, unskilled, and from poor rural backgrounds) were part of a growing underclass who moved from province to province in search of work. These workers were often anonymous, living on the fringes of society, with little oversight and few records tracking their movements. It was within this social invisibility that Yang would begin his descent into violence.

Between 2001 and 2003, a series of violent deaths began to surface in various provinces, including Henan, Hebei, Shandong, and Anhui. At first, the incidents were treated as isolated home invasions or robberies gone wrong. But a consistent pattern emerged. In each case, the victims were entire households, families attacked in their sleep, often in rural or semi-rural homes located on the outskirts of towns.

There was no clear financial motive. Money and valuables were often left untouched. The brutality was startling, but what baffled investigators even more was the apparent randomness. The victims had no clear ties to each other or to the perpetrator.

The randomness proved to be Yang's most effective cover. By choosing homes seemingly at random and moving frequently between regions, he avoided detection for years. There was no clear personal vendetta, no psychological connection to his victims. This lack of motive made profiling difficult. Traditional investigative strategies, which often rely on known associates, motives, or repeat locations, were largely ineffective. Even as public anxiety increased, there was little solid information to go on. In a country with a population in the billions and vast rural regions lacking surveillance infrastructure, Yang was able to operate with unsettling freedom.

What eventually led to his capture was not a breakthrough in the investigation itself but rather a routine identification check. In November 2003, Yang was stopped by police in Cangzhou, Hebei Province. Officers noticed that he was acting nervously and provided false identification. After further questioning, he confessed, first to a single crime, then to many more. What unfolded was a confession to one of the highest confirmed death tolls by any serial offender in modern times.

According to official reports, Yang confessed to the deaths of 67 people across 23 separate incidents between 2001 and 2003. He also admitted to injuring others who had survived his attacks. Authorities found forensic evidence and eyewitness accounts that corroborated many aspects of his statements. During interrogations, Yang reportedly remained calm and emotionally detached. He did not offer excuses or expressions of remorse. When asked why he committed the acts, his answer was chilling in its simplicity: he claimed to hate society.

This phrase ("I hate people") became a central theme in media portrayals of Yang after his arrest. It suggested a level of misanthropy and nihilism that set him apart from many other serial killers, who often act from personal compulsion or delusional belief systems.

Yang's response implied a worldview in which human life held no value, and destruction became a form of expression. Criminologists have debated whether this statement was a reflection of deep psychological disturbance, extreme social alienation, or a mix of both.

His behavior during the legal process added to his mystique. Unlike some offenders who seek attention or attempt to rationalize their actions, Yang remained largely impassive. Court proceedings were brief, and he offered no resistance to the charges. The trial lasted only one day. On February 1, 2004, he was sentenced to death and executed by shooting just over two weeks later. The speed of the trial and execution, while in line with China's judicial norms at the time, drew some international scrutiny, but there was no significant public outcry within the country. The public, already shocked by the details of the crimes, largely supported the swift outcome.

Yang's case prompted national discussions about public safety, mental health, and the challenges of policing a vast, decentralized population. It also raised questions about how social isolation, poverty, and displacement can contribute to a breakdown in empathy or the development of antisocial behavior. While Yang didn't undergo a formal psychological evaluation made public, some experts speculated that he exhibited signs of psychopathy or dissocial personality disorder. Others suggested that years of transient living and societal marginalization may have dehumanized him to the point where violence became an outlet for buried rage or nihilistic defiance.

There were also broader implications. In a society that places high value on family and community harmony, the revelation that someone could walk into a stranger's home and wipe out an entire household struck at the heart of cultural values. The randomness and scale of the attacks suggested that safety could not be taken for granted, even in tight-knit rural areas. This sense of vulnerability sparked renewed efforts in community policing, neighborhood watch programs, and rural surveillance, particularly in areas with high migrant worker populations.

In the years following his execution, Yang's case has remained a reference point in both Chinese media and criminal justice discussions. He is often cited in textbooks and criminology studies, not only for the sheer number of victims but for how he exploited mobility and anonymity in a rapidly changing society. His profile has become emblematic of the challenges modern nations face when individuals fall through the cracks of legal, medical, and social support systems.

Despite his notoriety, there is surprisingly little information about Yang's personal life beyond basic biographical details. He left behind no journals, manifestos, or detailed interviews. What little is known comes from his brief interrogations and statements to police.

His motivations, beyond his stated hatred of society, remain opaque. That lack of clarity has led to multiple interpretations. Was he driven by trauma, ideology, or simply a void where conscience should have been?

Yang Xinhai's crimes continue to stand out not only for their magnitude but for what they suggest about the human capacity for detachment and destruction. His case forced a reckoning in a country not often associated with high-profile serial crimes. It reminded the world that the conditions for such individuals (alienation, mobility, systemic failure) are not bound by culture or geography.

He remains a figure that defies easy explanation. There was no clear escalation period, no public warning, and no obvious trigger. His actions appeared methodical yet emotionally barren.

In the absence of remorse or ideology, what was left was a portrait of a man who moved through the world as a ghost: unseen, unrooted, and profoundly dangerous.

His name has since become synonymous with predatory anonymity, a haunting reminder of how individuals with no prior criminal record, no media presence, and no social ties can inflict massive harm under the radar of modern society.

Mikhail Popkov

In the cold expanse of Siberia, where cities stretch across frozen plains and police patrols are often thin, Mikhail Popkov committed a series of crimes that would take decades to fully unravel. Known by the media as the "Angarsk Maniac" or the "Werewolf," Popkov operated with a chilling level of confidence and familiarity with the very system meant to stop men like him.

What made his case stand out from other serial killings in Russia wasn't just the number of lives he ended, but how long he evaded capture, and the betrayal of trust that came with the uniform he once wore.

Popkov was born on March 7, 1964, in Norilsk, one of the northernmost cities in Russia, though he grew up in Angarsk, a city in Irkutsk Oblast. He came of age in the shadow of Soviet decline, a period of tightening resources and social instability. His father was reportedly an alcoholic, and Popkov would later speak of a home life shaped by tension and emotional distance. These early experiences likely contributed to his worldview, marked by control, order, and resentment, particularly toward women. Yet to most who encountered him in his youth, he appeared quiet and unremarkable.

He eventually joined the police force in Angarsk, where he worked as a patrol officer. His colleagues viewed him as dependable, if slightly reserved. He kept to himself and did not often socialize outside of work. At home, he was a husband and father. His wife, Elena, also worked in law enforcement as a forensic expert, and they had a daughter together.

By all outward appearances, Popkov lived a stable life. But beneath the surface, his views were warped by a growing hostility, particularly toward women he perceived as immoral or disrespectful to the conservative values he claimed to uphold.

Between 1992 and 2010, Popkov carried out dozens of attacks across Irkutsk and surrounding areas. The victims were mostly women, ranging in age and background, though many were targeted while walking alone at night or accepting rides. A few were men who had been with the women or happened to be nearby.

Over time, locals became increasingly aware of the rising number of deaths, but fear was mixed with confusion. The victims seemed unconnected. There was no public profile of a suspect, no footage, and no obvious pattern of method beyond the consistent targeting of women after dark.

Popkov exploited his badge and authority to earn trust. In many cases, he approached victims while wearing his police uniform or while driving a vehicle that resembled a patrol car. This created an illusion of safety. In Russia, as in many countries, citizens often instinctively trust the police, especially in isolated areas where law enforcement is the first and only line of protection. Popkov used this power not only to gain access to potential victims, but also to move through neighborhoods without suspicion, a calculated advantage that extended his freedom for nearly two decades.

When the first cases emerged in the early 1990s, the Russian police struggled to connect them. The collapse of the Soviet Union had left law enforcement agencies under-resourced, fragmented, and technologically behind. DNA analysis, at the time, was limited and inconsistently used. Popkov's knowledge of investigation procedures and crime scene management gave him a further edge. He understood what would be tested and what wouldn't, where evidence might be collected, and how to avoid detection. As his confidence grew, so did the frequency of his attacks.

Despite the number of cases piling up, there was little public acknowledgment of a serial killer operating in the region. Authorities were reluctant to stoke panic, and media coverage remained limited until the early 2000s. By then, families of victims had begun pushing harder for answers, forming support networks and pressing for more thorough investigations. Even then, Popkov's name did not surface. He had by then quietly left the police force and taken a job as a security guard at a local factory, still within the same community, still largely unnoticed.

The eventual break came not from a slip-up, but from advances in forensic science. In 2012, Russian authorities began a renewed push to investigate unsolved murders from the 1990s and 2000s. DNA samples were re-tested using updated technology, and investigators initiated mass screenings of men in the Irkutsk region. Popkov had previously avoided these rounds due to his police background, but eventually, his DNA was collected through a sample taken from a relative. The match was conclusive.

He was arrested that same year and confessed to dozens of murders during initial interrogations. At first, he admitted to 22 killings. Then, the number rose to 59. Eventually, he confessed to 83 murders, and investigators later tied him to at least 78 confirmed deaths. His demeanor during questioning was eerily calm. He offered detailed accounts of many cases and spoke without remorse. He claimed his actions were driven by a desire to "cleanse" society of women who were, in his view, promiscuous or disrespectful to their families. This twisted sense of moral judgment became a chilling trademark of his case.

The idea that someone could act as judge and executioner based on their personal beliefs, while using the shield of authority to do so, horrified the Russian public. His trial began in 2015 and spanned several months. Popkov sat in court behind reinforced glass, often silent. Survivors and family members of victims gave emotional testimony, describing years of grief, unanswered questions, and the shock of learning the man responsible had once sworn to protect them. He was convicted and sentenced to life in prison, though the scale of his crimes prompted continued investigations.

In 2018, he was convicted of an additional 56 murders, making his confirmed count the highest for any convicted killer in Russia. Popkov expressed no remorse. In rare interviews, he described his crimes with chilling detachment and sometimes referred to them as a "hobby."

He seemed to compartmentalize his violent acts from the rest of his life: his marriage, his parenting, his day-to-day routines. Psychologists and criminologists studying his case have noted this emotional duality: the ability to lead a stable domestic life while carrying out extreme violence in secret.

Popkov's wife and daughter were reportedly devastated by the revelations. His daughter, who once admired her father's discipline and intelligence, was left to reckon with a truth that shattered her understanding of him. His wife, who had worked in forensics, denied knowledge of his crimes and was never implicated, though some have questioned whether subtle signs might have been missed or dismissed over the years. Their reactions highlight one of the most unsettling aspects of such cases: the ability of individuals to hide their darkest impulses even from those closest to them.

His imprisonment has not ended interest in his case. In fact, the details continue to emerge. Authorities in Russia have reopened cold cases across Siberia, and Popkov has offered to assist in clearing up other unsolved murders, sometimes exchanging confessions for small privileges in prison. This has made him a grim but active figure in Russia's criminal justice system even years after his conviction. His cooperation has sometimes been self-serving, but it has led to the resolution of cases that had remained unsolved for decades.

The societal implications of the Popkov case are still being processed. His crimes exposed deep flaws in regional law enforcement practices, from fragmented investigations to misplaced trust in insiders. He was part of the very institution that should have stopped him. His status as a former officer discouraged deeper scrutiny, and his professional knowledge allowed him to exploit gaps in forensic methodology and administrative communication between jurisdictions.

For many Russians, Popkov's story is less about the twisted psychology of one man and more about the systemic vulnerability he exposed. A uniform can create complacency. A badge can shield. And when institutions fail to police their own, the consequences can be catastrophic. Popkov became a symbol not just of personal evil, but of bureaucratic blindness.

To this day, Popkov resides in a maximum-security penal colony in Siberia. He is allowed minimal interaction with the outside world. Journalists who have spoken to him describe a man who appears cold, rational, and entirely disconnected from the suffering he caused.

He sees himself not as monstrous, but as orderly, someone who enforced a set of personal rules in a world he believed had lost its way. This self-perception, perhaps more than anything else, offers insight into the danger he posed: not just a killer, but a man who believed he was justified.

Robert Ben Rhoades

For years, long-haul truckers have been a symbol of American freedom, solitary figures traveling vast stretches of highway, moving goods across the country while forming a hidden infrastructure of modern life. But in the case of Robert Ben Rhoades, the open road became something far darker. Operating under the radar for years, Rhoades used his mobility, privacy, and the perception of harmless professionalism to hide one of the most disturbing criminal patterns in American history. Often referred to by media as the "Truck Stop Killer," Rhoades is believed to have stalked, tortured, and murdered numerous victims while living a double life that only came to light by chance.

Born on November 22, 1945, in Council Bluffs, Iowa, Rhoades experienced a childhood marked by instability. His father, a military man, eventually took his own life while facing accusations of child molestation. Though Robert was never publicly linked to those accusations, the event cast a long shadow over his youth. Rhoades would later describe his upbringing as strict and isolating. After high school, he joined the Marines, only to be discharged for disciplinary issues. Over the years, he drifted between jobs, marriages, and small offenses, none of which hinted at what he would become.

By the 1980s, Rhoades had found stability as a long-haul trucker. The job allowed him to travel anonymously across state lines, staying just ahead of law enforcement jurisdictions. He customized his truck's sleeper cab into what authorities would later call a mobile torture chamber. Within that confined space, Rhoades transformed from trucker to predator. His method involved picking up hitchhikers, runaways, or women stranded at rest stops; individuals who, due to their circumstances, were less likely to be immediately reported missing. He took advantage of their vulnerability, his appearance as a working-class everyman, and the long stretches of rural isolation where few people paid attention.

One of the first cracks in Rhoades' careful routine came in April 1990. A state trooper in Arizona pulled over a truck parked on the highway shoulder. Inside, he found a terrified woman in chains. She had been abducted, assaulted, and held in captivity inside Rhoades' truck for days. The trooper arrested Rhoades on the spot, but the full scale of his crimes was not yet understood.

At first, he was charged with assault, false imprisonment, and other offenses. Only after investigators began digging into his background did a pattern emerge. The truck wasn't just a scene of one horrific crime; it was a traveling crime scene stretching back years.

As detectives searched his truck and home, they uncovered a disturbing collection of photographs. Hundreds of images showed women in various states of distress or restraint, many appearing unaware they were being documented. Some of the women were later identified, but many remain unknown. These photos became a key piece of evidence, not just in prosecuting Rhoades for specific crimes, but in establishing a behavioral profile consistent with serial predation. Investigators now had reason to believe they were looking at a serial killer who had operated undetected for nearly a decade or more.

Further inquiries tied Rhoades to the 1990 murders of Candace Walsh and her husband, Douglas Zyskowski, a young couple hitchhiking from Texas to Georgia. Walsh's body was found later that year in a shallow grave in Utah. Zyskowski had been discovered earlier in Texas, though at the time his death hadn't been linked to Rhoades. Once investigators matched Rhoades' fingerprints and photos to the couple, it became clear they had been picked up during one of his routes. These connections reinforced the theory that Rhoades targeted people on the margins: travelers, hitchhikers, or women with limited ties to any single location.

Perhaps the most notorious case associated with Rhoades involves Regina Kay Walters, a 14-year-old girl from Pasadena, Texas. She and her boyfriend, Ricky Lee Jones, had run away together in early 1990. Not long after, Jones was killed, and Regina vanished. Months later, her body was discovered in an abandoned farmhouse in Illinois. It wasn't until Rhoades' arrest that investigators uncovered photographs of Regina in his possession, including images taken just before her death. The photos were chilling not just because of what they depicted, but because they captured the final moments of a girl who had simply slipped through the cracks.

Rhoades' approach to killing was methodical. He didn't operate out of compulsion in the way many serial offenders are known to. Instead, he appeared organized, deliberate, and terrifyingly calm. His crimes were often spaced out across time and geography, making it difficult to establish connections. He rarely repeated the exact same scenario, which further hindered pattern recognition. This level of control, combined with his mobility and access to vulnerable populations, kept him off law enforcement radar for years.

Psychological profiles later described Rhoades as a narcissistic predator with sadistic tendencies. He sought power and control above all else and viewed his victims not as individuals, but as instruments for expressing domination.

The personalization of his truck cab into a confined torture environment suggested premeditation and a desire to create a world where he was the sole authority. While he has never publicly expressed remorse, Rhoades did not contest many of the charges brought against him, possibly as a legal strategy to avoid the death penalty.

His case also exposed a significant blind spot in how serial crimes were tracked across the U.S. at the time. Jurisdictional gaps between state and federal agencies allowed mobile offenders like Rhoades to exploit inconsistencies in law enforcement communication. In one state, he might have been viewed as a minor offender. In another, a murder suspect. Without modern databases or shared investigative platforms, it was easy for serial activity to go unnoticed, especially when victims were people often labeled as runaways or drifters.

The National Center for Missing and Exploited Children and the FBI's Behavioral Analysis Unit both took interest in Rhoades' case, viewing it as a cautionary tale about serial crime on the highways.

At one point, Rhoades was suspected in dozens of additional disappearances, though a conclusive link could not always be established. The number of victims he may have killed is still uncertain. Some estimates suggest over 50; others believe the number could be lower, given the lack of physical evidence in many cases. Rhoades has not provided full confessions, and many families remain without closure.

In 1994, he was sentenced to life in prison without the possibility of parole for the murder of Regina Walters. He was later extradited to Utah, where he pleaded guilty to additional murders. Though he avoided the death penalty, his incarceration ensures he will never again walk free. He is currently serving multiple life sentences in a maximum-security facility, his mobility permanently revoked.

Rhoades' crimes also sparked internal reviews within the trucking industry. While the vast majority of truckers are law-abiding citizens who play a crucial role in the economy, his case revealed how the job's inherent isolation and flexibility could be misused by predators. In response, rest stop surveillance, victim outreach programs, and interagency communication protocols have been improved across many states. Groups such as Truckers Against Trafficking have worked to train drivers and law enforcement to recognize signs of distress or potential exploitation, helping turn a point of vulnerability into one of prevention.

The long-haul routes that once offered Rhoades anonymity now serve as reminders of the thin line between ordinary life and the hidden world of the predator. His story is one of movement without detection, of a man who used the symbols of trust (a job, a uniform, a polite demeanor) as tools of deceit. The betrayal inherent in his crimes, particularly his calculated use of isolation and trust, makes his story especially unsettling in the broader context of American serial killers.

Rhoades remains a subject of academic study in criminal justice and forensic psychology. His ability to evade capture, maintain a public persona, and systematize his crimes provides a grim blueprint for understanding other mobile offenders. He has not granted interviews in recent years, and little is known about his daily life behind bars.

What endures is the legacy of fear he left on America's highways, and the lives of those who vanished without a trace, now remembered largely through photographs, case files, and the voices of families still searching for answers.

Donald Harvey

To the public and even his coworkers, Donald Harvey was quiet, polite, and diligent. He wore the unassuming uniform of a hospital orderly, carrying bedpans, preparing rooms, and tending to the most basic needs of the sick and elderly.

But beneath this facade lay a far darker reality, one that would only come to light years later and place him among the most prolific serial killers in American history. The scope of his crimes was staggering, not because of sensational violence, but because of their methodical, almost invisible execution, carried out in the very institutions meant to preserve life.

Harvey was born on April 15, 1952, in Butler County, Ohio. He grew up in an ordinary rural town with no early indicators of the infamy that awaited him. His upbringing was modest, and while later accounts suggest he may have experienced emotional neglect or bullying, there were no early red flags that set him clearly apart.

He performed well in school and was known to be intelligent and quiet. Like many young adults in the early 1970s, he looked for stable work in a field where job security was strong. He soon found his way into the world of hospitals, places built on trust, routine, and a presumption of care.

It was in 1970, while working as a hospital aide in Kentucky, that Harvey is believed to have committed his first murder. He would later claim that a patient in the intensive care unit was suffering terribly and that he acted out of what he described as mercy. This claim, whether true or not, set a precedent. Over time, the line between alleviating pain and asserting control over life and death seemed to vanish entirely. His role gave him intimate access to patients, their medications, and their vulnerabilities. He began to see himself not just as a caregiver but as an arbiter of fate.

Throughout the 1970s and 1980s, Harvey worked in multiple hospitals and care facilities across Kentucky and Ohio. His professional demeanor and willingness to take extra shifts made him a favored employee. Colleagues described him as quiet but helpful. He rarely drew attention to himself and did not display erratic behavior that might have triggered alarm. This invisibility was a key component of his success. While some co-workers occasionally noted a high number of deaths on his shifts, the hospitals at the time did not connect the dots. Mortality in medical settings is not uncommon, and few people thought to link them to a particular staff member.

Harvey later confessed to killing dozens of people during this period. His methods varied: sometimes involving poison, sometimes involving tampering with medical equipment or drug dosages. He exploited the very systems that were designed to manage patient care: medication carts, access to oxygen and IV drips, and even the trust of family members. He often rationalized his actions, claiming that some victims were terminal or suffering. But others, by his own admission, were killed simply because they annoyed him or inconvenienced him in some way.

This blend of calculated indifference and warped justification made Harvey's case uniquely disturbing. He didn't fit the psychological mold of a killer driven by compulsion or a single emotional trigger. Instead, he acted out of a chilling blend of control, resentment, and convenience.

Psychologists who later assessed him described a man who felt powerless in many areas of life but found ultimate control in deciding who lived and who didn't. His crimes weren't acts of passion; they were exercises in authority.

One of the more confounding aspects of Harvey's story is how long he continued without detection. Part of the answer lies in the nature of medical institutions during the era. Hospitals were often understaffed and overwhelmed. Record-keeping was inconsistent, particularly when it came to internal investigations. Deaths were frequently attributed to natural causes, especially among elderly or chronically ill patients.

Moreover, hospitals had strong incentives to avoid scandals. The notion that a staff member could be intentionally killing patients was so unthinkable that administrators often looked for alternative explanations.

Still, over time, a few people began to notice. Rumors circulated within staff circles about strange coincidences and questionable deaths. At one point, Harvey was quietly let go from a hospital in Kentucky, but no report was filed. He simply moved to a new facility. This failure to act decisively allowed him to continue his crimes elsewhere. In this way, his case reflects not just an individual pathology, but institutional breakdowns in accountability, communication, and oversight.

In 1986, Harvey's run of near-total anonymity came to an end. Suspicion grew when a patient at Cincinnati's Daniel Drake Memorial Hospital, where Harvey had been working, died under circumstances that didn't align with medical expectations. An autopsy revealed cyanide poisoning. The hospital reported the case to the authorities, and police launched an investigation. When they began examining Harvey's behavior, they uncovered stolen medications, detailed journals, and other evidence that pointed toward a chilling secret life.

Harvey was arrested and soon confessed to dozens of murders. In interviews with police and later with journalists, he described his actions with a level of detachment that shocked even seasoned investigators. He was not remorseful in any traditional sense. Instead, he portrayed himself as someone who had brought "peace" to his victims. But as prosecutors pressed further, it became clear that his motives were far more complex, and far less noble, than he claimed. Some victims had been killed because they complained too much. Others had simply crossed his path at the wrong time.

In 1987, Harvey pleaded guilty to 24 counts of murder and received multiple life sentences. Later, in 1989, he admitted to additional killings and was handed more sentences accordingly. Over time, he confessed to more than 50 murders, and some investigators believe the real number may exceed 80.

These figures make him one of the most prolific serial killers in U.S. history by body count; yet his name is far less known than others whose crimes were more sensational or violent in nature. Part of this is due to the quiet, institutional setting in which his crimes occurred. There were no high-speed chases, no dramatic standoffs. Just quiet deaths that blended into the rhythms of daily hospital life.

Harvey's case has had significant implications for the medical profession. It prompted reforms in how hospitals track patient deaths, how staff access and administer medications, and how whistleblowers are protected when they raise concerns. It also forced a reckoning within the healthcare system: a recognition that not all threats come from outside the institution. Some, like Harvey, hide within it, shielded by trust and bureaucracy.

His psychological profile has been studied extensively. Experts have pointed to signs of antisocial personality disorder and narcissistic traits, as well as a potential desire for dominance rooted in early feelings of powerlessness.

His ability to function undetected for so long suggests a high degree of self-control and planning, characteristics not always seen in serial killers. He didn't lash out impulsively. He bided his time, studied his surroundings, and chose victims who couldn't speak for themselves.

Despite his incarceration, Harvey remained a disturbing figure. He gave several interviews during his time in prison, where he continued to downplay the evil of his actions. In 2017, Harvey was attacked by another inmate at the Toledo Correctional Institution. He died from his injuries a few days later. His death brought an abrupt end to one of the most chilling chapters in American medical history, but the questions his life raised have not faded.

What drives a man like Donald Harvey is difficult to answer definitively. There are elements of resentment, control, disaffection, and possibly even warped altruism. But perhaps more disturbing than the motive is the method: the quiet, untraceable way he moved through hospital corridors, making life-and-death decisions without oversight. His crimes are not just a story of pathology, but of systemic failure: the failure to question assumptions, to follow up on doubts, and to believe that harm can come from within.

In many ways, Harvey's story is a cautionary tale not only about a singularly dangerous man, but about the blind spots that exist in even the most trusted environments. He didn't need to lure victims into his world. They were already in it, sick, sedated, and dependent on his care. And he used that trust not to heal, but to destroy.

William Bonin

In the shadow of Southern California's sprawling freeway network, William Bonin lived a double life that for a time escaped both public suspicion and law enforcement scrutiny. By all outward appearances, Bonin was a hardworking delivery driver, quiet and unremarkable. His job gave him flexibility, mobility, and a cover that allowed him to cross large distances without raising eyebrows. But behind this unassuming facade, he orchestrated a chilling series of crimes that would later place him among the most dangerous serial offenders of the late twentieth century.

Bonin was born on January 8, 1947, in Willimantic, Connecticut. His childhood was marred by instability, neglect, and dysfunction. Raised in a household rife with alcohol abuse and emotional volatility, Bonin spent parts of his early life in institutional care. Reports from later psychological evaluations suggested that he may have experienced trauma during his time in state-run facilities, experiences that likely shaped his emotional and behavioral development. Despite a turbulent adolescence, he managed to function within the framework of society. He graduated from high school and enlisted in the U.S. Air Force, where he served in the Vietnam War as an aerial gunner. His military service earned him several commendations, but it also introduced new psychological stressors that compounded his existing difficulties.

After his discharge, Bonin returned to California and attempted to build a life marked by routine employment and social stability. But his past had not been left behind. He had prior convictions related to serious misconduct, and despite multiple parole violations, he remained largely under-supervised. Over the years, he transitioned between jobs, often working as a truck driver or warehouse employee. His ability to blend into the background, combined with a cooperative attitude at work, helped him avoid sustained scrutiny. Yet his public persona was only part of the story.

Beginning in 1979, a pattern of disappearances and unsolved deaths began to emerge in the Los Angeles area. Young men and teenage boys were vanishing, their remains later discovered near freeway exits or in remote brush areas. Initially, the cases were handled separately by different jurisdictions. It wasn't until a growing number of incidents began to display striking similarities that a task force was assembled. The victims tended to be hitchhikers, runaways, or individuals with few family connections, demographics that made them especially vulnerable and delayed the urgency of some investigations. Each case bore certain behavioral hallmarks that, while not identical, followed a methodical pattern. Law enforcement officers were soon confronted with the possibility that they were dealing with a highly organized offender, one who was calculating, mobile, and difficult to profile.

Bonin was not working alone in every instance. Unlike many serial offenders, he occasionally acted with accomplices (most notably Vernon Butts): men he had befriended or manipulated into helping him. This element of his behavior was particularly unusual. It suggested a personality capable not only of coercion and deception but also of cultivating loyalty from individuals who may have feared or idolized him. These partnerships varied in their roles and levels of involvement, but their very existence complicated both the investigative and prosecutorial processes. It also added another layer of psychological complexity to Bonin's profile. He wasn't merely acting out compulsions in isolation; he was at times orchestrating multi-person operations, a chilling testament to his control and confidence.

As the body count increased and media attention intensified, Bonin's name eventually surfaced as a person of interest. His criminal record and geographic proximity to several of the incidents raised red flags. Authorities began monitoring his movements, setting up surveillance and quietly gathering evidence. A critical breakthrough occurred when police observed him in the company of a young man in circumstances that triggered immediate concern. He was detained, and further investigation uncovered physical evidence linking him to multiple crime scenes. A search of his van and residence yielded additional items of evidentiary value. At the same time, interviews with associates began to paint a clearer picture of the scope and timeline of his actions.

Upon arrest, Bonin initially denied involvement. But as evidence mounted and accomplices began cooperating with prosecutors, he ultimately faced trial for multiple counts of murder. The judicial process was long, complex, and emotionally charged. Prosecutors relied on physical evidence, behavioral patterns, and eyewitness testimony to build their case. Bonin's demeanor in court was largely flat, unsettling jurors and observers alike. His defense team attempted to raise questions about his mental health and the reliability of witness statements, but these efforts were ultimately unsuccessful. He was convicted and sentenced to death.

(Bonin (left), Butts (right))

Bonin's trial was one of the first in California to make use of certain forensic advancements and multi-jurisdictional coordination strategies. The scale of the case required prosecutors and investigators from multiple counties to cooperate across institutional boundaries, an effort that set a precedent for future task forces. The trial also prompted new conversations about parole systems, particularly in cases involving repeat violent offenders. Critics questioned how an individual with multiple prior convictions had been able to remain at large for so long. In response, state lawmakers proposed reforms to parole supervision, record sharing, and risk assessment procedures for released inmates.

While awaiting execution, Bonin granted several interviews to journalists and authors. In those conversations, he rarely expressed remorse. Instead, he spoke in abstract terms about control, opportunity, and the motivations that drove his behavior. Psychologists who reviewed his case noted a consistent absence of empathy, a lack of emotional regulation, and traits consistent with antisocial personality disorder.

Yet Bonin didn't fit every expected mold. He was intelligent, organized, and capable of long-term planning. He showed little interest in fame or notoriety, contrasting with other high-profile offenders. His crimes appeared to be more about control and detachment than about recognition or attention.

Bonin's final years on death row were spent at San Quentin State Prison. After exhausting appeals, he was executed by lethal injection in 1996, becoming one of the first inmates in California to be executed using that method. The execution drew national media attention and reopened public discussions about capital punishment. For many of the families involved, it marked a painful but final chapter in a long and agonizing story. For law enforcement and legal experts, Bonin's case became a foundational study in both criminal behavior and systemic oversight.

Today, William Bonin remains a case study in criminology programs and law enforcement seminars. His ability to operate with stealth, his manipulation of others, and the logistical planning behind his crimes offer important lessons for understanding modern serial offenders. The geographic sprawl of his actions, facilitated by the freeway system, also contributed to changes in how agencies coordinate cross-county investigations.

In this sense, Bonin's legacy is one of reform and vigilance. His crimes served as a wake-up call that predators do not always fit neatly into expected categories, and that institutional assumptions can sometimes enable their worst impulses.

Though his name is less well known to the general public than other high-profile serial offenders, Bonin's impact within law enforcement circles is profound. His case challenged assumptions, exposed vulnerabilities in the justice system, and contributed to real-world policy changes. In the end, William Bonin is remembered not only for the horror he inflicted but also for the hard-earned lessons his case forced society to confront.

Patrick Kearney

In the history of American serial crime, Patrick Kearney stands out not just for the number of victims attributed to him, but for how long he avoided detection while living an unremarkable life. Known by investigators as one of the "Freeway Killers" active in California during the 1970s, Kearney's crimes were ultimately overshadowed in media coverage by the more chaotic and violent cases of his contemporaries. Yet his methodical behavior, high victim count, and quiet demeanor placed him among the deadliest serial offenders of the twentieth century.

Born on September 24, 1939, in East Los Angeles, Kearney was the eldest of three boys. By all available accounts, his childhood was turbulent. He was described as quiet, highly intelligent, and socially withdrawn. Family accounts and psychological assessments suggest he was bullied both at school and at home.

In his early years, he reportedly developed a vivid inner world, often retreating into fantasy when social environments became overwhelming. By adolescence, Kearney had become increasingly introverted, and he demonstrated signs of emotional detachment that would later be of interest to criminal psychologists.

Despite these early challenges, Kearney was intellectually gifted. He enrolled in college-level courses and later worked as an engineer. He eventually settled in Southern California, living with a long-term partner in a modest home in Redondo Beach. Those who knew him described him as polite, soft-spoken, and punctual, a picture of normalcy that masked a darker undercurrent. The seeming ordinariness of his life would later shock neighbors and coworkers, who had no inkling of the crimes he was committing under their noses.

Kearney's criminal activities came to light only after several years of operation, during which he exploited his access to California's vast freeway system to avoid detection. His pattern involved targeting vulnerable individuals, often young men and boys, whom he encountered in transient areas like bus terminals or along highways.

Unlike offenders driven by chaotic impulse, Kearney operated with meticulous control. He maintained a consistent method, avoided leaving forensic traces, and adapted his tactics when he sensed increased law enforcement attention. His crimes, though brutal, were calculated, often leaving little behind for investigators to work with. This made his identification far more difficult than in many high-profile serial cases.

What made Kearney particularly difficult to profile was the contrast between his behavior in private and public settings. At work, he was competent and efficient. At home, he maintained a stable domestic relationship and upheld a routine that offered few red flags. He didn't present as threatening. He didn't draw attention to himself. This camouflage, whether intentional or not, allowed him to remain hidden from authorities for years, even as the bodies of unidentified young men began to appear along roadways and in rural areas across Southern California.

Eventually, Kearney's name emerged in connection with several disappearances. A critical turning point came in 1977, when a young man went missing after being seen in Kearney's company. The investigation gained traction after a witness came forward and identified Kearney's vehicle. As detectives began to look deeper into his background, they uncovered inconsistencies and timelines that suggested he might be involved in more than one case. Faced with mounting pressure, Kearney turned himself in to authorities before a warrant could be executed. He arrived at the police station alongside his partner and, in a remarkable departure from most serial offenders, confessed voluntarily to a long series of killings stretching back nearly a decade.

His confession stunned law enforcement. Kearney calmly described his actions in chronological order, offering details about victims, dates, and disposal locations with chilling precision. He admitted to more than 20 murders, and eventually that number rose to over 30. Investigators were struck by how matter-of-fact he was; there was no apparent remorse, no emotional agitation, only a desire to cooperate and provide clarity. This behavior raised questions among psychological experts. Unlike many violent offenders who exhibit signs of impulsivity, rage, or delusion, Kearney appeared calm, rational, and entirely aware of the consequences of his actions. He admitted to knowing that what he was doing was wrong, yet he continued for years without any apparent compulsion to stop.

This blend of detachment and method marked Kearney as an unusual figure in criminology. He did not fit neatly into the existing categories of psychotic or compulsive killers. Instead, he seemed to operate within a calculated framework of decision-making that allowed him to balance his criminal life with a stable domestic existence. When questioned about his motives, Kearney provided vague answers. He said he often felt a need for control, for the removal of perceived threats or discomfort. These justifications, while disturbing, lacked the dramatic narratives sometimes found in serial offender cases. There were no grand delusions or messianic claims. Just a quiet man who methodically removed others from the world for reasons that remained elusive even under scrutiny.

In the legal proceedings that followed his confession, Kearney pleaded guilty to 21 counts of murder. This spared the state a lengthy trial and led to his sentencing to multiple life terms without the possibility of parole. His demeanor in court was the same as during his confessions: quiet, unemotional, and composed. There were no outbursts or attempts to shift blame. He accepted the sentence, and shortly after, was transferred to a state correctional facility where he remains to this day.

The aftermath of Kearney's case prompted important shifts in investigative practices within California. Law enforcement agencies began sharing information across jurisdictions more proactively, recognizing the challenges posed by mobile offenders who operated across city and county lines. Advances in forensic science would later be applied to unresolved cases with possible links to Kearney, though many of the victims he confessed to remained unidentified, their names lost to the margins of recordkeeping and the limited resources devoted to transient or at-risk populations.

Kearney's ability to evade detection for so long also highlighted systemic vulnerabilities. At the time, many victims were misclassified, their deaths considered isolated events rather than part of a larger pattern. Some were mischaracterized due to their age, background, or lack of family advocacy. Kearney himself avoided suspicion in part because of his quiet lifestyle and lack of overt warning signs. This combination of social invisibility, on the part of both victim and perpetrator, became a central focus of criminologists who later analyzed the case.

Psychologically, Kearney remains a point of interest in the study of serial offenders who defy traditional profiles. Unlike offenders who seek attention, media coverage, or symbolic meaning in their actions, Kearney maintained a low profile and expressed no interest in notoriety. His emotional detachment, high IQ, and logistical sophistication place him in a rare category of serial predator who relies on precision over compulsion. These qualities make him a particularly unsettling figure; not only for what he did, but for how easily he moved through the world while doing it.

Within academic circles, his case is frequently cited in discussions about the evolution of profiling techniques, particularly in distinguishing between different subtypes of organized offenders. While the broader public tends to associate serial killers with erratic or flamboyant personalities, Kearney exemplifies the opposite: an unremarkable man with a stable job, a clean home, and a routine that allowed him to evade suspicion for years. That contrast, between normalcy and horror, is perhaps what makes his story so enduringly disturbing.

Patrick Kearney is currently serving life in prison without the possibility of parole. His story has never received the same sensational media coverage as some of his contemporaries, perhaps because of his calm demeanor or because his victims, like himself, lived on the margins of mainstream awareness.

Yet his case remains one of the most prolific in California history. It underscores how methodical cruelty can exist beneath even the quietest exterior, and how vital it is for investigative systems to evolve, collaborate, and remain alert to patterns that might otherwise go unnoticed.

Joseph DeAngelo

For decades, a series of unsolved crimes haunted communities across California. The cases bore distinct and disturbing patterns; break-ins followed by assaults, stalking behaviors, escalating violence, and eventually, murder. The unknown assailant taunted police and left behind a trail of fear across Northern and Southern California. Investigators and journalists gave him various names over the years: the Visalia Ransacker, the East Area Rapist, the Original Night Stalker. It wasn't until 2018 that these identities were finally linked to one man (Joseph James DeAngelo) who would come to be known as the Golden State Killer. His arrest brought closure to more than a dozen families, but it also raised difficult questions about how a man could live for so long in plain sight while leaving such devastation in his wake.

Joseph DeAngelo was born on November 8, 1945, in Bath, New York. His early life was marked by family instability, including reported abuse and dysfunction in the home. He spent much of his youth moving from place to place as his family settled in California. As a teenager, DeAngelo was described by peers as quiet and intense, someone who did not easily fit in but rarely stood out in a disruptive way. He graduated from high school in Auburn, California, and eventually enlisted in the U.S. Navy, serving during the Vietnam War. After his military service, he returned to California and studied criminal justice at Sacramento State University, later working as a police officer in Exeter and Auburn.

That law enforcement background would become a chilling irony in hindsight. DeAngelo was employed as a police officer in the very communities where he committed many of his early crimes. This duality, upholding the law by day, violating it with chilling precision by night, underscored the complexity of his case. As an officer, he had insight into police procedure, investigative techniques, and how to manipulate evidence or avoid leaving incriminating traces. His knowledge contributed to his ability to evade capture for decades, and it also compounded the betrayal felt by communities who later learned that the man responsible had once sworn to protect them.

His criminal activity began in the early 1970s with a series of residential burglaries in Visalia, where a masked intruder became known for stealing small items, vandalizing property, and escaping before law enforcement could arrive. The behavior escalated over time, culminating in the killing of a man who attempted to confront the intruder. Shortly after that incident, the Visalia Ransacker appeared to vanish. Unbeknownst to investigators at the time, DeAngelo had simply moved on, his crimes shifting both in geography and intensity.

By the mid-1970s, attacks began occurring in the Sacramento area. The offender targeted single women and couples, often entering homes at night, binding victims, and terrorizing them for hours. He showed signs of elaborate pre-planning – cutting phone lines, stalking residences ahead of time, and bringing tools to control his victims. The crimes sparked mass panic. Neighborhood watches were formed, hardware stores saw a surge in lock and security system sales, and many families refused to sleep in their bedrooms. Police departments, overwhelmed and lacking leads, struggled to contain public fear.

Despite hundreds of tips and a massive investigative effort, the East Area Rapist continued to elude capture. His ability to disappear without a trace after each attack baffled detectives. He moved quietly through neighborhoods, often escaping on foot or by bicycle, and rarely left behind usable physical evidence. Forensic DNA was not yet a reliable tool in the 1970s, and investigators were left with incomplete sketches, partial footprints, and a growing sense of frustration. The case eventually went cold, though it remained one of the most infamous unsolved crime sprees in California history.

In the 1980s, a new series of violent crimes began in Southern California. This time, the offender focused on couples in their homes, killing them in ways that suggested premeditation and a lack of hesitation. The MO shared several eerie similarities with the earlier attacks, but it would take years before the connection was confirmed. The offender, now dubbed the Original Night Stalker, struck with precision, leaving few clues. For a long time, the two crime series were considered separate, pursued by different jurisdictions with no shared suspect.

It wasn't until 2001 that a breakthrough came through DNA technology. Advances in forensic science allowed analysts to link evidence from the East Area Rapist crimes with that of the Original Night Stalker, revealing that both sets of offenses had been committed by the same person.

This composite offender was then given a new moniker: the Golden State Killer. The realization stunned law enforcement and reignited interest in solving the now decades-old mystery. Task forces were reassembled, evidence was re-examined, and victim advocates continued pushing for resolution.

Years passed without a suspect, until in 2018, a combination of modern DNA analysis and genealogical research pointed to Joseph DeAngelo. Investigators had used publicly available genetic databases to identify familial connections from old crime scene DNA. From there, they constructed a family tree, narrowing down potential suspects until DeAngelo emerged as a prime candidate. Undercover officers obtained a DNA sample from discarded items, which confirmed the match. The arrest came as a shock to his neighbors and community. DeAngelo had been living a quiet life in a Sacramento suburb, retired and maintaining a low profile.

Following his arrest, DeAngelo was charged with multiple counts of murder and other crimes spanning from the 1970s through the 1980s.

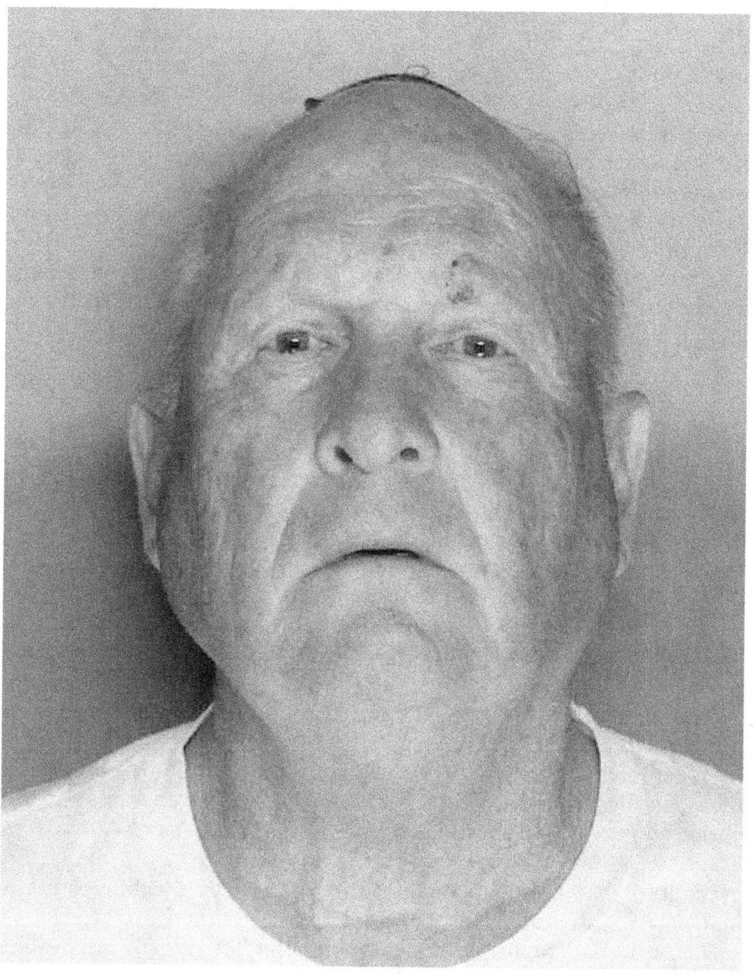

(Joseph DeAngelo mugshot)

The legal proceedings were extensive. Given the passage of time, some charges could no longer be brought, but prosecutors moved forward with the most serious counts supported by physical evidence. In a courtroom packed with survivors and family members of victims, DeAngelo entered a guilty plea in 2020 as part of a plea agreement that spared him the death penalty. He was sentenced to multiple consecutive life terms without the possibility of parole.

His behavior in court drew widespread attention. Once a seemingly confident and elusive figure, DeAngelo appeared frail and subdued. He spoke in a low voice, often seeming distant or vacant. Yet during the sentencing hearing, when allowed to address the court, he briefly uttered an apology, a statement that many found hollow given the magnitude of his crimes.

Victims and survivors gave powerful testimonies, describing decades of trauma, fear, and the long shadow cast by unanswered questions. The hearing became not just a moment of justice, but a collective reckoning with a chapter of California's criminal history that had remained unresolved for too long.

In the years since his sentencing, DeAngelo has remained incarcerated in a high-security prison. His case has continued to attract public and academic interest. It is studied in law schools, criminology courses, and forensic programs as a landmark example of how modern technology, especially genetic genealogy, can solve cases once thought unsolvable. It also raises important ethical and legal questions about privacy, the use of public DNA databases, and the balance between individual rights and public safety.

DeAngelo's case is notable not just for the crimes themselves, but for how long he avoided detection and how thoroughly he compartmentalized his life. As a husband, father, and neighbor, he presented a calm and ordinary exterior. As a former police officer, he once upheld the very laws he would later violate so completely. His ability to maintain this dual existence for decades, evading justice while watching news coverage of his own crimes, adds to the psychological complexity of his profile. Experts continue to debate the motivations behind his behavior, with some pointing to early trauma, power dynamics, or deeply embedded personality disorders. But in many ways, DeAngelo defies simple explanations. He is an example of the type of predator who can function in society, mask his deviance, and blend seamlessly into the everyday.

The Golden State Killer's story is also a story of endurance. Survivors, family members, and detectives refused to give up. Their persistence kept the investigation alive and ultimately led to his capture. In that sense, the case represents more than tragedy; it stands as a testament to human determination and the evolving power of science in service of justice.

Joseph DeAngelo's crimes left a lasting scar on California and on the many lives he impacted. Yet his eventual unmasking also marked a turning point in forensic investigation. He was not caught by luck, but by the patient application of new tools and techniques to old questions.

And while no sentence can reverse the harm he caused, the resolution of his case closed a chapter that had been open for too long. His story remains a chilling reminder that the past doesn't always stay buried, and that even the most elusive offenders can eventually be found.

Bruce McArthur

The arrest and conviction of Bruce McArthur shocked Canada and reverberated across the global true crime community. Not only was the case unusual in its scope and duration, but it also forced difficult conversations about systemic failures in how marginalized communities are protected and how violent offenders can go unnoticed for years. McArthur operated in Toronto, one of North America's largest and most diverse cities, and lived most of his life as an unremarkable figure, a self-employed landscaper with ties to the LGBTQ+ community, known by some as a kind, grandfatherly man.

The revelation that he was responsible for the deaths of multiple men over nearly a decade shattered any illusions about his outward persona and brought to light a story shaped as much by cultural blind spots as by calculated predation.

Born in 1951 in Lindsay, Ontario, Bruce McArthur grew up in a conservative, rural environment. He married young, had children, and for many years lived a seemingly conventional life. It wasn't until midlife that McArthur came out as gay, after separating from his wife. He moved to Toronto and embedded himself in the Church and Wellesley neighborhood, the city's historic gay village. There, he became known to some as friendly and unthreatening, occasionally participating in local events and working steadily in his landscaping business. He built relationships with clients, many of whom welcomed him into their homes and yards. There was little to suggest anything sinister in his daily behavior.

Yet beneath that benign surface, McArthur was harboring secrets. His eventual victims were primarily men of color, immigrants or refugees, some living on the margins of society. Many had limited support networks, precarious immigration status, or strained ties to their families. They were not invisible in their communities, but they were vulnerable in ways that made them easier targets for someone like McArthur. Between 2010 and 2017, several men from the Church and Wellesley area disappeared without a trace. Posters were put up. Vigils were held. Loved ones demanded answers. But early investigations yielded few results.

As disappearances continued, members of Toronto's LGBTQ+ community began to express frustration with what they perceived as a lack of urgency from law enforcement. In the absence of concrete leads, speculation grew that a serial predator might be responsible. Still, no official link was drawn between the missing persons cases for years. It wasn't until 2017, following the disappearance of Andrew Kinsman, a well-known community member, that significant progress was made. Kinsman had left behind a clue in the form of a note with the name "Bruce" written in it. This single detail, coupled with digital surveillance and cell phone data, allowed detectives to narrow in on McArthur.

Police began covertly monitoring him, ultimately obtaining a warrant to enter his residence. What they found confirmed their worst fears. In January 2018, Bruce McArthur was arrested. In the days that followed, investigators uncovered evidence that he had concealed human remains in planters at properties where he worked. Over time, the remains of eight men were discovered, all linked to victims who had disappeared in the preceding years. Each revelation shocked the city further. The idea that someone could operate so brazenly, and so long, while living in the heart of a close-knit neighborhood, challenged assumptions about how and where danger hides.

McArthur's method of operating was calculated and methodical. He targeted individuals he knew or had met through dating apps or social networks within the gay community. Several victims were last seen with him, and he used familiarity and perceived safety to gain their trust. He didn't operate impulsively or with visible instability.

His crimes were deliberate, concealed, and repeated over time, suggesting a level of control and planning that set him apart from many other violent offenders. Investigators later discovered that he kept trophies from his victims, including photographs and digital files, a grim reminder of his need to assert dominance and revisit the crimes in private.

In 2019, Bruce McArthur pleaded guilty to eight counts of first-degree murder. The plea deal spared the victims' families a lengthy trial and guaranteed that McArthur would spend the rest of his life in prison without the possibility of parole for at least 25 years.

At the sentencing hearing, victims' family members and community leaders gave statements describing their loss, their pain, and their frustration at the long delay in justice. The presiding judge called McArthur's crimes "pure evil," noting the callous disregard he showed for the humanity of his victims. McArthur, for his part, showed little emotion. He offered a brief apology but provided no substantial insight into his motives or mindset.

The case sparked a national reckoning in Canada about how marginalized communities are treated within the justice system. Many critics argued that the disappearances would have received more immediate attention had the victims been from more affluent or visible backgrounds. The delay in connecting the cases, despite community advocacy, was seen as evidence of systemic bias. A subsequent independent review examined how Toronto Police handled the investigations and recommended several reforms aimed at improving communication with vulnerable populations, enhancing data-sharing across jurisdictions, and prioritizing missing persons cases more effectively.

Psychologically, McArthur presents a rare and troubling profile. He did not fit the popular image of a serial killer. He was not socially isolated or visibly disturbed. He had no significant criminal record, no history of overt violence, and no known childhood trauma that would readily explain his behavior. He lived in a densely populated area, maintained stable employment, and had ongoing personal relationships. This ordinariness made him more dangerous, not less. Experts who examined the case noted that McArthur's ability to compartmentalize his actions was indicative of a deeply ingrained capacity for deception and manipulation. He understood how to appear harmless, and he used that perception as a shield against suspicion.

What also makes McArthur's case distinct is how long he was able to continue offending despite signs that something was wrong. The disappearances were clustered, the victims were demographically similar, and community members raised concerns early. Yet those warnings were not acted on with the speed or seriousness required. In many ways, McArthur exploited the very structures meant to protect people. His victims were targeted precisely because they lived in a gray area of social visibility, known to their peers but not prioritized by institutions.

The landscape of accountability changed following McArthur's conviction. Toronto Police introduced new protocols for handling missing persons cases and expanded outreach programs with the LGBTQ+ community. The city acknowledged the pain caused by institutional delay and pledged to do better. However, the scars from the case remain deep, not just for the families of the victims but for a community that felt unheard for far too long.

In terms of criminal history, McArthur was not completely invisible to law enforcement before the killings. In the early 2000s, he was involved in a minor assault case that did not lead to jail time. The incident was not pursued in a way that would have flagged him as a potential threat.

This pattern, early warning signs that fail to result in meaningful consequences, echoes in many serial offender cases. It raises important questions about how information is stored, shared, and weighed within the justice system, especially when the individuals involved do not fit stereotypical profiles.

Since his incarceration, McArthur has remained largely silent. He has not granted interviews, written accounts, or expressed remorse beyond his brief courtroom statement. He now resides in a maximum-security facility, aging in relative isolation. His silence has left many questions unanswered, particularly about how he viewed his victims and how he rationalized his actions to himself. Forensic psychologists continue to debate whether he should be categorized as a psychopath, a narcissist, or an opportunist shaped by late-life psychological shifts. What remains clear is that he maintained a chilling level of self-control, methodically covering his tracks and maintaining a double life for years.

The public legacy of the McArthur case is still unfolding. Books, documentaries, and public inquiries have examined it from multiple angles: criminal, sociological, psychological, and institutional. It has become a case study in what happens when warning signs are missed, when biases influence the pace of justice, and when someone leverages trust and appearance to devastating effect.

For Toronto, it served as a breaking point and a call to action. For the broader criminal justice field, it offered sobering lessons about offender typology, victim profiling, and the role of community pressure in advancing investigations.

Bruce McArthur did not operate in secret because he was invisible. He operated in secret because he was trusted. His demeanor, age, and occupation all contributed to a perception of harmlessness that helped him avoid scrutiny. This discrepancy between appearance and reality lies at the core of his story. It reminds us that danger doesn't always announce itself with menace. Sometimes it smiles, offers a business card, and asks for access to a backyard garden.

Dennis Nilsen

For years, the quiet hum of North London life moved on, unaware of the horror unfolding behind the closed doors of a seemingly ordinary apartment. Dennis Nilsen lived in modest flats, kept to himself, and gave off little impression of menace. Yet his arrest in 1983 uncovered one of the most disturbing criminal cases in British history.

Known as the "Muswell Hill Murderer," Nilsen was responsible for a string of killings that shocked the nation and revealed a complex psychological portrait of loneliness, control, and detachment from human life.

Born on November 23, 1945, in Fraserburgh, Scotland, Dennis Andrew Nilsen was the second of three children. His early life was marked by instability. His parents' marriage was troubled, and they eventually divorced when Nilsen was a child. He was especially close to his grandfather, whose sudden death when Nilsen was just six years old left a deep emotional scar.

Years later, Nilsen would describe seeing his grandfather's corpse during the wake, a moment that reportedly left him fascinated by death and permanence. That fascination would take on darker forms as he matured.

Nilsen's adolescence was largely uneventful on the surface. He kept to himself, struggled with his s**ual identity, and later confessed to feeling isolated. In his early twenties, he joined the British Army, where he served as a cook. His time in the military gave him a sense of structure and routine but did little to ease his internal conflict. He traveled, maintained a clean appearance, and was viewed by colleagues as efficient and capable.

But underneath the discipline, his loneliness deepened. After leaving the military, he worked briefly as a police officer and then held various civil service positions. His life, by most external markers, appeared ordinary.

What distinguished Nilsen was not a chaotic descent into crime, but a gradual, methodical emergence of a secret life. Between 1978 and 1983, he committed a series of murders in two North London residences, first in Cricklewood, then in Muswell Hill. His victims were typically young men, many of them transient or estranged from family. Some were drifters, others struggling with poverty or housing insecurity. Nilsen often met them at pubs, bus stops, or on the streets, offering a place to stay. The interactions began with gestures of kindness or companionship, but ended in violence and concealment.

What startled investigators and the public was not only the number of victims, believed to be at least fifteen, but the fact that Nilsen lived with the remains. His need for control and continued possession of the deceased indicated an extreme level of psychological disturbance. He made no effort to dispose of the bodies in a timely fashion and instead attempted to maintain a sense of connection to the victims. When plumbing issues in his building eventually led to his arrest, police found evidence of remains clogging the drainage system, prompting a full-scale investigation.

The arrest in February 1983 was almost accidental. A complaint by a plumber led to a grim discovery, and Nilsen calmly invited police into his flat. What followed was a confession so detailed and unemotional that it stunned detectives. Nilsen admitted to the crimes with chilling calmness, speaking at length about each case. He expressed little remorse, focusing instead on the emotional states that led him to commit the acts.

His statements revealed a compulsive need for companionship, paired with an inability to cope with abandonment or rejection. He often described his motives in abstract, philosophical terms, highlighting a profound detachment from the human consequences of his actions.

At trial, Nilsen was charged with six counts of murder and two of attempted murder. Although he had confessed to more killings, the prosecution focused on those supported by the strongest forensic evidence. The trial in 1983 became a media spectacle, with intense public interest in how someone so unremarkable in appearance could carry out such sustained violence. Nilsen's defense attempted to argue diminished responsibility, suggesting he was mentally ill and therefore not criminally liable. However, the jury rejected this claim, and he was convicted and sentenced to life imprisonment, with a recommendation that he never be released.

Psychiatrists and criminologists have since studied Nilsen extensively. He did not kill out of impulse or for profit. His crimes were deeply rooted in issues of isolation, identity, and fantasy. He often spoke of wanting his victims to stay with him, fearing abandonment above all else. This need for connection, distorted by a lack of empathy and an absence of normal emotional development, manifested in the most extreme form of control, taking life and refusing to let it go. Experts debated whether he was a psychopathic personality, a narcissist, or suffering from a dissociative disorder. Ultimately, his psychological profile resisted simple classification.

Nilsen remained in prison until his death in 2018. While incarcerated, he kept detailed journals, wrote volumes of reflections, and corresponded with academics and journalists. His writings revealed a self-awareness that bordered on the obsessive. He often portrayed himself as misunderstood, even as he acknowledged the horror of his actions.

Yet he showed little true remorse, framing his story as a tragic narrative rather than a series of calculated choices. These documents, later archived, provide a window into a criminal mind shaped by detachment rather than chaos, a personality more orderly than erratic, more cold than impulsive.

One of the lingering impacts of the Nilsen case is how it highlighted the vulnerability of certain populations. Many of his victims were never officially identified, in part because they lived on the margins of society. Without strong family ties or support systems, their disappearances were not always noted. This lack of visibility made it easier for Nilsen to continue his crimes without detection. The case raised important questions for police services and social institutions about the need to better track missing persons and respond quickly when individuals from disadvantaged backgrounds vanish without explanation.

In the decades since Nilsen's conviction, public fascination with the case has remained high. Documentaries, books, and dramatizations have explored various angles of the story, from the psychological complexity of the killer to the failures of the justice system. While many true crime cases evoke shock and horror, Nilsen's story resonates because of its banality. He didn't operate in darkness or wilderness. He lived in densely populated neighborhoods, shopped at local stores, and held stable employment. He was, by all appearances, part of the fabric of ordinary life. That illusion of normalcy was precisely what enabled him to continue for so long without scrutiny.

For many in the UK, Nilsen's name became synonymous with deception. He represented a version of evil that did not require theatrics. His crimes were not the result of rage or external provocation, but a reflection of an inner void, a psychological vacuum where empathy should have existed. He created routines, played roles, and constructed a double life with terrifying efficiency. He reminded the public that danger does not always come with visible warning signs, and that some of the most serious threats may be hidden behind soft voices and polite conversation.

In later years, Nilsen himself seemed to court the narrative. He corresponded with writers and attempted to publish his memoirs, which were ultimately blocked. He sought, in his own way, to shape how history would remember him.

Yet the facts stood firmly against that revisionism. His victims were real people with families, dreams, and futures cut short. Their names, where known, were remembered not for how they died but for the lives they tried to live. Advocacy groups and surviving relatives ensured that the focus remained on justice, not spectacle.

Dennis Nilsen's story is now part of British criminal history, taught in courses on forensic psychology and cited in debates about criminal profiling and offender management. His case influenced how missing persons reports are handled and contributed to the evolution of investigative techniques that rely more heavily on pattern recognition and community outreach. In a tragic but important way, his actions forced institutions to adapt and become more sensitive to the quiet signals that something is amiss. While the lessons came at a high cost, they have helped to improve future protections.

Ultimately, what makes the Nilsen case stand out is not just its brutality, but its dissonance. He was not the monster hiding in shadowy alleys. He was the man next door, trimming hedges, greeting neighbors, and blending in with the rhythm of city life. That incongruity, the coexistence of normalcy and horror, continues to unsettle, even decades later.

Nilsen remains a case study in how pathology can wear a mask of order, how loneliness can metastasize into destruction, and how the ordinary can sometimes be the most dangerous disguise of all.

Carl Panzram

Carl Panzram occupies a grim place in the annals of American criminal history, not merely for the scale of his offenses, but for the unflinching clarity with which he expressed them. Unlike many serial offenders who masked their intentions or showed signs of remorse, Panzram left behind a written confession that was as cold and deliberate as it was articulate. His life and crimes spanned a volatile period in early 20th-century America, during which prisons were brutal, justice was inconsistent, and criminal profiling was in its infancy. His legacy is disturbing, not only for what he did but for what he revealed about the systems that shaped him.

Born on June 28, 1891, in East Grand Forks, Minnesota, Carl Panzram was raised in poverty on a struggling farm by German immigrant parents. His father abandoned the family early on, and Panzram's relationship with his mother and siblings was strained. He ran away from home by age 11 and was soon entangled in a life of petty theft, vagrancy, and defiance.

His first serious institutionalization came shortly thereafter, at the Minnesota State Training School, a facility meant to reform delinquent boys. Instead, it became the crucible for his rage.

Later in life, Panzram claimed that the abuses he endured at the reform school shaped his contempt for authority and humanity. Whether exaggerated or not, the claims he made were consistent with known conditions at such institutions during the time, where corporal punishment was rampant and young inmates were often subject to violence. For Panzram, these formative years were marked not by rehabilitation but by trauma, humiliation, and the internalization of a philosophy rooted in revenge.

After escaping the school, he began a criminal trajectory that escalated steadily. By his late teens, Panzram was traveling across the country under false identities, stealing, robbing, and occasionally working as a laborer. He joined the U.S. Army in 1907 by lying about his age but was quickly discharged after being court-martialed for theft. That incident landed him in Leavenworth Federal Penitentiary, where he served a sentence and developed a deeper hatred for confinement and those who imposed it.

Over the following two decades, Panzram would serve time in numerous prisons across the United States and commit crimes in multiple countries. His movements were erratic but methodical, driven by an almost philosophical belief in destruction. He viewed institutions as corrupt and hypocritical and considered his actions as a form of vengeance against society at large. He developed an ideology in which trust was weakness, compassion was a flaw, and the world was divided into predators and prey. This worldview was reinforced with each arrest and release, each encounter with brutality, and each perceived betrayal.

Panzram's most infamous years came in the 1920s, when he claimed to have traveled through the United States, Mexico, and parts of Africa, committing violent crimes along the way. Though the full extent of his offenses is impossible to verify, his written confessions outline a staggering range of actions, from burglary to arson to murder. He claimed responsibility for over 20 killings, although he was only formally charged with one. Some investigators believe the number may have been inflated, but others point to the consistency and detail in his writings as evidence of credibility.

Regardless of the final count, his admissions painted a portrait of a man driven by hostility, not compulsion, a person who killed not out of impulse but out of principle.

What made Panzram's case particularly unique was his level of introspection. After being arrested in 1928 for a burglary in Washington, D.C., he confessed not only to that crime but to a litany of others. He told police that he had no desire for a trial or mercy. While awaiting sentencing, he befriended a young prison guard named Henry Lesser, who encouraged him to write about his life. Panzram agreed, and over time produced a handwritten autobiography detailing his upbringing, crimes, thoughts, and worldview. The result was one of the most chilling documents in criminal history, not because it was sensationalized, but because of its unflinching honesty.

In his writings, Panzram doesn't ask for sympathy. He describes his actions in blunt, matter-of-fact language, rarely embellishing or moralizing. He presents himself as someone who was forged in cruelty and who chose to return cruelty tenfold.

He claims that any good impulses he may have once had were beaten out of him by the age of 15, and that from that point forward, his only joy came from inflicting pain. Whether these claims represent his genuine psychology or a cultivated persona is debated by scholars, but the consistency of tone suggests that he saw himself not as a tragic figure, but as an avenger without remorse.

Carl Panzram's trial for the murder of a prison employee in 1929 was swift. He pleaded guilty and demanded the death penalty. He refused all appeals, mocked his defense team, and warned the court that sparing his life would only prolong the suffering of others.

On September 5, 1930, he was executed by hanging at the United States Penitentiary in Leavenworth. His final words, according to witnesses, were characteristically defiant.

In the decades that followed, Panzram's life has been the subject of books, documentaries, and academic studies. Criminologists have studied his writings as a rare primary source into the psyche of a serial offender who was both self-aware and unrepentant. Unlike many serial killers who construct elaborate justifications or deflect responsibility, Panzram fully embraced his role as an antagonist to society. That clarity makes him an unsettling figure, one who removes the ambiguity often associated with criminal minds and instead offers a portrait of purposeful destruction.

His confessions are not easy to categorize. Some view them as the result of deep-seated psychological trauma, others as evidence of an antisocial personality disorder taken to its extreme. What is certain is that Panzram's worldview did not include space for empathy or social reintegration. He did not see himself as curable or misunderstood. His acts were deliberate, and his writings make clear that he understood their consequences. In his mind, he was a reflection of the world's brutality, shaped by it, responding to it, and mirroring it back.

From a criminal justice standpoint, Panzram's life underscores the failures of early 20th-century penal systems. The institutions that were supposed to correct behavior often inflicted further damage. Prisons were punitive rather than rehabilitative, and the frequent beatings, overcrowding, and isolation contributed to cycles of rage and recidivism. Panzram's life was an extreme case, but it illustrated systemic patterns that reformers would spend decades trying to address. His case became a cautionary tale about what can happen when cruelty is institutionalized and individuals fall through every possible crack in the system.

There is also a philosophical dimension to Panzram's legacy. His writings raise uncomfortable questions about accountability, moral development, and the nature of evil.

Can someone who has been brutalized from childhood be held fully accountable for the person they become? Does recognizing the roots of violence excuse it? What happens when someone refuses redemption?

These questions remain unresolved, but Panzram's story ensures they are never ignored. He forces readers and researchers alike to confront the possibility that some individuals do not seek rehabilitation, do not feel regret, and do not conform to the narratives we prefer about crime and punishment.

Today, Carl Panzram is remembered less as a criminal mastermind and more as a symbol of nihilism in its purest form. He did not kill for money, fame, or even pleasure in the conventional sense. He killed because he believed it was the only true response to the pain he experienced and the hypocrisy he perceived in others. His clarity, paradoxically, made him one of the most terrifying figures in criminal history, not because he was chaotic, but because he was so ordered in his hatred. He lived by a code, albeit one rooted in destruction.

The notebooks he left behind, preserved and studied for decades, remain among the most detailed confessions ever written by a serial offender. They are used in criminal justice education to highlight the limits of psychological profiling and to demonstrate how dangerous intelligence, articulation, and bitterness can be when combined. His interactions with Henry Lesser, the guard who encouraged him to write, also show that even in the darkest figures, there can be glimpses of humanity, however fleeting.

Carl Panzram's life is not one to romanticize or sensationalize. It is a warning. A stark reminder that beneath the surface of failed systems and ignored trauma can emerge something irreparably damaged. His case demands that we look not only at individual pathology but at the broader contexts that allow such pathology to fester unchecked. He is not a figure of mystery. He made himself clear. That, in many ways, is what makes him so chilling.

Anatoly Slivko

Anatoly Slivko's crimes stunned the Soviet Union not only for their disturbing nature but for how long they went unnoticed by authorities. A respected youth leader with an image of community service and moral responsibility, Slivko spent years cultivating a carefully constructed double life. By the time his actions came to light in the mid-1980s, the realization that such acts could be carried out in plain sight, under the guise of mentorship, shattered public trust in institutional safeguards. His case remains one of the most infamous in Soviet criminal history, not merely for its brutality but for its methodical deception and the long-term systemic failures that allowed it to persist.

Slivko was born in 1938 in the Soviet republic of Dagestan. His early life was marked by a deep need for structure, identity, and validation. The postwar Soviet environment in which he came of age emphasized conformity, discipline, and loyalty to the state. For many, these values became a source of stability.

But for Slivko, they seemed to evolve into a desire for control and hidden power. He presented himself as an ideal citizen: a model party member, an enthusiast of youth development programs, and a leader in the Soviet Pioneers, a state-run organization akin to the Boy Scouts. This role granted him access to vulnerable populations and social credibility.

By the late 1960s and early 1970s, Slivko had moved to the city of Nevinnomyssk in southern Russia. There, he began organizing adventure clubs, film screenings, and camping expeditions for young boys. His programs appeared to be wildly successful, winning the praise of local officials and parents. For many families, entrusting their children to someone like Slivko felt safe. His uniforms, awards, and enthusiasm made him appear trustworthy, even admirable. But beneath that façade was a meticulous predator who was using his position not only to build a narrative of public service, but also to conceal calculated acts of violence.

The key to Slivko's success in evading suspicion for so long was his mastery of compartmentalization. He kept his criminal activities tightly bound to a separate realm from his public identity, ensuring that few would question his motives. When young boys went missing or were found injured, his name rarely came up in investigations. Some of the boys he approached were from troubled families or vulnerable backgrounds, and their disappearances did not always prompt immediate concern. In a state bureaucracy where paperwork was often inefficient and law enforcement resources limited, Slivko exploited institutional blind spots with astonishing success.

Authorities would later discover that Slivko maintained detailed journals, photographs, and footage documenting his activities. These materials were not discovered by chance, but through persistent police work following a tip-off from a concerned mother and a teacher who noticed inconsistencies in Slivko's interactions. As the case unfolded in the early 1980s, investigators began to piece together a horrifying timeline of abuse and murder that stretched over nearly two decades.

What made Slivko especially dangerous was the calm, rational way in which he carried out his crimes. He planned extensively, selecting victims with care and using his role as a mentor to lower their defenses. His ability to manipulate not just individuals but entire systems (schools, police departments, and youth organizations) underscored the limits of traditional methods of oversight.

In the Soviet context, where criticism of the state or its institutions could be seen as subversive, even well-meaning officials were often hesitant to raise concerns. This dynamic made it easier for figures like Slivko to operate without meaningful scrutiny.

As the investigation deepened, Slivko's pattern of offending came into focus. He was not driven by opportunistic violence, but by a structured set of fantasies and compulsions. Experts brought in to assess his psychological profile described him as organized, intelligent, and emotionally detached. Unlike impulsive offenders, he maintained a calculated control over his environment and was adept at projecting normalcy. Even after his arrest, he remained composed and willing to cooperate with investigators. In interviews, he explained his motivations with dispassionate clarity, a characteristic that both disturbed and intrigued criminal psychologists.

His trial was one of the most closely watched in Soviet legal history. Though the media coverage was limited due to censorship policies at the time, word of his crimes spread quickly through unofficial channels. In closed court proceedings, the prosecution presented an overwhelming body of evidence. Slivko admitted to multiple murders, and his confession aligned with the records found in his possession.

These included photographs, written notes, and personal effects taken from victims. His cooperation, while seen as an attempt to control the narrative, did little to reduce the public's shock.

The legal outcome was swift. Slivko was found guilty and sentenced to death in 1985. He was executed the following year. But even after his death, questions lingered. How had such a person operated so openly for so long? Why did institutions fail to act on warning signs? And what did this say about the limits of public trust in authority figures?

In the years that followed, criminologists, journalists, and human rights advocates studied the Slivko case as a critical failure of institutional vigilance. It exposed weaknesses in centralized control structures where social status and state loyalty could serve as a shield against suspicion. It also emphasized the importance of listening to dissenting voices (teachers, parents, and concerned individuals) who raised red flags even when it was uncomfortable to do so. The case contributed to quiet reforms in how background checks, reporting systems, and psychological screening were handled in youth programs throughout the country.

From a psychological standpoint, Slivko's profile falls into a category often described as organized offenders. He was methodical, employed strategic manipulation, and rarely left immediate evidence. These traits made him harder to detect but also helped authorities, once they understood his patterns, construct a thorough behavioral profile. His confessions became required reading in some Russian criminal psychology courses, not because they offered sensational material, but because they demonstrated the intellectual rationalization of predatory behavior. For modern profilers, the case offered insights into how some offenders build elaborate moral justifications for their actions, often invoking ideas of science, control, or personal philosophy.

Slivko's manipulation of institutional systems also speaks to a broader theme in criminal justice: the risk posed by charismatic individuals who use social roles to deflect suspicion. Like other notorious figures in this category, Slivko blended into his environment precisely because he appeared to serve it. He didn't merely act out criminal impulses; he disguised them beneath a layer of civic engagement. This ability to use trust as a weapon remains a chilling reminder of the limits of surface-level assessments in safeguarding vulnerable communities.

The legacy of the Slivko case is complicated. On one hand, it sparked internal reviews within Soviet administrative circles and youth organizations. On the other, it exposed a kind of collective denial: that certain individuals, if properly credentialed and socially embedded, were above suspicion.

In some ways, Slivko represented a rupture in the official Soviet narrative that crime was primarily a symptom of Western corruption. His crimes were homegrown, systemic, and deeply psychological. They challenged the notion that authoritarian control alone could insulate a society from internal threats.

In post-Soviet Russia, renewed interest in the case emerged during the 1990s and 2000s. As archives were opened and censorship loosened, researchers began to reconstruct the full timeline of Slivko's activities. Documentaries, academic papers, and journalistic investigations revealed just how extensive his network of deception had been. One particularly troubling discovery was how often suspicions were dismissed or ignored, whether due to institutional inertia, misplaced trust, or bureaucratic fragmentation.

Survivors and families of victims, many of whom had been silenced or marginalized during the initial proceedings, gradually began to share their stories. Their testimony helped humanize a case that had long been shrouded in clinical descriptions and state-controlled messaging.

They demanded reforms, not just in background checks or psychological screening, but in fostering a culture of accountability within public institutions. Some of these changes were eventually codified, while others remain aspirational.

For those studying criminology, the Slivko case is more than a cautionary tale. It is a blueprint of how some offenders cultivate entire personas to evade detection. His story teaches that violence isn't always chaotic or unstructured; it can be planned, rehearsed, and concealed behind masks of order and professionalism. In many ways, that makes it harder to detect and even harder to accept.

At the same time, the case also demonstrates the importance of persistence in investigative work. It was not a single tip or a dramatic confession that led to Slivko's downfall. It was the accumulation of small inconsistencies, local suspicions, and the courage of individuals who chose not to remain silent. The eventual unraveling of his double life was a victory not for technology or surveillance, but for attention to detail and human vigilance.

Anatoly Slivko's crimes are not widely known outside of Eastern Europe, but they stand among the most chilling examples of how psychological manipulation, institutional blind spots, and charismatic deceit can combine into a long-term threat. His case is studied not because of sensationalism, but because it exposes critical vulnerabilities in how societies protect, or fail to protect, the vulnerable. It forces us to question how much we really know about the people we trust the most, and whether systems designed to nurture can also become vehicles for exploitation.

As with many high-profile offenders, the lessons from Slivko's life extend far beyond his personal story. They ask how we can better detect red flags, create systems of accountability that don't rely solely on credentials, and encourage environments where speaking up is not just permitted, but expected. The case leaves behind a legacy not of mystery, but of warning. And perhaps most importantly, it underscores that evil can wear a smile, carry a clipboard, and speak with authority, making it all the more important that we remain vigilant, even in places where safety appears to be guaranteed.

Lonnie Franklin Jr.

Lonnie Franklin Jr. operated in the margins, moving through a sprawling city that rarely stood still long enough to notice what had gone missing. For years, he led an unremarkable life in South Los Angeles, working on cars, chatting with neighbors, barbecuing in the front yard, and offering advice to people who passed by. To most who knew him, Franklin seemed like a friendly, quiet man, a reliable presence in a neighborhood where chaos could come and go without warning.

But beneath this surface existed a dark reality that law enforcement would take decades to uncover. When they finally did, the story that emerged was one of chilling patience, institutional failure, and a city that had, knowingly or unknowingly, looked the other way.

Born in 1952, Lonnie David Franklin Jr. came of age during a time of extraordinary change in Los Angeles. The civil rights era, economic transformations, and rising tensions between communities and police shaped the landscape of his youth. Franklin served in the U.S. Army, and though his military record was largely unremarkable, it included at least one serious blemish, an overseas conviction related to assault.

By the time he returned to civilian life, his trajectory was relatively anonymous. He held a number of jobs: sanitation worker, mechanic, and city employee. These positions placed him inside the workings of the very systems that would later try to capture him.

Franklin's crimes spanned more than two decades, beginning in the mid-1980s and allegedly continuing into the early 2000s, with a long break in between. This pause in activity would earn him the name "Grim Sleeper," a moniker created by the media to reflect what they believed was a 14-year gap between killings. The idea of a serial killer who took a long hiatus only to return later added a surreal layer to the case. In reality, investigators would later question whether the pause was real at all. Perhaps he had never stopped. Perhaps he had simply become better at hiding.

The story of how Franklin's crimes were discovered is a testament to perseverance, community concern, and the role of forensics in modern policing. In the early years, his crimes went largely unnoticed by the public. Many of the victims were marginalized: Black women from impoverished areas, some with histories of substance use or transient living. These facts contributed to the widespread sense that authorities weren't treating the disappearances or deaths with urgency. Families of victims raised alarms, but their pleas were often ignored or deprioritized. In some cases, they were told their loved ones had simply left or that the circumstances didn't warrant deeper investigation.

Throughout the late 1980s and early 1990s, the city faced a surge in violence due to gang conflicts and the crack epidemic. This chaos created a perfect cover for a serial predator operating with surgical precision. It also revealed a tragic divide in how victims were perceived. When certain lives are viewed as expendable, killers who target those individuals can thrive. That was the reality in South Central Los Angeles, where Franklin's trail of destruction continued without major media coverage, without intense public outcry, and without effective law enforcement response for many years.

But even as the case went cold in public memory, behind the scenes, a group of detectives never fully let it go. In 2007, the Los Angeles Police Department created a special task force to reexamine unsolved homicides that shared common features. The cold case unit, supported by advances in DNA technology, began identifying patterns that pointed to a single individual.

Key breakthroughs came when forensic evidence linked several crimes separated by years. What had once seemed like unrelated acts of violence were, in fact, connected through minute biological traces preserved at crime scenes.

The key turning point in the case was the use of familial DNA, a groundbreaking but controversial investigative tool. Investigators had DNA from the crime scenes but no direct matches in the national database. Instead, they found a partial match to someone who had recently entered the criminal system: Christopher Franklin, Lonnie Franklin Jr.'s son. This partial match led police to consider the possibility that a close relative of Christopher was their suspect. From there, they began surveilling Lonnie Franklin Jr., collecting items he discarded in public to obtain a sample of his DNA without a warrant.

When the forensic team tested the new sample, it was a match. The man who had walked the streets of South Los Angeles for decades, waving to neighbors and tinkering with cars, was now the prime suspect in at least ten murders.

In July 2010, Franklin was arrested outside his home. The news shocked his neighborhood. Many couldn't believe the man they had known for years, who had helped them fix their bikes or offered advice about local repairs, was being accused of some of the city's most chilling crimes.

Inside Franklin's home, police found a trove of material: hundreds of photographs and videos of women, some of whom were never identified. The images spanned years and depicted women in various states of vulnerability. The volume of this evidence suggested a far greater scope to the crimes than initially believed. While only a handful of cases had forensic confirmation, the discovery of these items hinted at dozens of additional victims. It was a haunting archive that raised even more questions about who had gone missing, who had never been reported, and how many families were still waiting for answers.

Franklin's trial was delayed multiple times due to the sheer complexity of the case and the amount of evidence to be catalogued. In 2016, he was convicted on ten counts of murder and one count of attempted murder. Jurors heard testimony about the forensic techniques used, the stories of survivors, and the detailed investigative work that led to his capture. The verdict was swift: guilty on all counts. Franklin was sentenced to death, though he would die in prison in 2020 before the sentence was carried out.

The Grim Sleeper case catalyzed a wave of reforms and soul-searching within law enforcement and advocacy communities. The disparities in how cases were prioritized, the invisibility of certain victims, and the underreporting of violence in low-income neighborhoods all became points of national discussion.

Many believed that if the victims had belonged to wealthier or more politically connected demographics, the case would have been solved much earlier. Activists demanded not only justice for the known victims but systemic change in how missing persons cases are handled, particularly those involving vulnerable populations.

From a psychological standpoint, Franklin defied easy categorization. He wasn't a drifter or an outsider. He maintained a stable residence, had long-term employment, and presented a consistent image of ordinariness. This "everyman" persona often masks deeper compulsions and psychological divides. Interviews with people who knew him rarely yielded warning signs. He wasn't charismatic in the traditional sense, but he had a way of blending in; enough to seem safe, trustworthy, or simply forgettable. That camouflage was essential to his ability to offend for so long.

His crimes also exposed how systemic neglect can serve as a co-conspirator. When communities are over-policed in some ways and neglected in others, a paradox forms: residents may feel watched but not protected.

In such an environment, predators who target the vulnerable can exploit the disconnect between authority and community. The fear that reporting a crime may lead to more harm than good further silences those at risk. Franklin operated in this space, just present enough to seem normal, just quiet enough to avoid scrutiny.

In the wake of Franklin's conviction, city officials launched initiatives to improve response times to missing persons reports and to modernize cold case investigations. But the question of how many more like him may have existed, or may still exist, remains open. The case also triggered renewed debates about the use of familial DNA. While some praised it as an essential tool for modern policing, others raised ethical concerns about privacy, consent, and the scope of surveillance. In Franklin's case, the technique undeniably worked, but it also opened up broader conversations about the boundaries of investigative power.

The families of Franklin's victims continue to fight for recognition, closure, and dignity. Many have criticized the city's slow response, the lack of media attention, and the obstacles they faced in simply being heard. Their persistence, however, helped keep the case alive during years when it could have easily been forgotten. Their voices are now central to any discussion about the legacy of the Grim Sleeper and what it teaches us about justice delayed and justice denied.

Franklin's ability to disappear into his environment, to live a quiet life while carrying out acts of profound violence, forces us to reevaluate assumptions about what a criminal looks like. It also highlights the limits of traditional investigative profiling, which often centers on deviance from social norms. In Franklin's case, the conformity was the mask. His crimes challenge the idea that danger comes with visible warning signs. Sometimes, it comes with a smile, a friendly nod, or a neighborly hello.

The story of Lonnie Franklin Jr. is not just a story about a serial killer. It's about the stories that weren't told, the missing women who never made headlines, the families whose pain was not believed, and the communities whose fears were validated only after it was too late. It's a story about how violence can be obscured by indifference, and how predators can use the very fabric of daily life as a shield. But it's also a story about resilience, of investigators who refused to give up, of survivors who came forward, and of families who demanded to be heard.

In the end, Franklin died not at the hands of the state, but of natural causes in a prison cell. His death closed a legal chapter but not the emotional one. The city he haunted continues to grapple with what his crimes revealed: that even in a place as watched and wired as Los Angeles, silence can reign for years, and justice, if it comes, is often far too late.

The lessons of the Grim Sleeper remain etched not only in court records and police reports, but in the lives of those left behind, and in the ongoing efforts to ensure that the same mistakes are never made again.

Mark David Chapman

Mark David Chapman occupies a uniquely disturbing place in the public imagination; not just because of what he did, but because of who he did it to. The man responsible for the murder of John Lennon on December 8, 1980, didn't look like a hardened criminal or a figure of chaos. He appeared as just another man in the crowd, blending into the ordinary moments of one of New York City's most iconic streets. Yet within his mind, decades of unresolved psychological tension, identity confusion, and fixation had built toward one of the most infamous murders of the 20th century. Chapman's name, once obscure, is now forever tied to the loss of a musical legend and to a question that still haunts many: why?

Born in 1955 in Fort Worth, Texas, Mark David Chapman was raised in a middle-class household that, by outward appearances, offered stability. But as is often the case in these stories, appearances were deceiving. Chapman's childhood was marked by emotional upheaval and internal conflict. He later claimed to have experienced abuse at the hands of his father and described his early years as full of fear and alienation. From a young age, he struggled with self-worth and identity, often retreating into fantasy and adopting personas from books and music. By his teenage years, he had already developed a pattern of obsessive thinking, emotional instability, and an intense desire for significance. He longed to stand out, yet felt perpetually invisible.

Chapman's early adulthood did little to anchor him. He drifted through various jobs and underwent several religious awakenings. He once served as a counselor for Vietnamese refugee children in Georgia and even traveled internationally with the

YMCA. At one point, he considered becoming a missionary. These periods of apparent direction were often short-lived, quickly dissolving into disillusionment. Chapman would bounce between evangelical fervor and nihilistic despair, a pattern that mirrored his deteriorating mental state. Alongside these emotional swings, he developed a dangerous tendency to externalize blame and to see the world as full of phonies, people who pretended to be one thing while secretly being another.

This fixation on authenticity versus hypocrisy would later become a crucial part of Chapman's justification for the act that made him infamous. He began to direct this resentment toward cultural figures, particularly those who represented peace, love, or spiritual growth, yet lived in ways he perceived as contradictory. No figure encapsulated this contradiction for him more than John Lennon.

To Chapman, Lennon's promotion of peace, his famous declaration that The Beatles were "more popular than Jesus," and his immense wealth coexisted uneasily. Chapman, already battling mental illness, began to fixate on Lennon as a symbol of perceived hypocrisy, a public figure who represented everything that Chapman, in his darkest moments, believed was wrong with the world.

It wasn't just Lennon's fame or wealth that enraged Chapman. It was what he perceived as Lennon's betrayal of his own ideals. Songs like "Imagine" promoted a vision of a world without material possessions, yet Lennon lived in a luxury apartment building and was a global icon of affluence. To Chapman, this was unforgivable. But rather than turning away, he obsessed. He began reading everything he could about Lennon, studying his interviews, and examining his lyrics. Chapman's feelings evolved from disillusionment to a sort of violent moral mission: to hold Lennon accountable for what Chapman believed was cultural deception.

Complicating all of this was Chapman's deepening psychological fragmentation. Diagnosed later with schizophrenia spectrum symptoms and strong signs of psychosis, Chapman was not merely angry; he was unwell. His delusions grew more complex, intertwining fantasy, identity, and existential longing. At some point, Chapman began to identify with Holden Caulfield, the protagonist of J.D. Salinger's "The Catcher in the Rye." Like Holden, Chapman viewed himself as a protector of innocence in a world full of fakes. He saw his mission not just as personal vengeance, but as a symbolic act, a statement against a culture that celebrated inauthenticity. In his mind, Lennon's death would be a message, not a crime.

By late 1980, Chapman had begun actively planning. He traveled to New York City and visited the Dakota, the building where Lennon lived. On December 8, he waited outside the entrance. In a chilling moment that has since become part of popular lore, he approached Lennon earlier in the day and asked him to sign a copy of the "Double Fantasy" album. Lennon did, unaware that the man thanking him politely would return that night with a revolver. At around 10:50 p.m., as Lennon and Yoko Ono were returning home, Chapman stepped forward, pulled out the gun, and fired. Lennon was rushed to the hospital but pronounced dead on arrival.

Chapman did not flee. Instead, he remained at the scene, took out his copy of "The Catcher in the Rye," and began reading. When police arrived, he surrendered without resistance. His calm demeanor stood in stark contrast to the shock and horror erupting around the world. In an instant, one of the most beloved cultural figures of the 20th century was gone, and the man responsible was eerily composed.

(The entrance to the Dakota, the site where John Lennon was killed.)

The juxtaposition between Lennon's advocacy for peace and Chapman's cold execution of violence created a dissonance that would ripple through public consciousness for decades.

The aftermath was immediate and intense. Fans gathered outside the Dakota in tears, holding vigils and singing Beatles songs. Public memorials spread across continents. For millions, Lennon's death was more than a personal tragedy; it was the symbolic end of an era. The 1960s, with all its promise of love and revolution, felt definitively over. And Mark David Chapman became a cipher for modern madness: a seemingly average man whose internal collapse had global consequences.

Chapman was arrested and charged with second-degree murder. Though his defense team prepared to argue insanity, Chapman surprised many by pleading guilty, stating that God had told him to do so. In 1981, he was sentenced to 20 years to life in prison. He served decades behind bars and was denied parole multiple times before eventually being released, a decision that reignited debate about justice, remorse, and the lasting impact of his actions. During hearings, Chapman has expressed remorse, claiming he was "sorry for being such an idiot" and calling his actions "despicable." But whether his statements reflect genuine understanding or continued mental disorganization is debated.

One of the most chilling aspects of the case isn't simply the act itself, but its banality. Chapman didn't act out of spontaneous rage or overt chaos. He planned. He waited. He read a book. He surrendered.

In this way, his crime resembles other assassinations of high-profile figures throughout history, moments when an individual becomes obsessed with a public icon, not as a person, but as an idea. Lennon, to Chapman, was never truly human. He had become a projection screen for Chapman's own internal war. This dehumanization, this symbolic targeting, is what gives the case such disturbing resonance.

Forensic psychologists who have studied Chapman point to a combination of personality disorders, possible delusional thinking, and deep-seated narcissistic tendencies. He wasn't driven by monetary gain or political ideology, but by a need to matter. Chapman has admitted as much, telling parole boards that part of his motivation was the belief that killing Lennon would make him famous.

In this sense, his crime also fits within a disturbing pattern of violence performed for notoriety. He wanted the world to know his name, and in killing a global icon, he ensured that outcome. This aspect of the case has led to ongoing debates in media ethics about how much attention to give such individuals.

Yoko Ono, Lennon's widow, remained a consistent voice in opposing Chapman's release. She has written letters to parole boards urging them to consider the trauma his release would cause her and her family.

Lennon's sons, Julian and Sean, have also spoken about the long-lasting effects of the murder; not just the loss, but the permanence of the wound inflicted on popular culture. For them, and for millions of Lennon's fans, Chapman's name is inseparable from a day that redefined what it meant to be unsafe, even as a celebrity.

The cultural ripple effects of the murder extended far beyond Lennon's inner circle. It reshaped how public figures engaged with fans, how security was handled, and how society viewed parasocial relationships, the one-sided connections people form with celebrities. Chapman's obsession was extreme, but it grew out of a familiar cultural dynamic: the idea that public figures exist for consumption, scrutiny, and judgment. When that dynamic collapses into violence, it forces a reevaluation of fame itself.

In a broader context, the killing of John Lennon became a case study in the intersection of mental illness, media, and celebrity. It prompted discussions about gun access, the treatment of psychiatric disorders, and the limits of personal responsibility in the face of psychosis. But above all, it became a symbol, a reminder that the age of innocence, if it ever existed, could be shattered by a single act of violence carried out not by a mastermind or a revolutionary, but by a troubled man with a book and a gun.

Mark David Chapman was incarcerated at Green Haven Correctional Facility in New York for decades following his 1981 sentence. Over the years, he was denied parole numerous times as public debate resurfaced at each hearing. Those proceedings repeatedly raised difficult questions about remorse, accountability, and whether the passage of time can lessen the impact of irreversible harm.

In 2023, Chapman was granted parole and released, a decision that reignited widespread discussion about justice, forgiveness, and the lasting consequences of his actions.

Since his release, Chapman has largely remained out of public view. Yet his name continues to carry weight, not because of any life he built afterward, but because of the cultural figure whose life he ended.

In killing John Lennon, Chapman permanently linked himself to one of the most significant moments in modern music history, not as a cause or crusader, but as a man whose personal turmoil resulted in a loss felt around the world.

Conclusion

The final pages of a book like this can feel heavy. Fifty one individuals. Dozens of communities affected. Hundreds of lives lost. Years of fear, unanswered questions, and long investigations. It's not light reading. And it isn't meant to be.

But this book was never just about listing crimes. It was about understanding patterns. It was about seeing how certain behaviors repeat across time and place. It was about looking carefully at what went wrong, what was missed, and what eventually led to justice.

Across these profiles, you have seen very different people. Some were outwardly charming. Some were isolated and withdrawn. Some were married with children. Others drifted from place to place. Some were respected professionals. Others struggled with addiction or unstable work. There is no single "type" that fits them all.

That is one of the most important lessons. Serial killers don't all look the same. They don't come from one background. They don't share one personality. What connects them is repetition and intent. It is the pattern of targeting, harming, and repeating over time. That pattern is what separates a single act of violence from something more organized and sustained.

You may also have noticed how often warning signs appeared long before the crimes reached their worst point. Early aggression. Obsession with control. Manipulation. A history of violence that did not lead to serious consequences. In many cases, small red flags were ignored or explained away.

At the same time, you have seen how difficult it can be to detect someone who hides well. Many of the offenders in this book blended into their communities. They worked regular jobs. They paid bills. They had neighbors who described them as quiet or helpful. Some even volunteered or held positions of trust.

That contrast between appearance and reality is unsettling. It reminds us that danger does not always come with a warning label.

Another theme that runs through these pages is vulnerability. Many victims lived on the margins of society. They were poor, isolated, elderly, undocumented, struggling with addiction, or otherwise overlooked. In too many cases, their disappearances were not treated with urgency. Families had to fight to be heard. Communities had to demand attention.

Studying these cases shows how inequality and indifference can create opportunities for predators. It also shows the power of advocacy. When families and communities refused to stay silent, investigations reopened. Cold cases were revisited. DNA evidence was tested again. Justice, even delayed, became possible.

You've also seen how law enforcement has changed over time. Early cases relied on witness statements and basic detective work. Later cases used fingerprint databases.

Then DNA testing transformed investigations. In the most recent cases, genetic genealogy connected suspects to crime scenes decades later.

Technology didn't eliminate violence. But it made hiding harder.

Certain similarities stand out. A need for control. A tendency to escalate. A focus on specific types of victims. Periods of calm followed by bursts of activity. You may also notice differences. Some offenders sought attention. Others avoided it at all costs. Some confessed freely. Others denied everything.

Understanding these similarities and differences matters. It helps criminologists build profiles. It helps investigators spot patterns earlier. It helps communities recognize when something is wrong.

It also reminds us that these crimes didn't happen in isolation. They happened in neighborhoods. In cities. In small towns. In hospitals. On highways. Behind closed doors. Every case involved real people with families, dreams, and futures that were cut short.

That is why this book has aimed to avoid sensationalism. There is no need to exaggerate. The facts are powerful enough. The goal has been clarity, not shock. Education, not entertainment.

Serial killers represent a rare but extreme form of human behavior. Most people will never encounter someone like the individuals described in these chapters. But understanding how such offenders think, operate, and hide gives us critical context. It sharpens awareness. It reinforces the importance of listening to instincts, reporting concerns, and taking missing persons seriously.

If there's one lasting takeaway from these stories, it is this: patterns matter. Small details matter. Every life matters.

Communities that stay connected, institutions that respond quickly, and systems that treat every victim with equal importance are stronger and safer. The failures in these cases offer lessons. The breakthroughs offer hope.

As you close this book, you may feel unsettled. That reaction is understandable. But you may also feel more informed. More aware of how investigations work. More conscious of how easily appearances can mislead. More respectful of the resilience of victims' families who never stopped searching for answers.

Knowledge doesn't erase tragedy. But it does help prevent repetition.

The *Most Notorious Serial Killers in History* has brought together stories from different eras and continents. Each case stands alone. Together, they form a larger picture of how violence evolves, how systems adapt, and how justice, though sometimes slow, can prevail.

The final pages don't end the conversation. They simply close this collection of profiles. The lessons remain. The patterns remain. And the responsibility to learn from history remains with all of us.

Works Cited & Recommended Readings

References

Aamodt, M. G. (2014). *Serial killer statistics.* Serial Killer Information Center, Radford University.

Bardsley, M. (2007). *Jack the Ripper: The definitive history.* Virgin Books.

Burgess, A. W., Hartman, C. R., Ressler, R. K., Douglas, J. E., & McCormack, A. (1986). *S**ual homicide: Patterns and motives.* Free Press.

Carlo, P. (1996). *The Night Stalker: The life and crimes of Richard Ramirez.* Pinnacle Books.

Douglas, J. E., & Olshaker, M. (1995). *Mindhunter: Inside the FBI's elite serial crime unit.* Scribner.

Douglas, J. E., Burgess, A. W., Burgess, A. G., & Ressler, R. K. (2013). *Crime classification manual: A standard system for investigating and classifying violent crime* (3rd ed.). Wiley.

Hickey, E. W. (2016). *Serial murderers and their victims* (7th ed.). Cengage Learning.

Holmes, R. M., & Holmes, S. T. (2009). *Serial murder* (3rd ed.). Sage Publications.

Jones, J. (1992). *Let me take you down: Inside the mind of Mark David Chapman.* Villard.

Keppel, R. D., & Birnes, W. J. (2004). *The riverman: Ted Bundy and I hunt for the Green River Killer.* Pocket Books.

Kessler, R. (2018). *The first family detail: Secret Service agents reveal the hidden lives of the presidents.* Crown Forum.

Larson, E. (2003). *The devil in the white city: Murder, magic, and madness at the fair that changed America.* Crown.

Leyton, E. (2005). *Hunting humans: The rise of the modern multiple murderer.* McClelland & Stewart.

Masters, B. (1985). *Killing for company: The case of Dennis Nilsen.* Jonathan Cape.

Masters, B. (1993). *The shrine of Jeffrey Dahmer.* Hodder & Stoughton.

McNamara, M. (2018). *I'll be gone in the dark: One woman's obsessive search for the Golden State Killer*. HarperCollins.

Michaud, S. G., & Aynesworth, H. (1989). *Ted Bundy: Conversations with a killer*. Authorlink Press.

Newton, M. (2006). *The encyclopedia of serial killers* (2nd ed.). Facts On File.

Pelisek, C. (2017). *The grim sleeper: The lost women of South Central*. Counterpoint.

Ramsland, K. (2016). *Confession of a serial killer: The untold story of Dennis Rader, the BTK killer*. University Press of New England.

Ressler, R. K., & Shachtman, T. (1992). *Whoever fights monsters: My twenty years tracking serial killers for the FBI*. St. Martin's Press.

Rule, A. (1980). *The stranger beside me*. W. W. Norton & Company.

Schechter, H. (2003). *The A to Z encyclopedia of serial killers*. Pocket Books.

Shipman Inquiry. (2005). *The Shipman inquiry: Sixth report*. The Stationery Office.

Silkman, W. (2011). *The Yorkshire Ripper case files*. The History Press.

Sullivan, T., & Maiken, P. T. (2000). *Killer clown: The John Wayne Gacy murders*. Pinnacle Books.

Tithecott, R. (1997). *Of men and monsters: Jeffrey Dahmer and the construction of the serial killer*. University of Wisconsin Press.

Tulloch, M. (2021). *Missing and missed: Report of the independent civilian review into missing person investigations*. Toronto Police Service.

Wickenheiser, R. A. (2019). Forensic genealogy, bioethics, and the Golden State Killer case. *Forensic Science International: Synergy, 1*, 114–125.

Recommended Readings

Beauregard, E., & Martineau, M. (2017). *The s**ual murderer: Offender behavior and implications for practice*. Academic Press.

DeFronzo, J. (2010). *Criminology* (8th ed.). Allyn & Bacon.

Douglas, J. E., & Olshaker, M. (1997). *Journey into darkness*. Scribner.

Fox, J. A., & Levin, J. (2015). *Extreme killing: Understanding serial and mass murder* (3rd ed.). Sage Publications.

Keppel, R. D. (2000). *Signature killers*. Pocket Books.

Ramsland, K. (2006). *Inside the minds of serial killers*. Praeger.

Turvey, B. E. (2012). *Criminal profiling: An introduction to behavioral evidence analysis* (4th ed.). Academic Press.

Wilson, C., & Seaman, D. (2007). *The serial killers: A study in the psychology of violence*. Virgin Books.

www.ingramcontent.com/pod-product-compliance
Lightning Source LLC
Chambersburg PA
CBHW050815260726
48660CB00004B/1445